# Willem de Kooning's Women:
# A Psychoanalytic Exploration

# Willem de Kooning's Women
## A Psychoanalytic Exploration

Graeme J. Taylor

**IPBOOKS**.net
International Psychoanalytic Books

International Psychoanalytic Books (IPBooks)
New York • http://www.IPBooks.net

Willem de Kooning's Women: A Psychoanalytic Exploration

Published by IPBooks, Queens, NY
Online at: www.IPBooks.net

ISBN: 978-1-956864-19-9

Willem de Kooning in his studio in New York, 1950
Photograph by Rudy Burckhardt

*For Helen, Paul, Ramzi, and Leila*
*and to the memory of my brother, Denis Taylor*

# Contents

# Acknowledgments

This project began as an essay that became too long to be considered for publication as a journal article. I thank my colleagues Ray Freebury, Jack Brandes, and George Boujoff for reading and discussing the essay and for encouraging me to expand the manuscript into a book. I am most indebted to my art historian friend John MacGregor, who kindly read an early draft and sent me detailed notes on each chapter. His advice and suggestions proved invaluable; he guided me toward finding the best way to structure the book, advised which parts I could eliminate, and where I needed to further develop my ideas. I was not able to follow all of John's recommendations, because they were leading me towards a terrain that requires a knowledge of art history and criticism that is far beyond my area of expertise. I therefore chose to explore my topic primarily from a psychoanalytic perspective.

In this regard, I thank Jack Brandes and Ray Freebury for carefully reading and commenting on two of the extensively revised chapters in the book, and also Peter Shoenberg in London for reviewing one of the revised chapters. I am grateful to philosophy professor Duff Waring for sharing with me his broad knowledge of creative writers and his interest in art, and for bringing to my attention Mary

Gabriel's book *Ninth Street Women*, which includes a section about Elaine de Kooning.

A special thanks to novelist Carolyn Taylor-Watts, who kindly edited several chapters and offered helpful guidance in selecting illustrations for the book. I am grateful also to Liz Konigshaus, who retyped Chapter 2, Jim Allan, who gave technical assistance and helped organize the digital images, and psychoanalyst Sarah Nettleton for directing me to a published interview with Christopher Bollas. I thank the librarians at the Robarts Library of the University of Toronto for organizing curbside pickup of books during the pandemic, and for providing online access to certain books from the Hathi Trust digital library. These resources prevented any major disruption to my writing.

I could not have written this book without important biographical information, which became known to the public through the extensive research on de Kooning's life and work by Judith Wolfe and by Mark Stevens and Annalyn Swan. Wolfe's 1996 doctoral dissertation (which I consulted many times online through ProQuest) provides detailed information about the artist's early life, training, and work in Holland. My well-thumbed copy of Stevens and Swan's superb and extensive biography of de Kooning gave me additional information about the artist's infancy, childhood and adolescence, as well as detailed information about his adult life in America, including his romantic relationships and slide into alcoholism. I thank Judith Wolfe for kindly sending me a digital image of de Kooning's drawing *Women and Tree*, which I was unable to locate elsewhere, and for obligingly responding to my questions about aspects of the artist's childhood.

I thank members of the staff at the Willem de Kooning Foundation for reading the manuscript and for drawing my attention to several factual inaccuracies, which I subsequently corrected. I also thank Winifer Skattebol for copyediting the final manuscript.

As always, my family provided emotional support, which I deeply appreciated while I was writing this book through the seemingly endless pandemic. I was sustained also by two small paintings on my study walls, which were given to me in 1966 by my Irish artist friend Vere Dudgeon. Perhaps influenced by de Kooning, Vere combines abstract and representational styles in these paintings.

# Illustrations

All quotations by Willem de Kooning © Estate of Lisa de Kooning

# Introduction

The Dutch-American artist Willem de Kooning (1951a) described painting as "a way of living"; it was a passion he pursued for most of his life. He showed an extraordinary talent for drawing in his early teens and continued to draw and paint until he was in his late eighties, one of his most productive years being 1985, when he was aged 81 and was showing some signs of an Alzheimer's-like dementia. Inspired by Cezanne, Miró, Picasso, and several other modern artists, and unwilling to let go of the Old Masters, de Kooning gradually developed his own personal style of painting. But his work often evoked strong criticism and continues to elicit mixed reactions among viewers. In a review of a retrospective of his work in 2011–2012, one prominent art critic rated him as "the greatest of American painters, and lesser only to Picasso and Matisse among all artists of the twentieth century" (Schjeldahl, 2011, p. 122). Commenting on the same retrospective, however, a distinguished art historian described de Kooning as abandoning the beauty of classical art and following "Picasso down [the] path of ugliness" and "destructiveness" (Kuspit, 2011). Such polar opposite opinions invite further inquiry about the artist and his work. Was there something in the psychology of the artist that might partly account for the contrasting reactions to his work?

De Kooning entered the United States illegally in 1926, having left Holland and crossed the Atlantic as a stowaway on a British freighter. For more than two decades, he feared being caught by the authorities and, until he became a registered alien, was concerned about having his status questioned (Stevens and Swan, 2004, p.132); he finally became an American citizen in March 1962 when he travelled to Canada and re-entered the United States legally. By that time, his reputation as a modern artist was firmly established. And two years later his contribution to American culture was recognized by the White House; President Johnson awarded him the Medal of Freedom, one of the two highest civilian awards in the United States (Stevens and Swan, 2004, pp. 468–9, 612). Although de Kooning did not like to be categorized as belonging to a particular art movement, he is generally considered an Abstract Expressionist painter. He is most widely known for his controversial series of images of women, which he painted in the early 1950s, although he also made a lot of drawings (including pastels) during this period. Art historians and art critics have written numerous articles and many excellent books about de Kooning's work, and several graduate students have made his work the subject of their master's thesis or doctoral dissertation. A dissertation that has proven to be an invaluable source of information is Judith Wolfe's (1996) study of the artist's early life, training, and work from 1904 to 1926. In 2004, Mark Stevens and Annalyn Swan published a comprehensive biography of de Kooning, a project that took ten years to complete. A decade later, art historian Judith Zilczer (2014) wrote an extensive and critically-informed account of de Kooning's art within the context of his life and times.

Most viewers of the Woman paintings of the early 1950s try to find meaning in the pictures; they wonder, 'Who does the woman represent?' The search for meaning has led a number of non-clinician scholars to propose interpretations of these paintings based on an application of certain psychoanalytic concepts. To my knowledge, however, no psychoanalyst or other mental health clinician has written an article or book that offers an in-depth exploration of the artist's life and/or aspects of his creative work. The web-based psychoanalytic electronic publishing library (PEP-Web) lists many articles by psychoanalytic authors who mention de Kooning by name, but only one article includes a short discussion of de Kooning's work; this is an essay by Steven Poser (2008) exploring the connection between modern art and the unconscious mind. In a published interview and in a book chapter about creativity and psychoanalysis, Christopher Bollas briefly describes a similarity he observes between de Kooning's method of painting and the psychoanalytic method of free association (Bollas, 2011; Molino, 1997). But neither Poser nor Bollas consider de Kooning's childhood experiences and how these might have influenced his paintings and his life as an adult.

As Poser (2008) points out, "Psychoanalysis and modern art are nearly contemporary movements in the twentieth century" (p. 128). Both disciplines involve engagement with the unconscious mind and the creative process, and much like artists, analysts are guided partly by their intuition. And just as styles of painting changed over the course of the century, resulting in different art movements, psychoanalytic theory evolved, and different schools emerged that

3

have each contributed to current understanding of the mind and important aspects of human behavior. The advances in psychoanalytic theory have also helped enrich the understanding of art and the creative process. Sigmund Freud provided an opening for applying psychoanalytic thinking to cultural and other phenomena in 1926 when he indicated that "the use of analysis for the treatment of the neuroses is only one of its applications; the future will perhaps show that it is not the most important one" (p. 248). The aims of applied psychoanalysis are to provide a deeper understanding of an individual and/or their creative work; in addition to writers and painters, its subjects include sculptors, political leaders, and religious leaders. The approach involves identifying behavior patterns of the individual, exploring information about their childhood, and postulating unconscious thought processes that together shed light upon the individual's character and suggest factors that helped motivate and contribute to their achievements. It is assumed that an understanding of the life of the person will provide a better understanding of their work. Freud demonstrated this approach in essays he wrote about Michelangelo's sculpture of *Moses*, Leonardo da Vinci's paintings of the *Virgin and St. Anne* and the *Mona Lisa,* and Wilhelm Jensen's *Gradiva*. Other well-known examples of this approach are psychologist Erik Erikson's studies of Martin Luther and Mahatma Ghandi, Bernard Meyer's psychoanalytic biography of Joseph Conrad, and in more recent years Jerome Frank's psychoanalytic portraits of Presidents George W. Bush, Barack Obama, and Donald Trump. Several other psychoanalytic authors have explored the influence of childhood trauma on the lives and works of well-known painters, including Vincent Van Gogh (Schnier, 1950), Egon Schiele (Knafo, 1991), Edvard

4

Munch (Turco, 1998; Viederman, 1994), Pablo Picasso (Blum, 2013), Mark Rotho (Turco, 1998), and Francis Bacon (Bose, 2005).

Applying psychoanalytic knowledge to artists and their work, however, is a risky enterprise, as it is prone to many errors. Indeed, Freud's interpretations of works by Michelangelo and Leonardo da Vinci have been harshly criticized for mistranslations, slender evidence, and failure to consider non-psychoanalytic factors (Abella, 2016; Glover, 2009; Kuspit, 2000; Spector, 1973; Wohl and Trosman, 1955). Freud probably anticipated making some errors; in a letter to Ernest Jones in 1921, he wrote: "Yet it is evident there is much slippery ground in many of our applications of psychoanalysis to biography and literature" (Freud and Jones, 1995, p. 408). A major limitation of applied psychoanalysis is that the data on which formulations and interpretations are based are not analogous with the data that emerge in clinical situations. Studies in applied psychoanalysis rely almost entirely on examination of the subjects' writings and artistic creations, as well as reported interviews with the subject and information in biographies. In clinical psychoanalysis, the data are the free associations of the patient on the analyst's couch as well as dreams recalled by the patient. In addition, aspects of the patient's early experiences with significant others, including traumatic experiences in infancy and childhood that underlie the psychopathology of the patient, are typically re-enacted in the relationship the patient establishes with the analyst—the "transference-countertransference" relationship. Identifying patterns of thinking and behavior within this relationship and linking them with early trauma minimizes the guesswork involved in constructing an understanding of the patient's inner world and its influence on the person's current life. Applied psychoanalysis not only lacks free associations of the subject and observations from a transference-countertransference relationship but is limited also by the absence of responses of the subject to the author's formulations of their character and interpretations of their work. The validity of the assumptions in an applied psychoanalytic study therefore rests upon how plausible the assumptions are, and whether there is consistency across interpretations and convergence of evidence gleaned from biographical material and other sources (Beres, 1959; Esman, 1998; Gabbard, 1986).

Aaron Esman (1998) makes the important point that in the absence of the artist to validate or refute interpretations of their work, there is "danger that the analytic investigator may, unimpeded, impose his biases on the data or that he will lack an adequate understanding of the terrain in which he is working (a risk presumably absent from the clinical situation), or that the humanist scholar will lack the full grasp of psychoanalytic principles that can come only from 'clinical immersion'" (p. 742). I am not an art historian or an art critic, but I have had more than forty years of experience as a research psychiatrist and as a clinician practicing psychoanalysis and psychoanalytic psychotherapy. My training and experience in different cities (Dunedin, New Zealand; Toronto; New York; London; Los Angeles) have given me knowledge of a broad range of psychoanalytic concepts and theories and kept me from the danger of becoming wedded to any single school of psychoanalytic thinking. Early in my career, I learned about the theoretical and clinical contributions of Ronald Fairbairn, Donald Winnicott, and John Bowlby, when I had a personal analysis with a senior colleague who had trained with the Independent Group in the British school of psychoanalysis. I then had a second analysis with a "training analyst" who was strictly Freudian in his approach. Later in my career I had a third analysis with a training analyst whose approach was strongly influenced by Wilfrid Bion and Melanie Klein. Over the years I had the privilege of treating many creative individuals, including actors, writers, painters, and musicians; they have all contributed to my way of thinking about artistic works and the relation between artists and their work. Prior to this book, however, my only publication about a work of art is a study of the iconography of a sixteenth-century painting with a unique pairing of Judith (from the apocryphal story) and the Infant Hercules, which is in the collection of the National Gallery in London. When I first saw this painting, I quickly recognized the unconscious symbolism, which led me on an investigative trail to further explore the pairing of the two figures from a psychoanalytic perspective (Taylor, 1984). The investigation gave me an appreciation for how artists sometimes unconsciously communicate the latent meaning in their work to the unconscious mind of the viewer.

Although I have taken courses on the history of art and about the works of several individual artists, art history and art criticism are not my usual terrain. I therefore offer this work not as something conclusive about de Kooning and his creative work, but rather as an exploration in which I make use of my psychoanalytic knowledge and insights gained from clinical practice. I am particularly interested in the Woman paintings from the early fifties. As many readers will know, this controversial series was preceded and followed by numerous other images of women, a subject the artist pursued in a seemingly compulsive way for nearly forty years. I was intrigued by art critic Rosalind Krauss' (2015) suggestion that de Kooning's apparent obsession with painting the female figure may have been motivated by an unconscious repetition compulsion, a phenomenon first described by Freud to indicate how the past may be brought into the present. Biographical accounts of de Kooning's relationships with women also suggest elements of an unconscious compulsion to repeat experiences from the past. De Kooning had multiple affairs and several long-term relationships with women throughout his adult life. Rather than being involved with one woman, and then with another, he was unable to commit to or completely leave a woman and vacillated between relationships. He could certainly be warm and loving with women, but at times he behaved ruthlessly toward some of them, who nevertheless remained deeply in love with him. I was left wondering what it was from his past that the artist may have been unconsciously repeating, both in his personal relationships with women and in his depiction of women in many of his canvases. And how might his addiction to alcohol be explained? Notwithstanding the limitations of applied psychoanalysis, after reviewing an extensive literature about de Kooning, I have written this book from a psychoanalytic perspective in an attempt to suggest possible answers to these questions.

# CHAPTER 1

# Paintings on the Theme of the Woman

Willem de Kooning's painting titled *Woman I* is considered one of the most controversial paintings of a woman in American art, and perhaps the most disturbing image of a woman in the history of art. The artist began work on this image in June 1950 when he was in his mid-forties, a project he then struggled with for almost two years. It became the first in a series of six paintings that were numbered *Woman I* to *Woman VI*, together with a seventh painting titled *Woman and Bicycle*. The seven images are generally regarded as alternate takes on the theme of the woman: as a critic commented after viewing six of the paintings in 1953, "the six paintings are really one, or, conversely, any one stands for the series" (Geist, 1953).[1] My discussion will focus primarily on the first painting in the series, since it has captured the most interest and commentary.

A few days before commencing work on *Woman I*, de Kooning completed a large, majestic and complex abstract painting titled

---

1 This critic saw only six of the seven paintings in the series, because *Woman VI* had not yet been completed. Some later critics describe significant differences among the images, which I discuss in the next chapter.

*Excavation* (Gaugh, 1983, p. 41). The painting was selected, along with works by Jackson Pollock, Arshile Gorky, and several other artists, to represent the United States at the Venice Biennale, which opened in mid-June that year. It subsequently won the top prize in the sixtieth annual exhibition of American painting and sculpture organized by The Art Institute of Chicago. And two years earlier (April 1948), de Kooning had his first solo exhibition, which was held at the Charles Egan Gallery in New York. The show comprised mostly black and white abstract works and was well-received; although few works sold, the reviews were mostly favorable. The influential art critic Clement Greenberg (1948) described the show as "magnificent" and de Kooning as "one of four or five most important artists in the country."[2] Having established a reputation for his abstract work, one wonders what motivated the artist to return to the figure and begin painting a large image of a woman on a canvas that is almost seven feet high.

De Kooning had been drawing and painting the female figure throughout the 1940s, including during his black-and-white period; it was a subject he pursued in a seemingly compulsive way. The seven images painted between 1950 and 1953 are just the third among six series of images of women that de Kooning painted over a period of nearly forty years.[3] He was once reported to have said, "I can't get away from the woman. Wherever I look, I find her" (Davis, 1972),

---

2 A second, smaller show of the unsold black and white paintings, as well as some works on paper, was held at the Egan Gallery in April 1951.

3 I hereafter refer to the seven images in the third series as the "Woman paintings of the early 1950s," or simply as the "Woman paintings." It should be noted that although Lauter (1976) and, before her, Thomas Hess (1968), grouped de Kooning's paintings of women into five or six series or types, it is no longer common practice to create categories for these paintings, as there are no clear boundaries for making distinctions between different series or types.

an admission that art theorist and critic Rosalind Krauss (2015) suggests "has the ring of a repetition compulsion that might demand explanation in the dimension of the unconscious" (p. 32).

In the late 1940s, de Kooning was among a group of New York artists who have come to be referred to as Abstract Expressionist painters or the New York School. He had developed friendships with several of these artists during the 1930s, some of whom were also émigrés from Europe. By the mid-1940s, they were meeting regularly to discuss philosophical theories and ideas about art and, to a lesser extent, the emerging popular interest in the unconscious and other psychoanalytic concepts. Although the styles of these artists differed, they developed a new approach to painting that emphasized freedom and abstraction and the qualities of brushstroke and texture. However, in contrast to abstract expressionist artists such as Barnett Newman, Jackson Pollock, Mark Rothko, and others in the group, de Kooning refused to give up representational painting and continued to blend figurative with abstract styles. Even some of the intertwined shapes in *Excavation* resemble deformed body fragments, including breasts, torsos, teeth, mouths, and eyes. De Kooning's reluctance to be part of a movement, and his conviction that "each artist can do what he thinks he ought to," annoyed Pollock, who had developed fame for his celebrated "drip" paintings. De Kooning's stance also puzzled Clement Greenberg and other supporters.[4]

---

4   At a symposium held at the Museum of Modern Art in February 1951, de Kooning gave a talk titled "What abstract art means to me." He said, "Personally I do not need a movement. What was given to me, I take for granted." He referred to Marcel Duchamp as a "one-man movement"

As described by museum curator John Elderfield (2011a, 2011b, 2011c) and art historian Judith Zilczer (2014), the painting of *Woman I* was preceded by numerous preliminary studies, some of which were documented in photographs taken by Rudy Burckhardt and Walter Auerbach while the work was in progress. De Kooning initially sketched two charcoal drawings of a standing nude woman on tall sheets of paper that were hung side-by-side on the wall. It is not known for certain if he then traced these sketches onto the canvas, but he soon decided to make his subject a single seated figure. He is thought to have also derived inspiration from three earlier works he had painted in 1948 and 1949. As he worked on the canvas, de Kooning repeatedly reworked or replaced the image, scraping away the figure and then beginning anew. According to his wife Elaine, herself an artist and art critic, at least 200 images had preceded the final state of *Woman I* (Elderfield, 2011c, p. 243; Gaugh, 1983, p. 41). De Kooning often used tracing paper to capture the outlines of a detail he liked; later, he would see if the detail fit into a new image, and then decide whether to trace the outline onto the canvas. This involved the Cubist method of fragmenting and dislocating the anatomy of the figure and then using collage to reassemble the figure. Sometimes he placed masking tape on the canvas and painted over the tape; once the tape was removed, it left a sharp line, which he then painted in various

---

which he considered "a truly modern movement because it implies that each artist can do what he thinks he ought to—a movement for each person and open for everybody" (de Kooning, 1951a). And as Bert Schierbeek (2005) concluded after interviewing de Kooning in 1967, "Bill will not serve any fixed conceptions of reality, or esthetics; he does not fit into anyone's pigeonhole; nor does he espouse any credo, political or professional, except that of the artist's will to freedom" (p. 55). Indeed, throughout his career, de Kooning followed his own creative interests and inspirations. His visual explorations included alternating between figure and abstraction, often merging figure with landscape, as I discuss further on.

widths. The photographs of early stages show that he had drawn a window in the upper right corner of the canvas; it was removed in the later stages. At some point Clement Greenberg, who had highly praised de Kooning's earlier abstract works, visited the studio and told the artist that, given the direction serious art was taking, it was a folly to return to the figure. This greatly annoyed de Kooning and made him even more determined to paint the figure.[5]

Judith Zilczer (2014) compared the extant painting with the photographic images and observed evidence that de Kooning had difficulty melding the face with the body and articulating the anatomy in *Woman I*. He also had difficulty drawing the hands. These difficulties may have contributed to his becoming dissatisfied and frustrated with the painting, and in the early months of 1952 he put it aside and began working on three other images of women, as well as several drawings and pastels. He received encouragement from art critic Harold Rosenberg, who supported the view that contemporary artists were free to depict the human figure. Rosenberg often visited de Kooning at his downtown studio, and they became friends. And, later that year, de Kooning was visited by the respected art historian Meyer Schapiro, who saw the abandoned canvas and is thought to have either encouraged him to complete it or reassured him that it was almost ready to exhibit. Stevens and Swan (2004) suggest that Schapiro may have inspired in the artist the thought that he should not make the picture look fully resolved—"that there should be something fundamentally broken in the image if [it] were to convey

---

5   Greenberg's visit to the studio is described by Cateforis (1991, pp. 60-62) and by Stevens and Swan (2004, p. 313).

**Figure 1:** *Woman I*, 1950–1952
Oil on canvas, 75 ⅞ x 58 inches (192.7 x 147.3 cm)
The Museum of Modern Art, New York

the ambiguous meanings of modernity" (p. 342). De Kooning made some additional changes to the painting, but did not complete it until after painting *Woman II* and *Woman III*, and he never considered it finished (Figure 1).

Willem and Elaine were invited to spend the summer of 1952 with Leo Castelli and his wife Ileana Sonnabend in their house on the outskirts of East Hampton, Long Island. They were glad to get away from the city for the season and knew that Castelli had recommended de Kooning to Sidney Janis, who owned a gallery in Manhattan (Gabriel, 2018, p. 444). The artist made a studio in an enclosed porch of the house, where he made several drawings, small oil paintings, and a series of pastels (Hess, 1968, p. 75) (Figure 2). It was a productive time, during which de Kooning also developed a deeper friendship with Rosenberg, who was a regular visitor at the Castelli house (Stevens and Swan, 2004, p. 334).[6]

---

6   The photograph in Figure 2 was probably taken in the summer of 1953 when Willem and Elaine spent another summer at Castelli and Sonnabend's house. As before, de Kooning made several pastels, but also worked on another large painting of a woman, which he struggled with and later destroyed (Elderfield 2011c, p. 244).

**Figure 2:** De Kooning contemplating one of his paintings in his improvised studio on the porch of Leo Castelli's house in East Hampton, New York in the summer of 1953.
Photograph by Tony Vaccaro

In December that year, Rosenberg published an article in *ARTnews* titled "The American Action Painters" that announced the arrival of a new kind of painter whose work embodied an "event" or an "action" that was inseparable from the biography of the artist and was therefore revelatory. Rosenberg (1952) named no individual artists in the article; and de Kooning did not fully qualify as an action painter because of his method of working and reworking his pictures. Nonetheless, readers of the article were aware that Rosenberg admired de Kooning's paintings and had seen his gestural and slashing brushstrokes when he observed him at work in the studio. Three months after Rosenberg's article appeared, Thomas Hess, who was managing editor of *ARTnews*, published an article titled "De Kooning Paints a Picture," in which he documented the evolution of *Woman I* (Hess, 1953). He compared the two years of work to a romantic voyage—"an exploration for a constantly elusive vision; the solution to a problem that was continually being set in new ways." The stages of the painting that were captured with the camera were memories of "some of the stops *en route*—like cities that were visited, friends that were met." Although *Woman I* took two years to complete, Hess observed that "De Kooning is a fast worker, and the entire picture frequently changed in a few hours' time. The voyage may have been long, but its tempo was hectic."[7]

---

7  It was not atypical of de Kooning to spend a considerable period of time working on a painting, even though there was a speed that might characterize any single gesture of the brush. Recalling his observations of the artist working on *Woman I*, Hess (1968) reported that "De Kooning paints fast and would cover the whole surface in a matter of hours. But then would follow weeks of analysis, dissection, drawing sections of the figure, moving the drawing to overlay another area" (p. 75). In 1955, de Kooning said, "I spend most of the time sitting there studying the picture and trying to figure out what to do next" (Shiff, 2011, p. 81). Three decades later, he still worked and reworked his paintings, but, according to his brother-in-law Conrad Fried, he said, "I might work on a painting for a month, but it has to look like I painted it in a minute" (Stevens and Swan, 2004, p. 591).

The slow progression of the work was attributed to the artist's wish to keep "off-balance" and maintain an open field "for studying an infinitely variable number of possibilities" that involved interchanging parts of the anatomy, as well as abrupt shifts caused by masking and overlays and the unidentified setting in which the woman is seated. Hess considered ambiguity a crucial element in this art. In stages of the work, a photograph of a mouth cut from a magazine advertisement was attached to the canvas as a focal point around which everything else moved. Within the metaphor of the voyage, Hess described the smile of the mouth as the "passport" that was needed at all times to continue the journey. In the final stage, de Kooning removed the collaged mouth and painted a snarling mouth with prominent teeth. Hess reported also that the artist told him that "his 'idolized' *Woman* reminds him strongly of a landscape—with arms like lanes and a body of hills and fields, all brought up close to the surface, like a panorama squeezed together (or like a Cezanne)" (Hess, 1953).[8]

In March 1953, the Sidney Janis Gallery in New York held a solo exhibition titled "Willem de Kooning: Paintings on the Theme of the Woman" with six large *Woman* oil paintings, as well as sixteen pastels and drawings on the same theme. As noted earlier, *Woman VI* was not included, because it was not completed until after the exhibition. The paintings shocked many of the people who attended the opening and generated intense controversy among art critics, except for the mainstream press, which gave somewhat guarded responses by focusing less on the content and more on the aesthetic

---

8   After completing *Woman VI* in 1953, de Kooning told Hess that "The landscape is in the Woman, and there is Woman in the landscapes" (Hess, 1968, p. 100).

aspects of the paintings. A review in the *New York Times*, for example, ignored the powerful emotions evoked by the paintings and suggested instead that one might feel that "the figures are the outcome of highly cerebral concepts rather than emotional reaction to them" (Devree, 1953). A critic for the *New Yorker* offered limited praise by commenting favorably on the colors in *Woman I* and *Woman III* and admiring two of the pastels. He considered the exhibition "moderately momentous," but only in the sense that de Kooning seemed to be turning to the representational, something this critic approved of, even though he was the person who had first applied the term "abstract expressionism" to this new American art. In his opinion, however, the artist did not commit himself to either the representational or the abstract possibilities of the images, but hesitated constantly between the two, resulting in "a splashy and confused muddle of pigment that obscures as much as it reveals of the subject" (R.M. Coates, 1953, p. 96).

Other critics of the exhibition expressed opinions about the images as well as de Kooning's technique.[9] Some of them, as Zilczer (2014) observes, "equated the seeming violence of de Kooning's expressionist technique with an assault on the subject" (p. 127).[10] Sidney Geist, a critic for *Art Digest*, wrote: "In a gesture that parallels a sexual act, he [de Kooning] has vented himself with a violence on the canvas,

---

9   A detailed description and commentary on the different critical reviews and interpretations of the paintings between 1953 and 1990 is provided by David Cateforis in a doctoral dissertation he submitted to the Department of Art History at Stanford University in 1991. A briefer and less complete account is provided by Judith Zilczer (2014, pp. 127–131).

10   Four decades later, Cateforis (1994) suggested that the violence in the *Woman* paintings was anticipated by the dissection of the woman's anatomy in *Queen of Hearts*, which was painted in 1943–1946; the arms are separated from the shoulders, hands are missing, and the breasts are rendered as detachable ovals. In *Pink Angels*, 1945, "the violence increases, as flesh-colored serpentine forms hurl themselves through space, twisting and writhing, lacerated by sharp lines of charcoal and cut by shards of yellow space" (p. 4).

which is the body of this woman, in what is a desperate effort to find an image. . . . He has gone too far, but that is the only place to go." Commenting on the artist's technique, he opined that "the paint has been pushed and dragged and stretched; it has been piled in rich layers or been allowed to drip in the haste of execution. . . . The color is dry, acid, shocking" (Geist, 1953, p. 15). And, like most of the critics, Geist wondered who the woman represented. He suggested:

> She could be Miss America, vulgar, blowsy, 20 years after Atlantic City. Or the woman opposite you on the subway. Or is she the muse of painting, on whom de Kooning is wreaking a revenge? We know little about her, but she is certainly not anonymous; her eyes and breasts bulge and her teeth could bite . . . her image exists in the vast area between something scratched on the wall of a cave and something scratched on the wall of a urinal (Geist, 1953, p. 15).

In a review for *Arts and Architecture,* James Fitzsimmons, who had an interest in Jungian psychology, proposed an interpretation suggesting that the *Woman* is a "goddess" or "evil muse" who has her origin in prehistory. "I see manic excitement, near-hysteria, and a terrible struggle with a female force who, like certain Greek and Indian divinities, never drops her vapid smile." He declared that the *Women* are "the ugliest and most horridly revealing" he had seen, not in regard to their physical appearance, which he found repellent enough, but in the woman herself, "the creature or goddess they depict." He thought that de Kooning had painted the woman "in a fury of lust and hatred, and with all the skill at his command." In his opinion, "This is a bloody, hand-to-hand combat which can only end in the artist's defeat—unless the goddess be transformed, for she cannot be stabbed to death" (Fitzsimmons, 1953, p. 8). Fitzsimmons mistakenly assumed that three dabs of red paint on the torso of *Woman III* represented "bloody stab wounds." In de Kooning's mind, the dabs of red paint represented rubies. And as Shiff (2011) points out, Fitzsimmons failed to mention "the possibility that de Kooning added the three red marks to enliven part of the pictorial surface—not in aggression, hostility, but as animating, painterly rhetoric" (p. 129). Fitzsimmons further suggested that the *Woman* might be perceived as the Medusa and that her fascination to viewers might be because she is a "female personification of all that is unacceptable, perverse, and infantile in ourselves . . . all that is undeveloped." Cateforis (1991) suggests that the argument that de Kooning's female images "represented the basic instinctual forces that the unsocialized infant has not yet learned to repress," implies that for Fitzsimmons, the figures "stood for the primal libidinal power of the id" (p. 128).

Hubert Crehan, in a review for *Art Digest*, focused on the boundary between art and psychology. He wrote: "These paintings of the *Woman* are, in the strictest sense, monstrous—half symbol, half fact. They are too closely coupled with the emotions of practical life; like the shamelessly self-expressive personages of a dream, they are psychological, rather than iconographic, symbols." Crehan thought that de Kooning had failed to fuse his feelings and ideas about the *Woman* and had been traumatized by the subject, "a fatal mistake for an artist, art and psychology being mutually exclusive. Striving after an apocalyptic vision of the *Woman*, he has produced for us a Medusa and for himself a dilemma." He believed this dilemma resulted from de Kooning's decision to return to the figure after previously leaving it; but he insightfully recognized that "He can't paint without the *Woman*, yet he can't connect with her." In Crehan's opinion, "it [the paint] is applied with a contemptuous, overriding, almost orgiastic impulsiveness; the color is raw when it isn't ugly." Yet, despite the image and despite the paint, he thought that "something does come through." He concluded that de Kooning was struggling with "the new American Woman, a formidable type, who is in the *avant-garde* of her sex in the contemporary world" (Crehan, 1953). Although most men and women observed strict gender roles and complied with society's expectations during the 1950s, some women were discontented with being wives and mothers and were finding new job opportunities and a different place in society; patterns of sexual behavior were also changing, especially a rise in premarital sex that led ultimately to the "sexual revolution" of the 1960s (https://www.khanacademy.org/humanities/us-history/postwarera/ *1950s*).

William Seitz discussed the Woman paintings in a doctoral dissertation on abstract expressionism that he was writing at the time of the exhibition and submitted to the Faculty of Art History at Princeton University in 1955. His poetic interpretation of the paintings was largely overlooked until it appeared in a book almost three decades later. As Cateforis (1991) points out, Seitz found a way to weave together "the contemporary aspects of the *Women* and their supposedly timeless or mythic ones"; he also gave attention to the "erotic charge that surged from the canvases" (pp. 146–147). Seitz writes:

Huge eyes dilated and teeth set, the full-blown figures struggle against recession, flatness, and structure. The mood, established

22

in small color sketches by the central placement of a lipsticked Coca-Cola mouth clipped from periodical advertising, could not be farther from Motherwell's tenderness. De Kooning's heroine is not wife, mother, or even mistress but darling of the bar stool and barber-shop magazine, ideal of a million cinema-going males, the indulgent strumpet, a carnal product of wish-fulfillment and commercialism, frightening in her orgiastic gaiety. Excoriated with blood-reds and ugly slashes of charcoal, her effect is unprecedented. But, from the very violence and intentional vulgarity of the image, another woman takes form: a goddess of fertility. Rising from the darkness of the past or the atavistic depths of consciousness, she stands, like the ancient Cybele castration, a cult image of the eternal female (Seitz, 1983, p. 126).

Cateforis points out also that, like the proposals of Crehan, Geist, and Fitzsimmons, Seitz's interpretation evokes the dynamic of attraction and repulsion operating on de Kooning as he painted the *Women*. The artist's starting point is the image of the sexually desirable and available female seen on calendars, pinups, and *Playboy* magazine; but de Kooning violates that image to discover beneath it "the awesome, devouring goddess, with the power to destroy the male's sexual potency. The Phrygian myth of Cybele, whose demonic and insatiable sexuality drove the young god Attis to madness, leading him to castrate himself, is a powerful metaphor for the threat to male sexuality embodied in de Kooning's females" (Cateforis, 1991, pp. 147–148).[11]

This threat to the male was also discerned by Alexander Eliot; in a review in *Time* magazine titled "Big City Dames," he described the *Women* as "mighty ugly, with ox eyes, balloon bosoms, pointy teeth, and vaguely voracious little smiles" (Eliot, 1953). He considered them the inverse of the All-American Girl, and more like the women who appear in the pages of crime magazines and detective novels. They were thought to represent *femme fatales* and, therefore, a threat to male potency and social dominance.

Only Thomas Hess and another New York commentator for *ARTnews* recognized humor and an element of caricature in the paintings. Jackson Pollock, who usually got along well with de Kooning, even though there was intense rivalry between them, certainly did not see humor in the Woman paintings. In an unpleasant exchange at a party after the opening of the exhibition, Pollock, who had been drinking heavily, accused de Kooning of betrayal for having never given up being a figure painter.

A few weeks after the Janis exhibition, a retrospective of de Kooning's works from 1935 to 1953 was held first in Boston and later in Washington. Similarly to some of the New York critics, a male reviewer for the *Washington Post* described the *Women* as "huge, totemic female figures seated in squat vulgarity, seeming like idols of some obscene religion, some cult of the ugly. Their power is majestic; their brutality sublime." He asserted that *Woman II* and *Woman IV*

---

11   According to Thomas Hess, there was usually a pinup calendar hanging on a wall of de Kooning's studio during the early 1950s (Hess, 1967, p. 10).

portrayed "monstrous harridans, dripping with venom, huge with hate" (Portner, 1953, p. L3). Two years later, after *Art Digest* had been renamed *Arts*, the magazine published a more favorable review of the Woman paintings written by Leo Steinberg, who commented on images from the 1953 exhibition as well as some later images shown at the Martha Jackson Gallery in New York. Steinberg was working on a doctoral dissertation in art history at New York University Institute of Fine Art during the 1950s and had previously studied at the Slade School of Fine Art in London. He wrote that whereas "some have seen hatred or the caricature's gibe in this de Kooning apparition . . . I am unable to see ugliness or hate in these marvelous paintings. To me they suggest, on the contrary, a fierce generosity" (Steinberg, 1955, p. 46). He associated the grotesque imagery of the *Women* with de Kooning's Netherlandish background, noting that "Dutch painters alone had the stomach to love real things, to accept men and women without idealizing, Platonizing, and Italicizing them." Steinberg also commented admiringly on the artist's technique:

Much of the power of those abstract paintings derived from the compelling force with which his forms sped through a hindering medium, not merely gliding across unresisting canvas. The artist's method of constant revision and adjustment—but with each correcting stroke applied at the same blinding speed— built up his ground in deposits of stratified color, deep as the shimmer of mother-of-pearl, and suggesting, between lines of stress, the sudden baring of some split-second geology (Steinberg, 1955, p. 46).

25

Unlike Crehan's narrow interpretation that the images reflect the "new American woman," Steinberg placed *Woman* within an historical context and gave her multiple meanings: "She is a first emergence, unsteeped from a tangle of desire and fear with some millennia of civilizing evolution still ahead of her." He described her as "disastrously erotic in some remote paleolithic way. Like the Venuses of Willendorf and Mentone, she is all vulgar warmth and amplitude..." Steinberg further opined that de Kooning is not concerned with nature once removed:

His *Woman* is at once more old and young than the beauty whose appeal is to our waking taste. She is the fluid, touch-determined image of the newly-born, the remembered flesh that yielded at all points to the lover, the succubus that lies too heavy on the drifting consciousness of sleep. She is shameless and innocent, as yet too female to be feminine, part witch, part farmer's daughter, part mother, and part whore, a power too comprehensive and immediate to be wisely watched and rendered with controlling skill (Steinberg, 1955, p. 46.)

In contrast to earlier critics, Steinberg thought that de Kooning painted the *Women* out of love rather than hate. Yet, as Cateforis comments, by allowing the artist to admire "not only the nubile physique of the 'prettiest chorus girl' but also the ample, corpulent flesh of a Rubensian nude," Steinberg "sees de Kooning's images as emblems of the masculine privilege of conceiving of women purely as objects for the male gaze, to be judged by their physical appearance and sexual attractiveness, rather than by their personalities, abilities or achievements." In Cateforis's opinion, Steinberg saw de Kooning and Rubens "united in their erotic desire for the woman's welcoming flesh that will yield at all points to the male lover" (Cateforis, 1991, pp. 156–157).

The first female critic to comment publicly about the Woman paintings was Dore Ashton, who wrote a review for *Arts and Architecture* after attending the exhibition at the Martha Jackson Gallery in 1955. Unlike the male critics, she avoided linking the images to sexual violence or to the new American woman or the "eternal woman." In her opinion, "The ladies, however prepossessing they were, were instrumental works leading to this apogee of abstract power." She focused on the aesthetic aspects of the paintings and proposed an humanistic interpretation, characterizing de Kooning's work as impelled not by mythological expressions of the relations between men and women, but as a "quest for clarification of relationships . . . of man to space, time, and environment" (Ashton, 1955, pp. 33-34).[12] Cateforis (1991) suggests that "Ashton's designation of the *Women* as 'ladies' can be read as a calculated, ironic refusal to engage in the kind of discourse that Steinberg and the others had established, and from which Ashton, as a woman, felt excluded" (p. 179).

Another woman who viewed the Woman paintings in the early 1950s was a young artist named Audrey Flack, whose response at the time was similar to that of the male critics. Writing about her impressions more than six decades later, she recalls that although she loved de Kooning's work, she was upset by those paintings:

---

12  In 1960, Ashton was fired as an art critic for *The New York Times* because of her continuing positive support for abstract expressionism.

The women looked ripped apart with eviscerated body parts, one breast here, another there. They stare at you with huge terror-filled eyes, crazy grins, and clenched Chiclet teeth. Some of them have two mouths and they all look insane. When I first saw *Woman and Bicycle* in 1952, I hated it (Flack, 2016).

Over the intervening years, however, Flack went back to the paintings and studied them, and her impressions changed. For example, she says that when she stood before *Woman and Bicycle* at the Whitney Museum (Figure 3),

[I] marveled at the beauty and exciting complexity of the paint that de Kooning moved around the surface of the canvas. It kept me riveted. These paintings have continued to vibrate through the years with the hatred and love that de Kooning had for all women, and that pulsation has given them a powerful afterlife. I am still fascinated (Flack, 2016).

Although the Janis exhibition was considered a success, only a few works sold, one to Mrs. John D. Rockefeller, who bought *Woman II*, which is currently in the collection of the MoMA. More than three months later, *Woman I* was bought by the MoMA. How do we account for the mostly negative reactions to the paintings? The responses of most of the early male critics may have been determined, at least in part, by pre-existing ideas about women and long-held views as to what art should be. It is not unusual for viewers to be unsettled by new art that violates ingrained assumptions. Some of the critics may have defended themselves against the emotions the images might

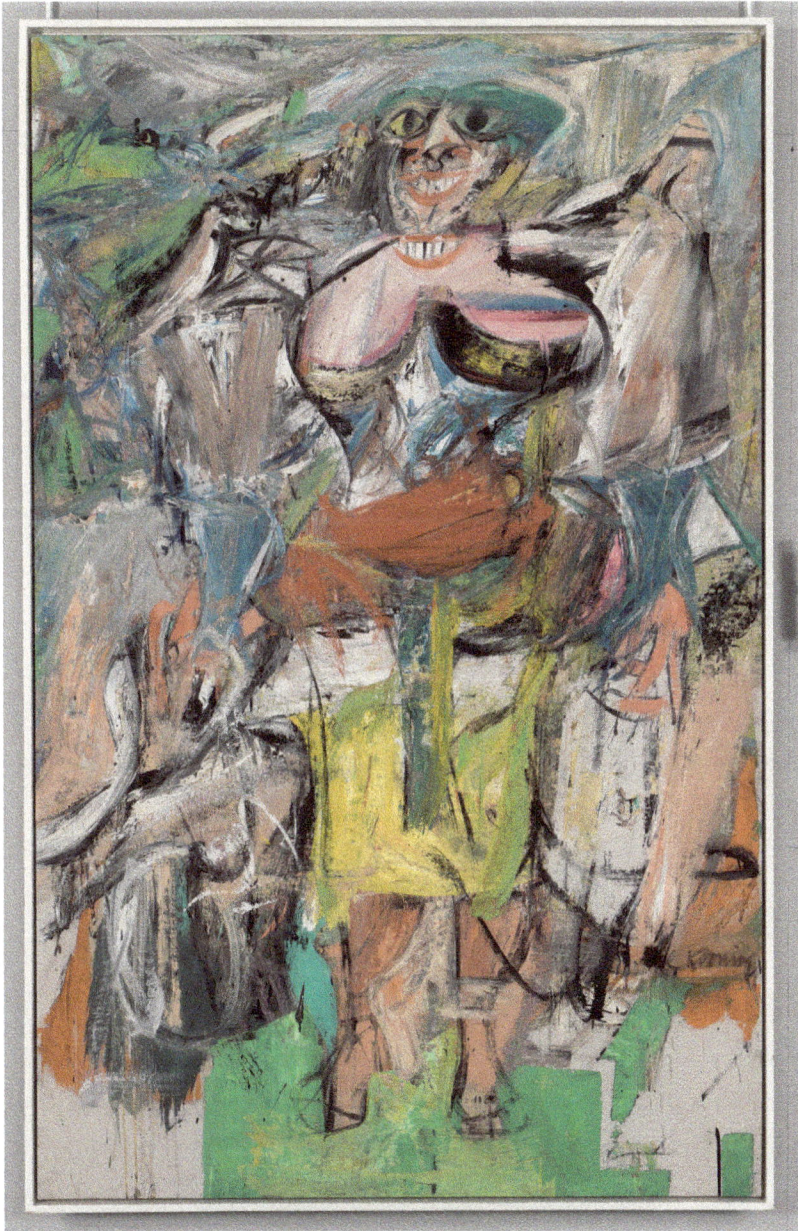

**Figure 3:** *Woman and Bicycle*, 1952–1953
Oil, enamel, and charcoal on linen, 76 ½ x 49 ⅛ inches (194.3 x 124.8 cm)
Whitney Museum of American Art, New York

elicit, whereas others may have projected their own fantasies onto the canvas and attributed them to the artist. Interpretation, as Cateforis (1991) emphasizes, is always a process of construction, which relies on both the visual properties of the work and the preexisting beliefs and conventions of the interpreter. I would add to this roles both for the unconscious and the ability of the viewer to identify with something in the internal world of the artist that influenced him to paint the way he did. I elaborate on the process of finding meaning in the paintings in later chapters.

## De Kooning's Response to the Critics

As reported by biographers Stevens and Swan (2004), and by John Elderfield (2011d) who curated a retrospective of de Kooning's work at the MoMA in 2011-2012, the ferocious intensity of the Woman paintings opened the artist to charges of misogyny. De Kooning must have been surprised and distressed by these accusations and he strongly defended himself. In a literary newspaper of the arts published in October 1955, he is reported as saying, "About my Woman series . . . they say that I hate women, that I am a homosexual, that I got the idea from one of Philip Wylie's books on Momism. Never read him until he was called to my attention by the critics . . . I have no opinion on women . . . I do not particularly stress the masculine or feminine. I am concerned only with human values" (de Hirsh, 1955). [13] As Cateforis

---

13  The only critic I found who thought that de Kooning's *Woman* bears some resemblance to the Mom made infamous by Philip Wylie was Alexander Eliot in an article in *Time* magazine, in

(1991, p. 181) points out, de Kooning made this declaration only two months before Ashton's review, in which she offered a powerful argument for his artistic humanism.

In a conversation with Selden Rodman in 1956, de Kooning suggested:

Maybe in that earlier phase I was painting the woman in *me*. Art isn't a wholly masculine occupation, you know. I'm aware that some critics would take this to be an admission of latent homosexuality. If I painted *beautiful* women, would that make me a non-homosexual? I like beautiful women. In the flesh; even the models in magazines. Women irritate me sometimes. I painted that irritation in the 'Women' series. That's all. (Rodman, 1957, p. 102; quoted in B. Hess, 2012, pp. 41–42).

Although Greenberg was at first complimentary about the series, he kindled the flames in an essay published in 1955, in which he implied that the artist expressed violence in the paintings: "When [de Kooning] left outright abstraction several years ago to attack the female form with a fury greater than Picasso's, the results baffled and shocked collectors, yet the methods by which these savage dissections were carried out were patently Cubist" (Greenberg, 1955/1995, p. 222). Such remarks ignored the fact that de Kooning never indicated any violent intent when he painted the women. In an interview with the British art critic David Sylvester in 1960, de Kooning was asked if he were

---

which he discussed works on display at the 1954 Venice Biennale (Eliot, 1954). There may have been others whom I overlooked.

concerned to get a particular kind of drama or feeling in the Woman paintings. He said:

> No. I look at them now; they look vociferous and ferocious, and I think it had to do with the idea of the idol, you know, the oracle, and above all, the hilariousness of it. I do think that if I don't look upon life that way, I won't know how to keep on being around (Sylvester, 2001, p. 51).

De Kooning also told Sylvester that painting women was just a desire related to the female figure's having been painted throughout the ages. He said, "It is a thing in art that has been done over and over, the idol, the Venus, the nude." He denied that he had made any attempt to make a comment on the age but said, "It may be turned out that way, and maybe subconsciously when I am doing it. But I couldn't be that corny." He said that when he was painting the figures, he was thinking of Gertrude Stein, "like they were ladies of Gertrude Stein" (Sylvester, 2001, p. 50).[14] De Kooning also spoke about cutting the mouths from magazine photographs and placing them on his paintings:

> I cut out a lot of mouths. First of all, I felt everything ought to have a mouth. Maybe it was like a pun, you know what I mean, but maybe it's even sexual, or whatever it is. I don't know. But anyhow I used to cut out a lot of mouths and then I painted

---

14   It is likely that de Kooning saw Picasso's portrait of Getrude Stein at the Metropolitan Museum of Art. Stein is depicted as a large, hulking figure who stares blankly across the picture rather than at the viewer. It is noteworthy that in this interview de Kooning refers to the images as "ladies," which is the word Dore Ashton used in her review five years earlier.

those figures and then I put the mouth more or less in the place where it was supposed to be. It always turned out to be very beautiful and it helped me immensely to have this real thing. I don't know why I did it with the mouth. Maybe the grin. It's rather like the Mesopotamian idol, you know. They always stand up straight looking to the sky with this smile, like they were just astonished about the forces of nature; you feel—not about problems they had with one another. That I was very conscious of; and it was something to hang on to (Sylvester, 2001, pp. 51–52).

When his artist-scientist friend Alfred Copley (known as Alcopley) asked de Kooning why he chose to paint *Woman I* as he did when he knew so many attractive women, the artist directed him to go to the basement bargain center at Klein's department store on Union Square. Alcopley later reported that he saw elegant women in the store but how greedy and nasty they could become as they fought over clothing in the bargain bins. "I looked at their faces; he had painted from memory what he had seen. It was this woman. . . . Perhaps he [de Kooning] had some memories of certain women who were otherwise angelic and lovely and became like this" (quoted in Stevens and Swan, 2004, pp. 338-339).

By the mid-1960s, there was a slight change in de Kooning's thinking about the series. It was as though he recognized the aggressiveness in the images that most viewers reacted to, but perhaps he was not conscious of at the time he painted them. In an interview for the *Saturday Evening Post*, he said:

In a way, I feel the Women of the '50s were a failure. I see the horror in them now, but I didn't mean it. I wanted them to be funny and not look sad and down-trodden like the women in the paintings of the '30s, so I made them satiric and monstrous, like sibyls (Dickerson, 1964).

Three years later, in an interview for *Newsweek*, de Kooning said:

I once wanted to paint a Madonna because all great artists did at some point . . . so I started painting women. Some of my earlier women are violent. They even scare me. But I'm not a misogynist. I have no contempt or bitterness toward women. The women I paint now are very friendly and pastoral, like my landscapes, and not so aggressive. Women are the symbol of civilization, like the Venus of Willendorf. I can't get away from the femaleness—those breasts are such great shapes. I start out with a beautiful girl in mind, and she comes out being a portrait of her mother (Shirey, 1967, p. 80).

De Kooning also suggested to this interviewer that the paintings were self-portraits: ". . . you can't always tell a man from a woman in my paintings. Those women are perhaps the feminine side of me—but with big shoulders. I'm not so big, but I'm very masculine and this masculinity comes out on canvas." In the mid-1970s, however, he told art critic Amei Wallach that people's assertions that he hated women, or that these represented the woman in him, is a lot of nonsense. Presumably referring to the concepts of the *anima* and the *animus* in analytical psychology, de Kooning said, "I've read Jung and it put me to sleep." But he did acknowledge that when he finished *Woman I*, he noticed that it looked like him, "Not the woman in me, but me" (Wallach, 1994, p. 9).

Thomas Hess was one of the insightful early critics who thought that the Woman paintings were associated with the artist's mother, who had dominated and traumatized Willem during his childhood. In a monograph published in 1968, he proposed that the regal, ferocious Woman "represents many things, but one of her aspects, surely, is that of the Black Goddess: the mother who betrays the son, gets rid of the father, destroys the home." Hess added, "There is something comical about the evocation of the Black Goddess anyhow—like a fifty-year-old man complaining that when he was five, his mother broke his bow and arrows. He still may feel the punishment, but he has to laugh at the same time. Hilarity is a balance to horror—and so is banality" (Hess, 1968, pp. 75-76). De Kooning may have described some aspects of his childhood to Hess, who, most likely, also heard some anecdotes about the artist's mother from Elaine de Kooning, with whom he had a long affair in the late 1940s and well into the 1950s (Stevens and Swan, 2004, p. 346). His comment about the broken bow and arrows, however, clearly shows that he had not thought about the possible serious, long-lasting consequences of childhood trauma. Perhaps in response to this type of biographical interpretation of the Woman paintings, de Kooning told a Dutch journalist in 1968 that he had seen a picture of a Mexican goddess to whom hearts were being sacrificed. It is not clear why, but this picture led him to speculate, "Maybe it also has something to do with my mother ... and I've just seen her again. Christ, a quivering bird, 92 years old" (Bibeb, 1968, p. 3).[15]

De Kooning certainly associated the Woman paintings with his childhood. In an interview with Harold Rosenberg in 1972, he said:

Woman I, for instance, reminded me very much of my childhood, being in Holland near all that water. Nobody saw that particularly, except Joop Sanders. He started singing a little Dutch song. I said, "Why do you sing that song?" Then he said, "Well, it looks like she is sitting there." The song had to do with a brook. It was a gag and he was laughing, but he could see it. Then, I said, "That's very funny, because that's kind of what I am doing." He said, "That's what I thought."

Rosenberg then asked, "You mean you had the water feeling even in New York?" De Kooning replied, "Yes, because I was painting those women, and it came maybe by association, and I said, 'it's just like she is sitting on one of those canals there in the countryside.' In Rotterdam you could walk for about twenty minutes and be in the open countryside. Of course, in that time it still looked like the Barbizon School, the idea of farms and ... " (Rosenberg, 1972; reprinted in Yard, 2007, p. 151).

Hess (1968) emphasized that "If the Black Goddess image was subconscious, the artist worked consciously with a number of highly developed plastic concepts" (p. 77). He described some of these

---

15  De Kooning returned to The Netherlands for the first time in 1968 to attend a retrospective of his work at the Stedelijk Museum. While there, he visited his elderly mother, who was in a nursing home.

concepts in detail, including de Kooning's "invention of forms" out of which to make a body for *Woman*, his insistence on "intimacy" as a quality of his Women, and his concept of "no environment." Any shape or part of the anatomy could stand for another part of the body: the arms of *Woman I* for example, could be parts of legs. Thus, the Cubist method of fragmenting and dislocating the anatomy of the figure, and then using collage to reassemble the figure, can be considered a mutilation of the picture rather than a savage dissection of a body (Shiff, 2011, p. 125).[16] According to Hess (1968), "[M]any of the postwar American artists . . . planned very large pictures because they worked 'close' to the painting (physically and metaphysically) and the size could embrace them — and the spectator. 'Intimate' meant breaking through the aesthetic barriers of style and establishing a direct flow between the artist and his work, between the work and the viewer" (p. 78). Hess suggests that de Kooning may not have achieved his "intimate proportions" in *Woman I*, but did so triumphantly in the Woman paintings that followed. And in *Woman I*, the environment could be both specific and general; the visual clues to the figure's location are kept purposely ambiguous. Is she in a room or in front of a house or beside a canal? Hess comments that the landscape elements played an increasingly large part in the Woman paintings as the series progressed, and finally took over the image as de Kooning returned to abstractions in 1956. "As the sense of a landscape grew stronger, however, the environmental forms tended

---

16  In Chapter 5 I discuss some psychoanalytic ideas about this breaking up and reconstruction of the figure. But here I note that, several centuries prior to de Kooning's method of reassembling the figure, the German painter and printmaker Albrecht Dürer (1471–1528) "believed that the ideal nude ought to be constructed by taking the face of one body, the breasts of another, the legs of a third, the shoulders of a fourth, the hands of a fifth — and so on" (Berger, 1972, p. 62).

to develop a likeness to the intimate proportions of the Women's anatomy" (Hess, 1968, p. 79).

In the interview with Sylvester in 1960, de Kooning said that certain artists and critics attacked him for painting something overtly figurative, "But I felt it was their problem, not mine." Despite this view, however, he must have continued to feel misunderstood and deeply hurt by the lingering charge of misogyny because he denied it again in 1975 while he was commenting on the Woman paintings:

People don't see the humor in my 'Women.' They talk too much of their tragedy and violence. As for me, I've found them comical, but with a lot of pathos because they're so ugly. I had the same attitude that a caricaturist has. You know that I have always loved comic book art. It's both true and funny, serious and silly. My 'women' are like caricatures. I'm not a misogynist and I've never had problems with women. Many of my paintings of women have been self-portraits (Hunter, 1975, p. 70; quoted in Shiff, 2011, p. 126).[17]

Why did most viewers and critics not see humor in the paintings? Might they have intuited that the comical aspect masked some deeper emotional experience of the artist? De Kooning's earlier comment to Sylvester that if he didn't look upon the amusing aspect of life,

---

17  By asserting that he had never had problems with women, de Kooning denied the conflicts he had in several long-term relationships with women, which I discuss in Chapter 6. Shiff (2011) does not indicate who translated this quotation from the French journal in which Hunter's article is published, but it may have been David Sylvester.

he would not know how to keep on being around, suggests that he relied a lot on humor to help him survive. Perhaps he used humor as a defense against intense emotions from his past. A defensive element in the paintings can be recognized in comments of Carol Duncan, an art historian and Marxist-feminist scholar, who holds the view that patriarchal ideology underlies the canonical status of de Kooning's *Women* (Cateforis, 1991). Arguing that *Woman I* is built on a pornographic base, Duncan (1989) described *Woman I* as "a big, bad mama—vulgar, sexual, and dangerous" and compared her with the Gorgon of ancient Greek art and with the Medusa. Noting that "The suggestive pose is just a knee-movement away from the open-thighed display of the vagina," Duncan discusses the more explicit act of sexual display in the art of ancient and tribal cultures and refers to the display of genitals in an ancient Etruscan Gorgon, which evokes the terrible aspect of the mother goddess presumably "intended to conjure up infantile feelings of powerlessness before the mother and the dread of castration" (p. 173). But in Duncan's opinion, the vulgarity of the image of *Woman I* is rendered harmless by the "girlie" side to her, which denies the terror and dread of the Medusa features. She writes: "The ambiguity of the image thus gives the artist (and the viewer) both the experience of danger and a feeling of overcoming it" (p. 175). Commenting on *Woman and Bicycle* in an earlier article, Duncan (1977) suggested that the woman's pronounced teeth and the second set of teeth around her neck "speak of primitive and modern neurotic fears of the female genitals," and bring to mind the ancient fantasy of the *vagina dentata*. But she similarly noted that the mixture of comic improbability and terribleness mutes the fear. Although Duncan (1989) considered de Kooning's images an objectification

39

of women's bodies, and expressions of masculine superiority over women, in her opinion, *Woman I* conveys complex and emotionally ambivalent meanings—"the fear of and flight from as well as a quest for the woman" (p. 178). And as Cateforis (1991) explains, Duncan "understood de Kooning's struggle against the fictive Woman as a metaphor for the male's psychic quest to transcend and/or control the female, identified as an image of the Terrible Mother or the 'other within'" (p. 317). Both of these images approximate the psychoanalytic concept of a "bad internal object" which I will discuss in Chapter 4.

## The Views of Other Later Critics

Despite de Kooning's rebuttals to his critics throughout the span of almost three decades, the controversy over whether the images in the Woman paintings express hostility toward women was never adequately resolved. In his doctoral dissertation, Cateforis (1991) suggests that for the early critics who accuse de Kooning of attacking the canvas violently with powerful masculine brushstrokes, "the 'act' of painting becomes a sexual one, with the arena of the canvas functioning as a substitute for the body of a woman" (p. 138). He notes that virility and violence were implicit in Rosenberg's theory of action painting, which reinforced the metaphor of the painter as violent attacker or rapist (pp. 133-135). The continuation of this view into the late twentieth century seems to have been driven by writers with an interest in feminist art history. In 1993, for example, Cathie Matthews argued that de Kooning depicts women "in a mutilated, slashed, fragmented state." In her view, "[they] are presented as other to us—hateful, illogical, fragmented. Additionally, these images diminish the power of women by depicting women as evil and as victims. Finally, these works invite and perpetuate the exploitation of women" (Matthews, 1993, pp. 182, 185).

Several years later, Fionna Barber (1999), a reader in art history at the Manchester School of Art, began to challenge feminist viewers who made links between the paintings and actual violence toward women, arguing that meaning in visual culture is not static, but is "something continually enacted through the operations of art historians, critics, and other interested viewers. Interpretation, in this view, becomes an ongoing, performative process" (p. 119). Although Barber acknowledges that she is a feminist, she tries to understand why she takes pleasure in the paintings. She opines that feminist discourse should not be confined to just one subject position, but rather open to a range of positions, including recognition of desires for the forbidden. Whereas the degree of disjunction in the twisted pose of *Woman I* (reflecting a dismembered and then reconstructed figure) is often taken as evidence of violence done to the body of the woman, Barber sees *Woman I* "as constituting a body in process: one that is embodied through the slow additive means of brushstroke onto canvas, but also one that departs from more normative representations of femininity" (p. 125). She notes that although feminist critics during the 1970s interpreted misogynistic violence in the paintings, Grace Hartigan, one of the few female painters who attended the Janis Gallery exhibition, refused to agree, and stated that "the violence is in the paint. De Kooning's women are very loving" (p. 122). In her essay published at the turn of the century, Barber argued that a reappraisal of gender issues within de Kooning's work is long overdue. She suggested that

*Woman I* may be read as an exploration of the *grotesque*, involving a dialectical relationship between order and disorder, masculine and feminine in the depiction of the body, "a point of identification beyond normative femininity and a representation which, although both threatening and deviant, is also empowering for its spectators" (p. 125).

Barber extended her discussion of gender identity as performative in 2004. In an essay titled "Abstract Expressionism and Masculinity," she comments that the use of gesture and certain types of brush stroke as signifiers of masculinity helped establish dominant readings of masculinity in abstract expressionist paintings; but she proposes that the predominance of forms of masculinity within the culture of Abstract Expressionism are as much a feature of the artist's social identity as they are of his or her work. One example Barber gave for how de Kooning and some of his male contemporaries acquired connotations of masculinity was through their style of dress, such as the T-shirt, which de Kooning often wore as he worked; the T-shirt defines the muscularity of the body and was an important agent in the construction of positive gender roles. However, Barber recognizes that the categories of masculinity and femininity are less stable now than they were during the period of Abstract Expressionism. Though abstract expressionist artists enacted various forms of masculine identity within their paintings, Barber also draws attention to their engagement with fantasies of femininity, with the depiction of women usually referenced to the mythical figures established by Carl Jung. She suggests that de Kooning's Woman paintings "can be seen as ambivalent archetypal 'other'" (Barber, 2004, p. 183). In a review of the essay, Christopher Heathcote (2020) points out that while

Barber does not suggest de Kooning was actually abusive or violent to women, she does claim "both his paintings and manner of dress exude such 'hypermasculine' values." Heathcote correctly observes that "the feminist interpretation of Willem de Kooning's *Woman* series avoids any mention of his troubled childhood, or the works' potential reference to an abusive mother."

During the second decade of the current century, critics took a more empathetic approach to de Kooning and suggested a reversal of the male-female power dynamic. In an essay written for the retrospective of de Kooning's work at the MoMA in 2011–2012, Elderfield (2011d) indicated that the charge of misogyny was invited by the "muscled, masculine, strokes" that compose the paintings. He questioned the validity of the charge, noting that one could think the artist did more violence to the bicycle in *Woman and Bicycle*, and no one ever accused de Kooning of hating bicycles. Art critic Peter Schjeldahl sensed an anguish and trauma behind the brushstrokes. In a review of the retrospective for the *New Yorker*, he wrote: "Far from illustrating Picasso-like male dominance, the female subject gains power from every swipe de Kooning takes at her, until she is a goddess, and he is effectively nothing. Some complicated anguish—worth trying to imagine—moved de Kooning to throw out the seemingly unfinished picture . . . Look at it closely. It thrills in detail, from skirmish to skirmish of a war with itself, which becomes a dance" (Schjeldahl, 2011, pp. 122-124). And Richard Brody, a film critic for the *New Yorker*, wrote: "[it is] as if the artist were pulling each brushstroke from deep in his psyche, and each were another layer or another trauma, and, with each one, telling himself—and us—'You think that's it? There's still more,' and then, agonizingly, delivering it. These paintings are psychodramatic, wildly self-psychoanalytic, and they do invite thought of de Kooning's 'complicated anguish'" (Brody, 2011).

American novelist and essayist Siri Hustvedt also commented on the brushstrokes. In her opinion, "The shock in the viewer does not come from brawny paint strokes *in relation* to the figure but from her or his immediate perception of *someone with a face* — a variously grinning, snarling, monstrous woman on a canvas made from strokes that create an illusion of hectic motion. And she looks crazy" (Hustvedt, 2016, pp. 15-16). But the question to be asked once again is: Who might this monstrous woman represent? Whereas some of the early critics thought that the paintings reflect de Kooning's struggle with both desire and fear of the emerging new type of American woman, and others linked the images with the "eternal woman," Robert Hughes, in his 1997 volume on the history of art in America, proposed that "One of the sources of the vitality of the *Woman* series was, one can only surmise, the simultaneous desire for and fear of women implanted by Mama. Its icon is the first of the paintings, *Woman I*." Hughes (1997a) described this image as "a bad dream of nurture denied, rendered with immense pictorial verve — imposing and commonplace and full of power which flows from the slashing brushstrokes into the body. When upholders of 'pure' abstraction felt that de Kooning, by painting such a creature, was backsliding into 'conservatism,' they did not grasp the greater psychic daring that *Woman I* embodied then for him and still may for us" (pp. 478–479).

To explore the possible influence of de Kooning's Mama on her son's creative work we need to review what is known about the artist's childhood and to then apply some concepts and theories from psychoanalysis and developmental psychology: in particular, psychoanalytic thinking about the nature of children's relationships with parents and the impact of early trauma. Before doing so, I will review and comment on the contributions of several scholars who have previously applied some psychoanalytic concepts to inform their interpretation of the Woman paintings. To my knowledge, these scholars are not practicing clinicians or authorities on child development.

# CHAPTER 2

# Searching for Meanings in the "Woman Paintings": The Psychoanalytic Interpretations of Non-Clinician Scholars

De Kooning said that he had no particular woman in mind when he painted *Woman 1*. In an interview in 1964, however, his wife Elaine suggested that the depictions were inspired by his mother, whom she described as having a ferocious aspect (Zilczer, 2014, p. 129). Heathcote (2020) notes that Elaine thought the hard black eyes were a giveaway. And over the five decades since Thomas Hess (1968) made his insightful comment that the paintings might refer to a dominating and traumatizing mother, several other critics and writers have suggested that the images might be associated with the artist's mother, or at least with an archetypal mother. Although these authors usually apply psychoanalytic concepts or theories to support their interpretations, they do not identify themselves as psychoanalysts or psychotherapists, and presumably lack the benefit of clinical experience. Rather than focusing on *Woman I* only, some of them comment on differences among the seven Woman paintings of the early 1950s. I will consider their contributions in chronological order.

## A Jungian Perspective

In the mid-1970s, Estella Lauter, who founded the women's studies program at the University of Wisconsin, Green Bay, discussed the entire six series of de Kooning's paintings of women from a Jungian perspective. In her opinion, "The paintings are a record of de Kooning's various encounters with images of the feminine, images that lie behind and beyond actual experiences with women. The images exist within de Kooning's psyche; yet they are transpersonal, even ancient." She suggests that the women in the third series "are greater than the beings who view them, either inside the imagined world of the paintings, or outside it. . . . they belong to the realm of myth" (Lauter, 1976, pp. 426, 430).

Lauter accepts Carl Jung's idea of the *collective unconscious*, which comprises inherited ancestral knowledge and imagery common to all mankind that is expressed through universal concepts which Jung called *archetypes*. The archetypes include birth, death, child, *anima/ animus*, the hero, the shadow, the *persona*, and the mother; these may be represented in a literal form or expressed in a figurative/metaphorical form, such as the church, the sea, the garden, and the Mother of God. One of the most important archetypes is the mother, containing her positive aspects of love and warmth as the Good Mother, or her negative aspects as the Terrible Mother, or both good and bad aspects as the Great Mother. In her psychological interpretation of de Kooning's Woman paintings of the early 1950s, Lauter is guided by this typology as set out by Erich Neumann (1963) in his book *The Great Mother. An Analysis of the Archetype*. She also accepts Jung's view that every human being has both masculine and feminine dimensions, the *animus* being the unconscious masculine aspect of a woman and the *anima* the unconscious feminine aspect of a man.

Lauter (1976) quickly realized that *Woman 1* (Figure 1), which Hess labeled the "Black Goddess," fits the image of the Terrible Mother. The figure is seated and manifests great power residing in her torso, eyes, and huge breasts, which convey a danger of being smothered or of being transfixed by her all-knowing, triumphant gaze. Her huge, even teeth are "strong enough to tear apart raw meat.... Her size and transpersonal character mark her as an archetypal figure rather than an individual woman" (p. 430). Lauter describes *Woman II* (Figure 4) as a smaller, seated figure with a closed mouth. Her breasts are huge, and she has a lopsided smile which gives the appearance of smugness, but she shows no rancor. The focal point in this image is the shoulders, which are bare, smooth, and flesh-colored. Lauter proposes that, because of the seductive quality of this image, "she belongs to the family associated with the transformative young witch" (p. 431).

Lauter does not describe *Woman III* (Figure 5); this is a standing bikini-clad figure expressing an even stronger aggressive sexuality with her enormous breasts, long scissor-like fingers, and thighs spread slightly apart (Elderfield, 2011b). Describing *Woman IV*, Lauter (1976) observes that her gaze is still direct, although a bit wild; her breasts are just as prominent; and "The mouth is open in a gasp or cry, and the teeth are prominent." In this image, the woman's power has shifted to her arms, which "come from incredibly broad unseen shoulders..." In Lauter's opinion, "the lightness, brightness, and relative clarity of the colors suggest innocence rather than gaiety ... the light heroine of American fiction who is seductive without intent" (p. 431). *Woman V* (figure 6) is a bulky figure dressed seductively in a small, brightly colored dress. She has powerful broad shoulders, a toothy grin, and one eye gazes directly at the viewer, while the other looks to the right. *Woman VI* (Figure 7) is close to *Woman I* in size: the figure is standing and depicts a terrifying image with wide vacuous eyes and the mouth "open and sucking" (p. 432). The woman's bulk is massive, and the different parts of her body are not clearly delineated except for her head and thick arms; she is surrounded by solid-colored shapes that connote sky and landscape. "Of all the figures in the series, she comes closest to being the death mother, the devourer, she who dissolves form" (p. 432). In *Woman and Bicycle* (Figure 3) the woman has an obscene smile, and she stares directly at the viewer; her pendulous breasts "hang out like signs," and she has a second set of teeth around her neck like a choker. Yet, despite the second set of teeth, Lauter describes her as "a gay figure" (p. 432).

Although Lauter considers all of the women in this series of paintings archetypal, she emphasizes that they are not uniformly negative. And, unlike most of the earlier male critics, she does not accuse the artist of misogyny. Moreover, she reports that when she showed *Woman I* to her class, "the women students were fascinated and stimulated by her rather than angered or repulsed" (p. 427). In her opinion, in this series alone, "de Kooning explores several types of feminine power: that of the old mother, of the seductive and sometimes dangerous young witch, of the beautiful idol, the mad wench, and the terrible mother" (pp. 433-434).

**Figure 4:** *Woman II*, 1952
Oil on canvas, 59 x 43 in (149.9 x 109.3 cm)
The Museum of Modern Art, New York

**Figure 5:** *Woman III*, 1952–1953
Oil on canvas, 68 x 48 ½ in (172.7 x 123.2 cm)
Collection of Steven A. Cohen

**Figure 6:** *Woman V*, 1952–1953
Oil on canvas, 60 ⅞ x 45 in (154.6 x 114.3 cm)
National Gallery of Australia, Canberra

**Figure 7:** *Woman VI*, 1953
Oil on canvas, 68 ½ x 58 ½ inches (174 x 148.6 cm)
Carnegie Museum of Art, Pittsburgh

It is not known whether de Kooning became aware of Lauter's discussion of his work, or how he might have responded to her Jungian interpretations of his Woman paintings. Unlike some of his fellow artists, de Kooning was skeptical of psychoanalysis. As I mentioned in the previous chapter, he claimed that he had read Jung's writings, but they put him to sleep. He was also dismissive of Freud, saying that "Freud messed up all of modern thought because he made formulas out of it. There were other men such as Dostoevsky who knew much more and could go anywhere" (Dickerson, 1964). On the other hand, de Kooning's artist friend John Graham, whom he met in 1929, admired both Freud and Jung and thought that the unconscious had a liberating role in the creation of art (Stevens and Swan, 2004, p. 96). Jackson Pollock was also very interested in Jung's idea of archetypes; his early works are influenced by Jungian symbolism, and he considered his later drip technique a way of expressing his unconscious. Pollock had three years of psychotherapy with Jungian analysts, which included identifying hidden meanings in many of his drawings (Sedivi, 2009). According to Edwin Denby, a poet and long-standing friend of de Kooning, "His friends would say: 'Listen Bill, you have a psychological block about finishing; you're being very self-destructive, you ought to see an analyst.' He burst out laughing, 'Sure, the analyst needs me for his material the way I need my pictures for mine'" (Denby, 1964, p. 88). De Kooning once told artist Philip Pearlstein that he had a great interest in dreams, suggesting that he did place some value on communications from the unconscious mind (Pearlstein, 1989); however, I have not found a record of any of de Kooning's dreams to examine.

## Freudian Perspectives

In 1997, the year in which de Kooning died, art historian Sally Yard was prescient in bringing Freudian ideas directly into the discussions about the Woman paintings; she focused on *Woman and Bicycle* and associated the snarling mouths with the threat of castration, interpreting the second set of teeth as a Freudian displacement upwards. Yard (2007) repeated her interpretation a decade later, in a second book about de Kooning's work. As I mentioned in Chapter 1, Carol Duncan (1977) had previously suggested that the teeth around the woman's neck bring to mind the ancient fantasy of the *vagina dentata*; but she did not employ Freudian theory in her essay. Although de Kooning had commented to David Sylvester (2001) that there might be something sexual about his emphasis on the mouth in his paintings, his biographers disagree with Yard's interpretation and opine that "The teeth of *Woman I* are not the Latinate *vagina dentata*; they are smiling American choppers without a conscience" (Stevens and Swan, 2004, p. 339). However, the suggestions of Duncan, Crehan, and Steinberg that *Woman 1* might represent the Medusa imply that the images have the potential for evoking castration anxiety. Freud (1922) had proposed that the Medusa, with artworks depicting multiple snakes for hair, represented the terrifying genitals of the mother, thereby linking the sight of her with the terror of castration.[1] In the original myth, the spectator is turned to stone when he sees the Medusa, which Freud suggested offered consolation, since the stiffening could represent

---

1    Karen Horney (1932) made an argument for the *vagina dentata* being feared because of a dread of the vagina as a devouring organ rather than a fear of the phallic teeth.

an erect penis. The British psychoanalyst Anthony Storr (1957) later disagreed and argued that being turned to stone is not equivalent to having an erection, but instead represents "being 'petrified' in face of an overwhelmingly powerful figure, which possesses both masculine and feminine characteristics: in other words, the great mother in her most destructive aspect" (p. 165).

Art historian and critic Donald Kuspit (1998, 2011), also writing from a Freudian perspective, echoed the suggestion that *Woman I* stares at the viewer like a Medusa, ready to turn men into stone.[2] Similar to Lauter, he equates the women in the third series with the archetypal Magna Mater, which Freudians refer to as the phallic woman, a phantasy that is ubiquitous in sexual perversions and conceptualized as a defense against castration. As argued by American psychoanalyst Nancy Kulish (1986), however, the phantasy of a phallic mother is not only a defense against castration anxiety, but also an expression of preoedipal anxieties linked to phantasies of a powerfully aggressive and sadistic mother (*i.e.*, the archetypal devouring "Terrible Mother").[3]

In the late 1990s, Kuspit pointed out that the proposed association of de Kooning's images of women with his mother is supported by the artist's acknowledgment that he was influenced by the *Willendorf Venus* and the Venus-like, fleshy, voluptuous women painted by Rubens. Whereas the pregnant Willendorf Venus symbolizes "sacred

---

2   Donald Kuspit completed a four-year program as an Academic Associate at the Psychoanalytic Institute of the Psychiatry Department of the New York University Medical Center during the 1980s, but he never practiced as a psychoanalyst (personal communication, December 6, 2021).

3   Here I use the word "phantasies" rather than "fantasies." As I will explain further in Chapter 4, Melanie Klein and her followers define phantasies as the unconscious psychic representations of the instincts, the objects to which the instincts are directed, and various ego defense mechanisms. The more popular term fantasy refers to conscious derivatives of unconscious phantasies, such as daydreams. Despite this distinction, many American psychoanalysts use the terms interchangeably.

mother-love—nourishing, idealized love," Rubens' Venus "symbolizes profane love; her beauty is an announcement of her perfect eroticism, an invitation to vulgar sexual use of her body" (Kuspit, 1998, pp. 281-282). Kuspit opines that de Kooning's Woman paintings of the early 1950s reflect his effort to combine these contradictory views of woman in hopes of neutralizing both; he describes the artist's gestures as both aggressive and loving. He also suggests that they show his attempts, as well as his failure, to control himself under the spell of his lust for the Venuses and need of their love and tenderness. Kuspit writes: "De Kooning hates [woman] as much as he desires her. Indeed, the greater the desire, the greater the hatred" (p. 283). In my opinion, Kuspit fails to consider the possibility that a relation between hatred and desire might have originated in deficiencies in maternal care during Willem's infancy, which I discuss in the next two chapters. In his influential book on the origins of love and hate, the Scottish psychiatrist Ian Suttie (1935) considered an infant's hate a consequence of intense separation anxiety, the ultimate appeal of a child to preserve itself from isolation and restore the love relationship with the caregiving parent.

A very different psychoanalytic perspective on de Kooning's Woman paintings was offered in 2005 by Teressa Broll. Her contribution has been overlooked by subsequent critics, probably because it is an unpublished dissertation which she submitted for a Master of Fine Arts degree at the University of KwaZulu-Natal in Pietermaritzburg, South Africa. Broll first provides scholarly reviews of the classical Freudian approach to art and the approach of Melanie Klein and her followers; she then applies theoretical concepts from the Independent British Group of Psychoanalysts, in particular, the theories of Donald Winnicott and Christopher Bollas. In so doing, she offers a reinterpretation of the role of aggression in the Woman paintings that provides an interesting alternative to the more negative interpretations that prevailed during the 1950s. Because there is some overlap of Broll's approach with my own thinking, I will defer discussion of her contribution to a later chapter.

In 2015, the art critic and theorist Rosalind Krauss attempted to answer the perplexing question of why de Kooning was unable to desert the woman as the subject of his paintings. As I mentioned in the previous chapter, she thought the artist's declaration that wherever he looks he finds the woman suggests a repetition compulsion, the explanation for which might be found in the unconscious. In her book *Willem de Kooning Nonstop: Cherchez la femme*, Krauss (2015) proposes that "Compulsively finding Woman 'wherever he looks' makes it not inappropriate to say that *woman* had become de Kooning's fetish" (pp. 31-32). I agree fully with Krauss for bringing Freud's concept of the "repetition compulsion" into the discussion, and for directing attention to the unconscious mind of the artist; I comment on these processes in considerable detail in Chapter 4. However, I disagree with Krauss's application of the fetish concept to the Woman paintings of the early 1950s. She first uses the term in a general way to denote a preoccupation or obsession without its necessarily applying to an object used for sexual stimulation. And when she then uses the term with its more specific meaning, she states that "Freud's discussion of the development of the fetish takes place in the context of the uncanny" (p. 35) for which she cites Freud's (1919) essay on the uncanny, even though Freud did not refer to the fetish in that essay. Indeed, this is the only publication by Freud that Krauss cites or quotes in her entire book, which suggests that she may not be very familiar with his writings or the extensive psychoanalytic literature on fetishism. She has obviously read Freud's (1927) essay on fetishism, however, because she refers to his comment that the fetish is associated with the last thing the child sees before the fateful glimpse of the female genital when looking up mother's skirt; she also mentions Freud's example of a man whose fetish was a "shine on the nose" (the German word for "shine" being *Glanz*, which is homophonic with "glance"). Krauss proposes that, for Freud, such a glance "from the vantage upward from below ... makes it significant that de Kooning would organize his own vantage on the monumental Women upward from below" (p. 35). She prepares the reader for her proposal in a chapter titled *Totem and Taboo* by quoting de Kooning's biographers, who opine that *Woman I* is the depiction of a relationship: "The perspective is that of a child looking up at an adult" (Stevens and Swan, p. 339).

Freud (1919) described "uncanny" as a strange feeling—especially a feeling of horror and dread—related to something that is frightening yet feels both familiar and unfamiliar at the same time. He gave examples such as seeing one's double or ghosts, and the male child's experience of seeing a girl's genitals. Freud related the uncanny to the "compulsion to repeat" by suggesting that the uncanny is in reality not something new, but something that has been repressed and threatens to return to conscious awareness. His earliest discussion of fetishism is in 1905, in *Three Essays on the Theory of Sexuality*. There he describes the fetish as some part of the body, such as the foot or hair or a piece of clothing that acquires a sexual interest and may substitute for the sexual partner. He likened such substitutes to the fetishes in which some primitive tribes believe that their gods are embodied.[4] He thought that the situation only becomes pathological when the desire for the fetish becomes not merely a necessary condition but takes the place of normal sexual intercourse with the sexual partner.

Though Freud related the choice of a fetish to some sexual impression, usually made in early childhood, it was not until 1910, in a footnote he added to a second edition of the *Three Essays*, that he first asserted that the fetish stands for the "missing" penis of the woman. In 1927, in his essay on fetishism, Freud again made clear that the fetish could be a normal part of erotic life and a subsidiary finding in analysis, not one that brings a person into treatment. He again described the fetish as a substitute for the woman's (the mother's) illusory penis that the male child did not want to relinquish, because of the fear that if a woman has been castrated, he is in danger of losing his own penis. Freud (1927) concluded that the fetish is thus "a token of triumph over the threat of castration and a protection against it" (p. 154). It was in this essay that Freud suggested that the reason why the foot or shoe is often the chosen fetish is that an inquisitive boy peered at the woman's genitals from below, from her legs up, or a piece of underclothing might have been the child's last impression before the uncanny and traumatic glimpse of the female genital. He maintained, however, that it is not always possible to discover with certainty how a fetish is determined.

---

4   The word *fetish* is derived from the Portuguese word *feitiço*, which was used originally to refer to objects used in religious practices by indigenous peoples of West African countries. Nowadays, *feitiço* may refer to something benign, such as a charm or an enchantment, but also to something with supernatural qualities and magic power such as witchcraft, juju, or witchery (see https://en.wikipedia.org/wiki/Fetishism/).

Krauss is correct that once a fetish is installed as a safeguard against castration anxiety, it represents the "female phallus" and will be repeated over and over. She opines that most of the Woman paintings of the early 1950s "organize their vantage on the female body according to the fetish *Glanz der Nase*, upward from below. This is particularly prescient in *Woman IV*, where the blue hemispheres of knees and skirt rhyme with the heavy spherical breasts. In *Woman V*, the yellow parallelogram of her lap reinforces the perspectival glance upward and the distance between legs and body. Perhaps this fetish character explains de Kooning's determination to encode that perspective on the Women which made it so difficult for him to 'stop'" (Krauss, 2015, p. 36).

Krauss goes on to suggest that her "premonition of de Kooning's Woman-as-fetish" might explain not only the figure's compulsively repeated monstrous and threatening character, but also her exaggerated sexual attributes, such as her enormous breasts and splayed legs, which she observes in *Woman III*. She suggests that a triangular patch between the legs of *Woman I* may indicate the woman's genitals. And she considers even more significant "the way the neck and head surmount the prominent breasts to suggest the erect phallic form of castration denial" (p. 37).

By introducing the defensive function of the fetish, Krauss unintentionally extends Sally Yard's suggestion that the necklace of a toothed mouth in *Woman and Bicycle* represents the *vagina dentata*. However, Krauss' perception that "the woman swells into the fetish form of the phallus, with monstrous breasts and pubis" contrasts with the perception of critics who have suggested that *Woman I* could represent the Medusa (*i.e.*, the threatening female genitals). Of course, both perceptions could relate to the powerful aspect of the Great Mother, but Krauss does not make that suggestion. Moreover, she equates the whole woman with a phallus rather than limiting the fetish to a body part or inanimate object, such as a foot, shoe, bracelet, or piece of fur. Although in psychoanalysis the unconscious phantasy of a phallic woman is considered ubiquitous in sexual perversions (Bak, 1968), equating the whole "non-phallic" female body with a fetish is unusual, and to my knowledge found only in the perversion known as *macrophilia*, which involves using images of a giant-sized woman to attain sexual arousal. Websites on the Internet have helped advance the development of this perversion, but to date the only case reported in the psychoanalytic literature is an account of a male artist whom I treated with psychoanalytic psychotherapy (Taylor, 2019). Though my patient's fantasy of a giant woman functioned partly to overcome castration anxiety and ensure sexual arousal, the woman always had a vagina (and not a penis) which, in the fantasied scenario, devoured imaginary small men (an annihilation fantasy consistent with Horney's [1932] formulation). In the 1930s, Betram Lewin (1933), who was a highly regarded member of the New York Psychoanalytic Society and Institute, argued that there is a "symbolic equation" between body and phallus in the unconscious; he illustrated this interpretation with several vignettes from his analytic work with female patients. Lewin's view has been largely dismissed as Freudian theories of female sexuality have been revised and replaced by the contemporary psychoanalytic view that the equivalent of castration anxiety in a girl is a fear of an attack on her genital organs (internal reproductive organs and *introitus*) and is unrelated to fantasies about the loss of or wish for a penis (Balsam, 2018).

Krauss's interpretation of the *Women* as de Kooning's fetish (if she means a sexual fetish) could imply that the artist experienced significant castration anxiety. As I will describe in a later chapter, he did experience anxiety and panic attacks, but there is no biographical evidence that he experienced any difficulty with sexual potency or had a sexual deviation. De Kooning's biographers describe the artist having as many as seven long-term relationships and several short-lasting affairs, as well as multiple flings with women. Krauss also overlooks ways in which psychoanalytic thinking about castration anxiety in men has broadened and is currently used not only to signify fear of damage to or loss of the genitalia, but also metaphorically to indicate a threat to or loss of any valued human characteristic or function, including a person's creative talent (Taylor, 2016). Whereas the emphasis in classical psychoanalytic theory has been on the boy's fear of being castrated by the powerful father as punishment for his oedipal wishes, many contemporary psychoanalysts now use the term "castration" symbolically "to refer to feared punishment in general and to powerlessness at the hands of a powerful figure" (Eagle, 2011, p. 160). There were probably occasions when de Kooning experienced anxiety and doubts about his capability as an artist. Indeed, according to Curtis Pepper (1983), when the work was not going well, de Kooning "suffered from doubts, and from fears of losing his creativity"; he would then go for long walks during the night. However, he was a fiercely independent person and not intimidated by authority. He was quite capable of standing up to powerful men, as for example when he told Clement Greenberg to get out of his studio after being told that he should no longer draw the figure.

## An Unorthodox Perspective

A more complex interpretation of the Woman paintings was proposed in 2020 by Marlene Clark, who teaches in the Division of Interdisciplinary Studies at the City College of New York. In contrast to critics before her who made Jungian or classical Freudian interpretations, Clark (2020) takes an approach that abandons the binary models of sex and gender and recognizes a contemporary emphasis on the fluidity of sexual and gender identities, a shift in perspective that is also being discussed among many practicing psychoanalysts (*e.g.*, Blass, 2020; Katz, 2018; Saketopoulou, 2020). In Clark's opinion, these paintings should be read as *self-representational* rather than *self-biographical*; she thinks they are self-portraits rather than representations of de Kooning's mother or of his attitudes toward women. She regards interpretations linking the images to the artist's mother as pathographic readings and disagrees with earlier critics who attributed misogyny to the artist. In her book *The Woman in Me,* Clark (2020) declares that when she walked into the Abstract Expressionism annex at the MoMA and saw *Woman I* for the first time, she immediately burst out laughing. In those days, she was unschooled in the abstract expressionist movement and in the artist's career, but for more than a decade she had studied and written about transvestite theater as it was performed in medieval England and at Shakespeare's Globe. She writes: "Clearly what I saw before me was an image of one burly man, likely Willem de Kooning, in a dress and heels. I silently congratulated myself for 'getting it.' . . . there was not a doubt in my mind that I was standing before a painting that, despite its title, was a self-portrait of the artist, obviously a man" (pp. 17–18). Confident that her interpretation is correct, Clark asserts that "due to their own myopia regarding both biological sex and gender," previous critics (mostly male) see "what they superimpose upon the paintings based on their own tendencies and fear of or repulsion by homosexuality" (p. 15).[5] And even more strongly she writes:

> . . . it would seem the Medusa-like shock effect of *Woman I* froze the critics in their tracks, casting a spell that left them unable to respond to much more than de Kooning's retention of the figure and that toothy grin. Once their own mouths regained locomotion, they in unison sang as a chorus, conjuring up every image of every good-time girl they could raise in response. Alternatively, they thought of goddesses of all stripes, witches, prostitutes, and castrators. And eventually all eyes turned to Elaine de Kooning, and that woman of woman in the room—de Kooning's mother, Cornelia (Clark, 2020, p. 176).

Clark acknowledges that her proposal is somewhat "unorthodox" and firmly indicates that she makes no claims, guesses, or assumptions as to de Kooning's sexual orientation. She suggests that de Kooning released biological sex from its constricting binaries and "out of his reflection he paints a 'third thing,' one that could be either/or, or neither/nor" (p. 15). In her opinion, the artist represented himself as a cross-dresser in each of his six paintings, *Woman I to Woman VI*. She perceives a close resemblance of the faces of the Women, especially the

---

5 Clark (2020) states that Grace Hartigan and Elaine de Kooning, "themselves both artists, provide the only extant female reaction to the paintings" (p. 4, Fn. 11). She overlooks the reaction to the paintings recalled many years later by artist Audrey Flack (2016) and the early review of some of the paintings by writer and art critic Dore Ashton (1955).

face of *Woman III* ("The large 'bug eyes', the upturned porcine nose, those teeth!"), with the features of de Kooning's own face in his 1947 *Self-Portrait*. She asks, "Could it be that rather than deliberately making his Woman ugly, de Kooning, as a comic aside, just superimposed a less than flattering image of himself onto the front of their heads?" (p. 35).[6] It is quite possible, however, that de Kooning's distortion of the face was influenced by his interest in Chaim Soutine's paintings, including portraits and self-portraits in which Soutine often distorted the features. According to Zilczer (2016), de Kooning and Elaine had the opportunity to view the large collection of Soutine's work at the Barnes Foundation in early June 1952. As I mention further on, de Kooning would also have seen some of Soutine's work at earlier times.

In Clark's view, de Kooning consciously created the *Women* as comical images of himself as a way of being playful; she buttresses this opinion with his statement, "I think it had to do with the idea of . . . above all the hilariousness of it" (Sylvester, 2001, p. 51). However, Clark seems unaware of Zilczer's (2014) reminder that, during the 1930s, Gombrich and Kris (1938; Kris, 1936) proposed that caricaturists express hostility by deforming and degrading their subject and may introduce a comic element as a way of overcoming fear. In other words, the comical element may serve a defensive function, as Carol Duncan (1989) seemed to recognize. Clark offers further support

---

6  Clark fails to report that in de Kooning's earlier works in which male figures are thought to be self-portraits, the men's faces are not distorted (*e.g.*, a drawing titled *Self-portrait with Imaginary Brother*, ca. 1938; and an untitled painting of a young man and a boy with a framed painting of a woman's head between them, ca. 1937) (T. Hess, 1959; Zilczer, 2014, p. 40). Furthermore, as Shiff (2011) points out, the head of *Woman III* (and also *Woman V*) is concave at the left and convex at the right; the head in the 1947 *Self-Portrait* is convex all around. In addition, the large bulging eyes and flared nostrils in some of the Woman paintings can be observed in de Kooning's *Manikins*, ca. 1939–1942. Polcari (1991, p. 269) noted how the facial features resemble works from the *Picasso: Forty Years of his Art* exhibition in 1939.

for her interpretation by citing some of de Kooning's remarks to interviewers such as, "You can't always tell a man from a woman in my painting. Those women are perhaps the feminine side of me—but with big shoulders" (Shirey, 1967, p. 80); and "Many of my paintings of women are self-portraits. I never thought about which sex they would belong to" (Hunter, 1975).[7] Clark argues also that de Kooning only referred to the image as a "figure" or "thing" and never as a woman. But she overlooks part of the 1960 interview with Sylvester, in which de Kooning said that his desire to paint the *Women* "had to do with the *female* painted through all the ages, all those idols" (my italics) (Sylvester, 2001, p. 49). In the same interview, he said, "It became compulsive in the sense of not being able to get hold of it and the idea that it really is very funny, you know, to get stuck with a *woman's* knees, for instance" (my italics). Contrary to Clark's belief, these statements indicate that de Kooning regarded his subject as a woman, even though he gave her large shoulders and a massive torso. Recall also that he said, "I can't get away from the femaleness . . . I start out with a beautiful girl in mind, and she comes out being a portrait of her mother" (Shirey, 1967, p. 80). In a lecture titled "Clarity in Confusion," which de Kooning delivered in November 1952, he is reported to have argued that confusion is a normal state of development for all artists, which Zilczer (2016) suggests "likely reflected his struggles with the Woman series" (p. 86); the paintings he ends up with are something other than what he started out with.

Clark thinks that the massiveness of the *Women* is consistent with the images' being self-portraits, but as art historian Richard Shiff

---

7  According to Clark (2020, p. 36), this quotation was translated from French by David Sylvester.

points out, de Kooning mentioned Gertrude Stein a number of times and would have seen Picasso's portrait of her at the Metropolitan Museum of Art, "an image possessing the authority and power de Kooning associated with motherhood as well as comparable to his own *Woman I*" (Shiff, 2011, p. 230). As Shiff further notes, "the association of massiveness with motherhood is a common one, derived from the infantile experience of being very close to something very big" (p. 299, Fn. 502).[8] Referring to his mother in 1954, de Kooning quietly said, "She's only five feet tall, but to me she looms ten" (Lieber, 2000, p. 40). De Kooning also referred to the Venus of Willendorf, which is only 11.1 centimeters tall, but is carved to emphasize large breasts and rounded abdomen and hips that make this figurine a Mother goddess, or goddess of fertility.

Like Estella Lauter, Clark comments on several differences among the Woman paintings, but rather than reading them as different versions of the Great Mother, she proposes that de Kooning puts some aspect of himself into each one of them, both physical and metaphorically. In her opinion, "as we move from *I to VI*, the Woman evolves, from the transvestite (*Woman I* and *II*), to the non-binary body (*Woman III and IV*), to a return to the transvestism of *Woman I* and *Women II*, with yet another twist (*Woman V*) and finally to nothingness that follows bodily disintegration altogether (*Woman VI*)" (Clark, 2020, p. 37). Clark uses "transvestism" as an umbrella term for cross-dressing that occurs on a "spectrum of sexual identification" with those on one side "who are comfortable with their biological sex but still enjoy dressing as

---

8 I am reminded of some of Henry Moore's large sculptures of a maternal figure, some with a child.

the opposite sex on occasion, to those on the other, who feel sexual reassignment surgery marks their only path to authenticity, as well as any number of practices somewhere in between" (p. 22). Although cross-dressing may be multi-determined, Clark fails to adequately point out that in psychoanalysis transvestism refers to a specific form of cross-dressing which is engaged in by some heterosexual men to protect their masculine identity; dressing in woman's clothing enables them to become sexually aroused and achieve an erection, thereby triumphing over childhood trauma of being threatened with the loss of masculinity and being humiliated by powerful women (Stoller, 1975). In this regard, transvestism functions like a fetish to overcome castration anxiety, but it also involves an object relation; by way of a vertical split in the ego, the transvestite enacts a drama in which his identity oscillates between a powerful phallic woman and a helpless humiliated boy (Taylor, 1980). In contrast, homosexual cross-dressing may function to caricature the female, and to flaunt homosexuality. Other cross-dressers include bisexual individuals, and transgender and transsexual individuals. Transsexual males do not value having a penis and would prefer to have female genitals. Clark does make a distinction in her interpretation that *Woman I* is not just any transvestite; she is Willem de Kooning in drag" (p. 68). She comments that he is not attempting to depict himself as a real woman but presents a comic version of himself as a man in a dress.[9]

Clark points out that *Woman II* (Figure 4) is smiling, her breasts appear soft, she is wearing a small hat, and she has an open book

---

9   Clark proposes that de Kooning did not disclose that he was "playing" with gender or sexual identity in the Woman paintings because he knew that, in the 1950s, it would lead to questions about his sexual orientation.

turned upside-down in her lap. Her shoulders and arms appear immense. Noting that there is a tradition for artists to paint pictures of women reading a book, Clark gives examples of paintings by Rembrandt and Picasso that may have influenced de Kooning. But she is also struck by the areas of blue-green paint surrounding the woman, which give a "marine quality" to the painting. Like Clark, I observed the sea-like color of the environs in *Woman II* and also in the lower part of *Woman I*, and immediately thought of de Kooning's comment in his interview with Rosenberg in 1972 that *Woman I* seemed like a woman sitting by a canal, which reminded him very much of his childhood, being in Holland near lots of water.

Clark goes on to suggest that the hat worn by *Woman II*, with its top ending in upward points, resembles a crown, and that the shoulder area in the painting could be read as a mantle or back of a throne-like chair, further suggesting precedents in the European tradition. Even with parts of the face painted with the color blue, "...*Woman II* is a strikingly aquatic creature" and "As a nymph newly emerged from the sea, the figure's face displays the transparency found in much of sea life..." (p. 103). Clark then turns to the psychoanalytic concepts of introjection and projection and points out that among de Kooning's introjections would have been "childhood memories of waterlogged Rotterdam and stories of sea creatures, many images and impressions of his lived experience in New York City and on Long Island, the parts of his significant others who fed into his ego, and, of course, a large gulp of his mother" (p. 108). She correctly indicates that it would be a mistake to interpret the images in the Woman paintings as depictions of these objects, or even aspects of them, because a person fuses introjects with his or her own subjectivity and may then at times project some aspect of the self which is "constructed out of the flotsam and jetsam of innumerable introjections" (p. 108). Clark opines that "what *Woman II* expresses may be de Kooning's comic envisagement of his own interior life, *vis-à-vis* women yes, but including so much more, and not, as has been argued for decades, a comically misogynistic envisagement of women" (p. 109). She suggests that de Kooning consciously and unconsciously internalized not only the female models of Ingres as his inspiration, but also Ingres' painting of Napoleon, which she thinks in some respects resembles *Woman II*. Clark's point is that whatever de Kooning internalized was "recycled, so to speak, and then added to his own interior montage so that what is projected onto the canvas—including its color field—becomes a mirror reflecting himself back to him" (p. 109).

I largely agree with Clark's understanding of introjection and projection, but I believe that she fails to consider the internal object relations that arise from the internalization of experiences with significant others, especially during childhood. Her basic assumption that "He becomes her; she becomes him" (Clark, 2020, p. 59) needs further elaboration to explain the repetition-compulsion that Krauss (2015) suspects underlies de Kooning's inability to desert the woman as the subject of his paintings. I will discuss these concepts in more detail in Chapter 4 and offer my own interpretations.

Clark has the impression that, because of the popular interest in Freud and Jung in the early 1950s, psychoanalytic explanations of the Woman paintings were proposed almost from the outset. She believes that critics "most readily related the appearance of the Woman to subliminal images drawn from de Kooning's relationship/s with either his mother, his wife Elaine, or both" (p. 14). She states that some critics looked to aspects of the artist's childhood and his disrupted family relationships. However, detailed information about de Kooning's childhood and adolescence did not become available until 1996, when Judith Wolfe completed her doctoral dissertation on the artist's early life, training, and work in Holland. Mark Stevens and Annalyn Swan began their research for a biography of de Kooning in the mid-1990s, but their book was not published until 2004.[10] The review by Fitzsimmons (1953) in *Arts and Architecture* may have been influenced partly by his interest in Jungian psychology, but the earliest article I found that offered a psychoanalytic perspective on the Woman paintings was Lauter's 1976 paper, in which she applied Jungian ideas. And, as I mentioned, Sally Yard brought Freud into the conversation in 1997. Clark mentions that at the time of a retrospective of de Kooning's work at the Whitney Museum in 1983–1984, Elaine de Kooning again connected the Woman paintings of the 1950s with de Kooning's mother, and that "This insight sent Donald Kuspit, among others, running straight to Freud" (p. 14). She did not say how far or for how long Kuspit had to run, but his article, which Clark quotes, was not published until 1998. As I indicated earlier, Thomas Hess suggested a connection between the paintings and de Kooning's mother in 1968, but the minimal biographical information he relied on had probably mostly come from Elaine.

---

10   Some friends of de Kooning's wife apparently thought she was the model for *Woman I*, but Elaine was quick to dismiss this, and in 1953 had photographer Hans Namuth take a photo of her beside the painting to demonstrate that it had nothing to do with her. However, Namuth positioned Elaine before the painting in such a way that a painted hand (or claw) seemed to be resting on her shoulder, as though she was the Woman's daughter. Elaine apparently appreciated the photo for its joke (Stevens and Swan, 2004, p. 344; Zilczer, 2014, p. 129).

In her discussion of *Woman III* (Figure 5), Clark moves away from Freudian criticism, which she argues links de Kooning's mother with the artist's presumed hatred or disdain of women, and from Jungian criticism, which looks for signs of the artist's "anima animating" the paintings; she moves instead toward an "object-relations approach," with which she hopes to highlight "a speculative look into de Kooning's interior life" (p. 112). Clark applies Melanie Klein's ideas about the infant's phantasies of a "good" nurturant breast and a "bad" withholding breast; Otto Kernberg's synthesis of Freudian drive theory and object relations theory, and his notion of the splitting of both self and objects and the need for integration of "part-object" into "whole object" representations; Heinz Kohut's description of mirroring, idealizing and twinship transferences; and Janine Chasseguet-Smirgel's emphasis on the child's need to differentiate between the sexes and between generations.[11] Whereas in the first two Woman paintings the figure is sitting, *Woman III* is standing, which allows Clark to observe that she does not appear to be fully clothed or has pulled up her skirt to keep it from getting wet in the water in which she is standing.[12] She perceives the lower pelvic area as exposed; there is a large black V indicating the groin, and below it an inverted black V dangling between the legs and along the inner side of the thighs. Clark proposes that this part of the body abstractly expresses genitals "that are either/or, neither/nor" and thereby draws attention to the sexual ambiguity and gender ambivalence that she also observes in some of

---

11   It is highly doubtful that the French psychoanalyst Chasseguet-Smirgel would have considered herself an object relations theorist. She held the Freud Professorship at University College in London in 1982–1983, at which time she was preparing material for her book *Creativity and Perversion*, which Clark cites as her source.

12   Perceptions vary; John Elderfield (2011b), for example, thinks the woman is wearing a bikini.

the other paintings (p. 126). In her view, this canvas reveals "a turn from transvestism to transsexuality" (p. 112).

Clark (2020) then draws on Stevens and Swan's account of de Kooning's childhood upbringing and argues that earlier interpretations of the Woman paintings focus only on the negative experience with his mother, and "[leave] aside the other half of the equation, the 'good breast,' or even the 'good-enough' mother" (p. 129). She suggests that rather than interpreting the large breasts of *Woman III* as engulfing to the point of suffocation, and thus terrifying, "Could not these breasts just as easily represent endless nourishment to countless infants in perpetuity?" (p. 130). In Clark's opinion, "as the critical history highlights, some [critics] can see only one aspect, usually the 'bad' breast, and not the other, the 'good' breast" (p. 131). She suggests that both aspects are present in the Woman paintings, but critics mired in the "paranoid-schizoid" position of mental functioning see only the "bad" breast aspect and are unable to achieve an integration.[13] Applying what she refers to as the "Kernbergian triangle" of a subject (viewer or the artist), object (a good or bad breast), and affect, Clark proposes that the affect could flow not only from the internalized objects of the artist, but also from the internalized objects of the viewer. In other words, "it could be said that in addition to relating to the painting as an object based on one's own object/affect dynamic, one also participates in the artist's object relation by way of transference. Hence the 'split' reception by viewer as well as artist" (p. 132).

---

13  The paranoid-schizoid position was first described by Melanie Klein to denote a mode of mental functioning in infancy which involves the splitting of early experiences into good and bad and keeping them separate and distinct by linking them respectively with an idealized good object and a persecutory bad object. The splitting protects the infant's good pleasurable experiences from bad, frustrating, persecutory experiences.

I agree with Clark that a painting might activate an internal object relation in the viewer that has some resemblance to an internal object relation in the artist, but I would not necessarily label this as transference. It might simply be that the emotions expressed in the painting arouse certain affective responses in the viewer, just as one might experience when listening to music. De Kooning said: "I paint the way I do because I can keep putting more and more things in—like drama, pain, anger, love, a figure, a horse, my ideas of space. Through your eyes it becomes an emotion or an idea. It doesn't matter if it differs from mine, as long as it comes from the painting, which has its own integrity and intensity" (Schierbeek, 2005, p. 43).

Clark wonders if the tiny skirt of *Woman III* has "been hiked up flirtatiously, perhaps to keep it from getting wet in the water in which the figure stands on spindly pink legs" (p. 125). Zilczer (2014, p. 120) points out that de Kooning would have been familiar with Soutine's painting *Woman Wading*, ca. 1931, which was based on Rembrandt's *Woman Bathing in a Stream*, 1654. She suggests that the influence of Soutine's painting is most apparent in the frontal pose of *Woman V*; I think it is also apparent in the stance of *Woman III*. According to Israeli art historian and author Avigdor Posèq (2001), Soutine made three versions of this subject in the early 1930s, and a fourth version in 1942. Whereas in Rembrandt's painting the woman's chemise is raised high enough to display her intimate parts, the first two of Soutine's versions omit the lower parts of the woman's body; in the other two versions the women raise their dresses only to their knees, "their gesture evoking a sense of shame and modesty which is the very opposite of the suggestive pose of Rembrandt's version" (Posèq, 2001, p. 261). Soutine painted only one female nude (a three-quarter-length girl with

76

her arms pressed to her body and both hands covering her genital region). Posèq suggests that the artist's avoidance of depicting the female genitals reflects his being raised in an orthodox Jewish society with its harsh restrictions on any overt manifestations of sexuality. As I have already mentioned, de Kooning was a strong admirer of Soutine's work, especially the sensual way in which he applied the paint. Even prior to seeing the collection at the Barnes Foundation in 1952, he would have seen some of Soutine's paintings exhibited at New York galleries during the late 1930s and the 1940s (Zilczer, 2016); he probably also attended a retrospective of Soutine's work at the MoMA in October 1950. In Zilczer's (2014) opinion, Soutine's work influenced the caricature-like imagery of the Woman paintings of the early 1950s with their "seemingly unbridled gestures, active brushwork and expressive distortions of face and body ..." (p. 112). Carolyn Lanchner (2011), a former curator of painting and sculptor at the MoMA, notes that the hands of *Woman II* closely resemble the hands in Soutine's *Woman in Red*.

Continuing with her analysis of *Woman III*, Clark attempts to apply Kohut's concept of a mirroring transference by arguing that "de Kooning's mother did at times mirror Bill back to himself [that he was] the apple of her eye, the love of her life" (p. 133). Although she acknowledges that de Kooning was often beaten by his mother during his childhood, Clark is guided by a single anecdote mentioned in Stevens and Swan's (2004) biography of the artist, which leads her to claim that his mother "also taunted him with seduction, even in old age" (p. 133). According to the anecdote, when the artist's mother was visiting de Kooning in America during the summer of 1954, she apparently revealed to his friend Joop Sanders that she and

Willem used to go to the movies and hold hands. To me, it seems rather doubtful that much (if any) handholding occurred, given that the biographers and de Kooning's relatives describe the artist's mother as a tyrannical woman, who was not affectionate and lacked maternal feelings.[14] Moreover, as I will mention in the next chapter, based on conversations with the artist about his childhood, painter Robert Dash concluded that Willem naturally wanted his mother's love, but she "gave him anything but motherly love" (Hall, 1993, p. 20). Nonetheless, Clark opines that "de Kooning's mother's rancid hatred of her son was only one manifestation of their relationship, the other being her overweening, sexually suggestive love (an obvious confusion of generations)" (p. 136). Clark obviously exploits the anecdote to support her application of Chasseguet-Smirgel's theory that a seductive mother can contribute to a male child's failure to differentiate between the sexes and generations, a failure that the French analyst considered characteristic of perversions. She writes:

If we think of Abstract Expressionism as an historical rupture, and of de Kooning's Woman as an aperture through which to view the destruction of 'sexual reality and truth,' we have a fairly apt description of de Kooning's project with the figure throughout his career, based as it is upon a 'confusion' between the sexes, if not generations. Chasseguet-Smirgel would point to this conflation of the sexes as evidence of de Kooning's pregenital personality organization, which shows up in the 'confused' genitals of *Woman III* . . . (Clark, 2020, p. 136).

---

14    I describe de Kooning's mother's personality and other aspects of the family history in Chapter 3.

Clark brings de Kooning's father into her formulation by mentioning the artist's memories of "impressive, but forbiddingly high starched collars" his father wore and the stamping of the hooves of the horses or ponies that pulled the father's delivery wagons, and how de Kooning said he wanted to get their feel into his paintings. In her opinion, he achieves this wish in *Woman III*, the upper torso being "undeniably masculine, strong, almost omnipotent" (p. 134). What Clark omits from Chasseguet-Smirgel's theory of perversion is that it involves a *failure* of the boy to identify with the phallic father, a regression to the anal-sadistic phase of development and idealization of its derivatives, and the formation of a fetish representing not only the mother's phallus but also a fecal phallus, which the boy considers superior to his father's penis. Moreover, as I have reviewed elsewhere (Taylor, 2019), Chasseguet-Smirgel (1984a) regards the creative paintings or writings of perverse individuals as "false" or inauthentic. If Clark believes de Kooning were simply being playful and comical in depicting sexual ambiguity of the women, why would she apply Chasseguet-Smirgel's theory of perversion to suggest that the artist had a "pregenital personality organization, which shows up in the 'confused' genitals of *Woman III*"? There is also little to support her view that "the destruction of 'sexual reality and truth' [provides] a fairly apt description of de Kooning's project with the figure throughout his career . . . " (p. 136).

Addressing de Kooning's unwillingness to forsake the figure and join his fellow abstract expressionist painters, Clark (2020) argues that his paintings reveal as well as conceal:

What he conceals is his 'woman's' biological sex. What he reveals instead is a series of fusions: Klein's 'good' breast and 'bad' breast, Kernberg's 'split' between subject ('artist') and object (Woman), and Kohut's 'twinship' with the idealized father-figure and mirrored mother-figure are all portrayed on this canvas, made literal in the amalgamation of vagina and penis. For just as *Woman III* reveals the presence of these dualities in all of us, exposing as well in this melding the lifelong work of integration, so too does it conceal differentiation between the sexes, showing us all the fluidity of the male/female dyad (pp. 137-138).

Clark mostly agrees with Lauter's (1976) description of *Woman IV*, and considers this image a "positive" figure, but reads the smile as mirthful rather than innocent. She observes that, like *Woman I* and *Woman II*, *Woman IV* appears to be sitting; she holds a book which is closed and by her side, not on her lap as it is in *Woman II*. Although the lower part of *Woman IV's* legs are not depicted, there appears to be water at the bottom of the painting. The thighs are spread apart, giving the sense of an exposed genital area; and similar to *Woman III*, the genitalia are represented by an upright black V mirrored in an inverted black V above it. Clark argues that whereas Kuspit reads *Woman I* as biologically female, and therefore genitally "deficient," she looks to both *Woman III* and *Woman IV* and finds "genital plenitude, a human being with both penis and vagina" (p. 155).[15] She regards the Freudian idea of a phallic female as a symbolic reading which "adds the sex of the body, 'female,'

---

15   Although other critics do not report perceiving a penis in these paintings, it does not discount that genital plenitude is the way Clark herself sees the black V lines of paint; but as de Kooning said in an interview with Rosenberg, "All painting is an illusion." Rosenberg gave as an example an occasion when, for the fun of it, he found all kinds of images in a large painting of the side view of a cow, much like the various images one might see when looking at clouds (Rosenberg, 1972).

to the gender of the personality, 'masculine'" (p. 154). In Clark's opinion, to a female critic this combination adds up to female empowerment, whereas to a male critic, the phallic female becomes the "quintessential figurative castrator" (p. 155). Clark is critical of Kuspit and Fitzsimmons and others whose interpretations of the Woman paintings depend upon the assumption that these figures are female, whereas she reads them as *androgynous*. Although it might seem that Clark has taken up Barber's (1999) challenge to reappraise gender issues in de Kooning's paintings, she emphasizes that her argument "swirls around issues of biological sex rather than 'gender'" (p. 12, Fn. 27).

Turning to *Woman V* (Figure 6), Clark opines that this canvas moves the series slightly closer to total abstraction when compared to the four previous paintings. She comments that the way the breasts are demarcated indicates flatness rather than fecundity, that the bulky torso is held up by spindly legs, and that, unlike *Woman III* and *Woman IV*, the groin area is not exposed. She observes that beneath the skirt, which is suggested by a yellow parallelogram, the upper legs appear to be clad in shorts, and at the top of the chest area there appears to be the top of a white sleeveless undershirt that emerges from underneath a red garment. Clark suggests that *Woman V* seems to take viewers back to the earlier premise of a male body carelessly and superficially dressed in female attire—the transvestite. In her opinion, "this figure very well could be the rendering of a man in a white sleeveless T shirt and shorts, who just happened to throw on a bra and/or skirt atop them" (p. 199). As she proposes with *Woman I* and *Woman II*, Clark reads the image as de Kooning's having some fun by imagining himself as a woman. The difference she observes in *Woman V*, is that the artist moves to greater abstraction of the figure and the background.

In the last chapter of her book, Clark briefly describes *Woman VI* (Figure 7) and offers her interpretation of this image. In contrast to Lauter's (1976) reading of the face, she observes that both eyes are focused straight ahead and show an element of surprise rather than hollowness, the balloon breasts are absent, the genital area is not depicted, there are no teeth, and the woman's mouth appears to be closed rather than "open and sucking."[16] While for the most part Clark agrees with Lauter's comments about the figure's body, she argues that rather than representing the devouring "death mother," *Woman VI* is the passive recipient of a form that has been dissolved by the artist. She observes that "the dissolution of the body is not marked by brushstrokes indicating a melting away; rather, *Woman VI* is built like a box. Largely made up of segments, the figure that is as close to Cubism as one can get without being overtly Cubist . . ." (p. 208). She notes that while the segments add up to a whole figure, the eyes of the viewer quickly wander to the parts of the body delineated into segments by black lines. The figure is "neither particularly male nor particularly female, just a collection of body parts welded together" (p. 209). In other words, Clark considers *Woman VI* to be de Kooning's final statement about the fluidity of the sexed body—the form of the figure is dissolved, and the body barely distinguishable.

Clark supports her interpretation of *Woman VI* by referring to part of a conversation de Kooning had with the Dutch poet Bert Schierbeek, who visited and interviewed the artist in 1967. De Kooning briefly

---

16   It is difficult to tell if the mouth of *Woman VI* is closed or open, but to me it appears slightly open. The perceptions of Lauter and Clark and all of us who view the paintings are possibly influenced by our own theoretical biases and previous interpretations of the paintings of which we might be aware.

referred to the book *Two Serious Ladies* by Jane Bowles and said, "Well those ladies are my 'Women'. In a humorous or philosophical sense they're nut-ting." De Kooning then quoted some vacuous greetings between Theresa I and Theresa II in Gertrude Stein's play *Four Saints in Three Acts*, and said, ". . . you know this is 'nuttingness,' 'no content' " (Schierbeek, 2005, p. 33).[17] Clark takes this comment to possibly refer to "a truth about the 'nothingness' of sexual content, at least in de Kooning's mind. Both man and woman, neither man nor woman, in the final analysis, nothing" (p. 224). In her interpretation of *Woman VI* as the artist's final statement about the fluidity of the sexed body, however, Clark overlooks his concept of "no-environment" and Hess's (1968) observation that the landscaped elements played an increasingly large part in the Woman paintings as the series progressed. Recall that de Kooning told Hess that *Woman I* reminded him of a landscape, and after completing *Woman VI*, he said that "The landscape is in the Woman, and there is Woman in the landscapes" (Hess, 1968, p. 100). Indeed, the figure is almost entirely merged with the landscape in an unfinished abstract painting titled *Woman as Landscape*, which de Kooning permitted to leave his studio in 1955. Rather than interpreting the dissolution of the figure in *Woman VI* as referring to a truth about the nothingness of sexual content in the artist's mind, why not just regard this painting as a move toward greater abstraction as Clark observes with *Woman V*?

Summarizing her view that de Kooning was working something through in the six Woman paintings, Clark proposes that he initially

---

17   De Kooning also mentioned his interest in the writings of Jane Bowles in interviews he had with Sally Yard (2007) during the 1970s.

combines the male body with the female body through the figure of the "drag Queen" in *Woman I* and the dysmorphia of *Woman II*. In *Woman III* and *Woman IV*, he makes explicit what was before implicit, by depicting the anatomy of the exposed genital area to include "both the 'V' of female anatomy and the 'third leg' of the male" so that "these two figures appear to be a she-man or non-binary body" (p. 226). Clark suggests also that the biology of *Woman IV* mirrors the Mesopotamian idols, which the artist referenced in relation to the paintings. Without breasts or male genitalia, but with heads that often hint at their sexual duality, these idols are symbols of female fertility, though some have two heads, which are thought to represent testicles; they are assumed to have been "accepted in their culture as androgynes and, as such, they resemble individuals identifying as non-binary today" (pp. 226-227). Clark proposes that "finally, in *Woman V* and *VI* the body falls apart, an indication of what de Kooning calls the 'nothingness' of these figures" (p. 227). Whereas she views Woman V as "a fleeting image of a body in transit, to nothingness", she perceives *Woman VI* as having "no content"; "in her near total bodily abstractness . . . she is emptied of whatever content most people ascribe to biological sex" (p. 227). Clark concludes that previous meanings that have been given to the Woman paintings "miss the point of de Kooning's project, which [she] suspect[s] was to gradually empty these figures of any 'content' marking them either male or female, just as he empties the categories male/female themselves" (p. 227).[18]

---

18  Apart from mentioning that *Woman and Bicycle* is more abstract that the first five Woman paintings, but not as abstract as *Woman VI*, Clark does not discuss this image even though it was completed before *Woman VI*. She therefore fails to comment on the double mouths in *Woman and Bicycle* or note that the eyes gaze directly at the viewer as they do in *Woman VI*.

Clark considers the six numbered Woman paintings a philosophical project, "though not one without humor, if considered in the spirit with which it was offered" (p. 227). But while she argues that de Kooning was being playful in depicting sexual ambiguity in these paintings, she also refers to this playfulness as "his *need* to always include humor" (p. 197) (my italics). Apart from mentioning that the artist told Sylvester that he found a retreat into hilarity necessary to his survival, Clark does not tell us how she understands this need. What does she think underlies it? Is she sensing, like Duncan (1989), that the humor might have served a defensive function? And in addition to her comments about the artist's philosophizing and his need to include humor, Clark "can't help but see de Kooning probing into his own identity, as well as an interest in the ontological questions as to the nature of biological sex, if not a combination of the two" (p. 197). She does not provide any biographical information to support her proposal that de Kooning was probing into his own biological identity. He was comfortable acknowledging the presence of feminine as well as masculine elements in his personality, but in my opinion his statements about "the woman in me" and some of the paintings being "self-portraits" may have a deeper meaning than those pertaining to sexual or gender identity. I will present my own suggestions about a possible deeper meaning in later chapters.

Clark's proposal that the Woman paintings of the early 1950s reflect de Kooning's exploration of "the ontological questions as to the nature of biological sex, if not a combination of the two," is consistent with an argument made many years ago by the American psychoanalyst Lawrence Kubie (1974) that there is a drive in all human beings to become both sexes. Kubie did not consider anatomical parity the sole objective of this drive, but rather it is a wish to have both male and female identities, or alternatively, neither. He described various ways in which the drive is expressed, and also how the unattainability of this wish can sometimes result in psychological conflicts, and on occasion lead to psychotic disorganization. Two decades later, Joyce McDougall (1995) similarly argued that "every child wants to possess the mysterious sexual organs and fantasized power of both father and mother, man and woman." In her opinion, "The obligation to come to terms with one's monosexual destiny constitutes one of childhood's more severe narcissistic wounds" (p. xi). However, the integration of these bisexual demands into an individual's psychic structure contributes to the potential to be creative, which McDougall and other analysts suggest is to sublimate the wish to be both sexes and to create children in the form of creative productions. Rather than the Woman paintings reflecting a pregenital personality organization and confusion over biological sex, as Clark suggests, I apply McDougall's ideas and propose that de Kooning's creative productions involve an unconscious sublimation of pregenital (oral, anal, and phallic) drives and an ability to engage both masculine (a metaphorical phallus) and feminine (a metaphorical vaginal space) elements in his mind (Gentile, 2016).

A major criticism of Clark's book is that she gives only cursory attention to de Kooning's childhood trauma and to his apparent inability to get away from painting women. Despite her comment that he internalized "a large gulp of his mother," she fails to formulate a dynamic model of the artist's early attachments and their mental representations and how these may have influenced both the Woman paintings of the early 1950s and his personal relationships with women. Instead, Clark is dismissive of what she refers to as "the tired readings of these paintings as the return of repressed versions of his difficult mother and artist wife, Elaine" (p. 190). Her own reading of the six images of women is influenced by her background experience studying transvestite theater and probably also by the contemporary cultural attention being given to the binary-based structures of sexual identity, gender identity, and sexual orientation. As Cateforis (1991) pointed out several decades ago, the meaning of the Woman paintings, like that of other works of art, is inherently unstable, and changes as a result of interpretations, which are themselves influenced by historical and ideological situations. In the previous chapter, I mentioned that feminist readings of the Woman paintings, which reinforced earlier views that they expressed misogynistic violence, were challenged by Fiona Barber (1999), who argued for a reappraisal of gender issues; Clark extends this to the question of biological sexual identity.

Clark's readings of the paintings imply that de Kooning was consciously aware of the final content that he wanted to depict on the canvas. She omits the role of unconscious factors that could potentially explain the artist's statement about his approach: "I start out with a beautiful girl in mind, and she comes out being a portrait of her mother" (Shirey, 1967, p. 80). As David Sylvester (1994) points out, de Kooning's interaction with the paint is similar to that of Francis Bacon and Franz Kline: "Each situation in the duet between painter and paint was to be met and dealt with as it came along, and the painter's hope was that they would not impose their own will upon the situation but collaborate in the emergence of something with a life of its own" (p. 29). Sylvester quotes Bacon, who said: "If anything ever does work in my case, it works from that moment when consciously I don't know what I am doing" (p. 29).

Before offering my own psychoanalytic perspective and interpretations of de Kooning's compulsive painting of women, I will follow the approach that is customary for most practicing psychoanalysts and psychotherapists, which is to first obtain a detailed history of the person's childhood and adolescence. The biographical information, and the way it is recalled and described, aids therapists in formulating some initial hypotheses about factors that might have contributed to the person's psychological problems. Although we have very few statements by de Kooning himself about his upbringing, much more is now known about his formative years than was known prior to the late 1990s. In the next chapter, I review what is known about the artist's infancy, childhood, and adolescence. My main sources are the accounts provided by art historian Judith Wolfe (1996) and biographers Mark Stevens and Annalyn Swan (2004); these authors conducted extensive archival research and numerous interviews in The Netherlands, and the information is well-documented.

# CHAPTER 3

# De Kooning's Childhood and Adolescence: Traumas and Challenges

Willem de Kooning was born in 1904 in the Dutch port city of Rotterdam. The city is located at the mouths of two rivers (the Rhine and the Meuse) and is open to the North Sea via the New Waterway, which was constructed in 1890. Around the turn of the century, Rotterdam was a rapidly growing city with a large harbor and an expanding economy based largely on shipping. Willem's paternal grandfather, after whom he was named, worked as a ship carpenter and had ten children, four of them boys including de Kooning's father Leendert, who was born in 1876. After completing his schooling, Leendert began selling flowers from a cart on a street, and later from a stand at the railway station. At age twenty, he joined an older brother to start a beer-bottling and distribution business. Willem's mother Cornelia was from a large family living in Schiedam, a small town on the outskirts of Rotterdam. Her mother, also named Cornelia, married a skilled carpenter named Christiaan Nobel in 1873. They had nine children, five of whom died at a young age, leaving three girls and one boy. Their daughter Cornelia, born in 1877, had black hair and dark eyes and was quite pretty; but she was known to be a forceful child with a difficult temperament. When she was seventeen, Cornelia went to Haarlem where she most likely worked as a maid, only to return to Schiedam after one year. A few years later, at age twenty-one, Cornelia met Leendert and soon became pregnant. Although Leendert was only twenty-two, they decided to get married; it is not known whether they were in love and strongly desired the marriage, or if it were because the pregnancy was a result of a brief sexual encounter and the expectation that a man would take responsibility for a woman he impregnated. Six months after the wedding, Cornelia gave birth to a daughter, Marie.

During the next five years there was constant upheaval in the family. Leendert was extremely busy trying to develop his business, which included delivering beer by dog and pony cart, and the family moved to six different addresses as they kept seeking a nicer apartment at a lower rent. The apartments were very small, usually with two rooms connected by a passageway that served as the bedroom. The toilet was in a closet on the landing and shared with other tenants on the same floor, heating the apartment in the winter months was expensive, and hot water had to be bought at a nearby grocery store and carried back home (Stevens and Swan, 2004, p. 8). In July 1901, Cornelia gave birth to twin girls, who died one month later. The cause of their deaths is not known, but the usual causes of infant death in the early twentieth century were birth complications, respiratory infections, gastrointestinal illnesses, malnutrition, and what is now called sudden infant death syndrome. The infant mortality rate in Holland at the turn of the century was 14.7%, with the highest rate among poorer working families; most families had experienced the loss of at least one infant before age one (Wintle, 2000). Having come from a family in which five of her siblings died very young, it is possible that Cornelia became depressed after the death of her twins and fearful that she was destined to suffer a pattern of losses similar to what her parents experienced. Within seven or eight months, however, she was pregnant again; she gave birth to a fourth daughter in October 1902. This infant died the following June at only eight months of age. It is not known whether Cornelia and Leendert were grieving the dead infants and hoping for a replacement child; they might even have blamed themselves for the deaths. And what effect did the death of the baby sister have on Marie? After a lapse of only two months, Cornelia was once again pregnant. Willem was born on April 24, 1904 (Stevens and Swan, 2004, p. 7; Wolfe, 1996, p. 28).

Given the series of losses that Leendert and Cornelia experienced and the struggles and stresses of daily life, their emotional states could hardly have been conducive to providing an empathically responsive environment for Willem. Like other working-class families in Rotterdam, and those struggling to start a small business, they were desperately poor, lacked secure accommodation, and had to move frequently from one tiny apartment to another. Moreover, they were temperamentally different; Leendert is remembered as a "stiff and emotionally withdrawn man," Cornelia as a "fiery, impetuous, caustic, and outspoken" woman. She was known to have "a sharp temper and wicked tongue" and even her sister found her difficult to bear (Stevens and Swan, 2004, pp. 5–6). Since her marriage, however, the physical and emotional strain on Cornelia must have been enormous; she was constantly pregnant or taking care of infants or burying them, and apparently without help from her parents. And religion was not a source of comfort, for it meant nothing to the couple (Wolfe, 1996,

p. 37). Did Cornelia and Leendert appreciate the depth of each other's grief? Perhaps the birth of a son offered some hope.

By this stage, Leendert had expanded his business to include soft drinks; he was working long hours and under considerable stress, and disliked coming home in the evenings to a crying infant and an angry wife. As the tension in the marriage increased, Leendert and Cornelia argued frequently and probably fought physically (Stevens and Swan, 2004, p. 9). Cornelia had an explosive temper and could fly into screaming rages at her husband. One wonders how much of the arguing and fighting was a reaction to the deaths of the three infants, and how much can be attributed to Cornelia's personality. Many years later, Leendert wrote to Willem explaining that he had been unable to live any longer with Cornelia because she was "too hysterical" (Wolfe, 1996, p. 30, Fn. 35). On the other hand, Cornelia likely felt neglected by her husband; he had little energy to give to his family and was considered selfish by nature, a trait that Willem encountered in his father during his boyhood whenever he asked him for pocket money. Leendert was particularly upset over an incident when he was jailed for two days as a penalty for failing to obtain a license for his delivery cart dog. When he was released and returned home, he discovered that Cornelia had sold his business equipment. She claimed that she needed the money to feed their children (Stevens and Swan, 2004, p. 9). Soon after that incident, at which time Willem was only twenty-one months old, Leendert separated from his wife and filed for divorce on the grounds of ill-treatment and cruelty. Two months later, Cornelia filed for divorce on the grounds of ill-treatment, adultery, insults, and extravagance. The divorce had serious consequences for both Willem and Marie.

Accounts differ as to the immediate living arrangement for Willem. It seems that he was initially taken to live with his father, but after a short period retrieved by his mother who, together with her father and two of Leendert's married sisters, had been awarded full custody. The divorce had a significant impact on the standard of living for Cornelia and the children, especially when the alimony payments were reduced by fifty percent after the first year. According to Stevens and Swan (2004), Cornelia "began to take in washing and started moving to ever smaller and shabbier houses" (p. 10). When Willem approached his fourth birthday, his mother decided to remarry and sent him to stay with his father, keeping Marie with her. The separation of the children must have been extremely distressing for both of them, as Willem had developed a closeness with Marie, and she had become protective of him. Abandoned by his mother and separated from his sister, Willem no doubt felt anxious and very lonely. At his age, children do have not have the cognitive capacity to think logically about such events and are likely to develop an explanatory fantasy. What meaning might he have given to the separation? Did he have a "transitional object" (such as a favorite soft cloth or stuffed toy animal, which stands for the mother) to help comfort him and to make him feel more secure?[1]

Leendert's mother helped look after Willem, but according to some accounts Cornelia would come and grab the child when he was playing outside and take him home (Hess, 1968, p. 12). Was she missing her son and feeling guilty about giving him up, or was she acting out her anger with Leendert? She was living in a small apartment in a working-class neighborhood where people moved frequently. After

---

1 I discuss the concept of transitional objects and transitional phenomena in Chapter 4.

ten months, Willem was sent back to live with his mother, as his father had remarried and apparently the stepmother did not want the boy. Thus, in the first few years of his life, Willem experienced several significant disruptions to his primary attachments as he was moved back and forth between "a bewildering succession of households, parents, and small cold rooms lit by hot flashes of anger" (Stevens and Swan, 2004, p. 11). Could these disruptions so early in life have affected the development of de Kooning's sense of self? As I will propose in the next chapter, they most likely influenced the patterns of attachment he established as a child with the important adults in his life.

The absence of a safe home environment with reliable and loving maternal care extended into Willem's childhood, even though his mother's second husband, Jacobus Lassooy, did not engage in arguments with her and brought a certain peace and quiet to the household. According to Stevens and Swan (2004, p. 12), Cornelia was a tyrannical woman who physically and emotionally abused her children. She had an explosive temper and often flew into screaming rages slapping and beating Willem and his sister and a younger half-brother with her shoes. She sometimes locked Willem in a closet, and on one occasion she hid in a closet and then jumped out at him holding a knife. According to Lee Hall (1993), Cornelia at times boxed her son's ears and whacked or punched him for reasons not apparent to Willem. Hall reports also that de Kooning confided in a friend that "his mother once came upon him, then a toddler, playing on the floor with her shoes. He felt helpless and frightened, he said, when she became enraged and savagely kicked him for a wrongdoing he did not comprehend" (p. 7). Cornelia seems to have not realized that a young child playing with his mother's shoes is a way of feeling connected to her. Although physical disciplining of children was common in Dutch society in those days, Stevens and Swan (2004) opine that "Cornelia's behavior was almost certainly excessive even by the standards of the time" (p. 633, Fn. 12). Was her harsh treatment of the children an unconscious repetition of the quality of parenting that she was exposed to during her own childhood? There is certainly empirical evidence that parenting styles can be transmitted across generations (De Carli, et al., 2018), and we can assume that Cornelia's parents were deeply affected by the early deaths of five of their children. A mother has insufficient time to mourn the loss of an infant when she soon becomes pregnant again and is easily frustrated and angered as she struggles to take care of her other children. But why did Leendert not find some legal way to protect his children when he had been unable to tolerate Cornelia's aggressive behavior himself? And did Cornelia's second husband make any attempts to intervene when she behaved abusively toward the children?

According to Hall, the painter Robert Dash had several conversations with de Kooning about his childhood; he concluded that:

Bill was deeply, deeply marked by his mother's hostility toward him. You don't have to be a certified Freudian to suspect that that was *the* formative relationship in his life, especially in shaping his feelings about women. Bill naturally wanted Cornelia's love, and Cornelia gave him anything but motherly love. Today, one would describe Cornelia as a child abuser. I believe, everything in Bill's life was darkly shadowed by his early experience with that awful mother (Hall, 1993, p. 20).

95

Cornelia was not affectionate with her children; she had an aversion to kissing and was described in later years by a grandchild as having no maternal feelings. Willem sought solace from his sister, who loved him and provided some of the maternal care that he did not receive from his mother. Staying in bed was also a safe haven, although his mother would repeatedly shout out "Wimpy—get up!" Judith Wolfe (1996) mentions seeing a photograph of Willem with his sister when he was six years old and observing that his "serious little face had a taut and wary expression" (p. 38); she wondered if his expression was elicited by the occasion or was more ingrained. An ingrained wary facial expression suggests that the child may have been repeatedly hurt and is fearful of further physical attacks. From an early age Willem would have felt the melancholy of Marie and experienced significant loneliness that continued throughout his childhood.

Willem had some respite from the home environment at age seven, when his mother left him with one of her friends in Schiedam to stay for a few days. There Willem observed a more stable household and an appealing daily routine. He was particularly intrigued by one member of the family, a watchmaker, who got up late in the morning and established his own routine. Willem was fascinated by the "magic lens" the man placed in his eye to look at watches. Judith Zilczer (2014) suggests that "de Kooning associated the watchmaker from Schiedam with the freedom and independence he would later find with art" (p. 14). The following year, Willem's stepbrother Koos was born; it seems the two boys did not develop a close relationship, probably because of the age difference. I wonder also if Willem spent any time visiting and playing with cousins or getting to know the children from his father's second marriage, and whether he felt loved and valued by any of his grandparents. As he grew a little older, he sought refuge in drawing, mostly boats and workhorses pulling wagons (Hall, 1993; Wolfe, 1996). Going to the harbor and watching the reflections on the water appealed to him. Recalling those days many years later in a conversation with Bert Schierbeek (2005), he said: "As a kid I always hung around ships, the water, and the way the sea reflects the sky . . ." (p. 39). His interest in drawing was approved of by his mother and may have served partly as a "transitional phenomenon" that helped fill a void in his inner world and experience of the real world.

Willem's stepfather Jacobus was a likeable man and made few demands; however, he was a hapless character who often changed jobs, and the family moved twelve times when Willem was between ages four and thirteen (Stevens and Swan, 2004, pp. 13–14). Moreover, Willem behaved in a haughty manner toward his stepfather, displacing on to him the resentment he felt toward his father.[2] During World War I, the family's financial situation worsened, as fewer customers could afford to buy drinks at the bar Jacobus ran and he had to declare bankruptcy. Although Holland remained neutral during the war, the economic slump and shortage of food in the country caused widespread misery. The family was soon living on the margins of society with a diet of mainly potatoes and turnips (Wolfe, 1996, p. 61); but even the price of potatoes increased. When the supply of coal was depleted, Dutch people dug for peat as a source of energy. The unhealthy diet and lack of dental care during Willem's early adolescence limited the height to which he grew and led to dental

---

2　According to Wolfe (1996, p. 43), many years later de Kooning sent a letter to his stepfather asking for forgiveness for the way he had disrespected him during childhood.

problems throughout his adult life. But the hardships he and his family endured during the war years presented challenges they surmounted and may have given Willem the resilience and capacity to tolerate the deprivation of food and comfort he was to experience in later years, when he had very little money.

Marie left school at age twelve or thirteen and worked initially as a hairdresser and later as a seamstress. When she was sixteen, she left home and eight months later got married. Similar to her mother, Marie was pregnant at the time of her marriage; two weeks later she gave birth to a boy who they named Antonie (Stevens and Swan, 2004, pp. 17–18; Wolfe, 1996, p. 51). Willem, age eleven, must have felt deeply saddened, as he had now lost his defender and close friend. There was probably nobody with whom he could share his feelings about this loss. One year later he met a slightly older boy who also had an interest in art and painted in oils. This led Jacobus to buy Willem a set of artist's paints, which Willem used to paint at least two still-life pictures that are dated 1916 and ca. 1916.

Willem's gift for drawing had been noticed by his schoolteachers, one of whom inspired him and told him to draw as much as he wanted. At age twelve, when he was finishing his elementary schooling, his stepfather took him job-seeking. He was hired as an apprentice at an important decorating firm run by two brothers, Jan and Jaap Giddings, who took a paternal interest in the boy. For most of the first year he was required to work twelve-hour days. As was the custom in many working-class families, Willem handed his paychecks to his mother, who gave him an allowance (Wolfe, 1996, p. 64). After one year, his employers paid for him to enroll and take evening drawing classes at the Academy of Art and Technology in Rotterdam. Though Cornelia took some pride in her son's artistic gifts, she remained domineering, frequently bickering and battling with him. During a major argument when Willem was sixteen, his mother hit him across the face, and when Willem laughed in defiance, she knocked him across the room and kicked him after he fell to the floor (Stevens and Swan, 2004, p. 33). Many decades later, as I will mention in the next chapter, de Kooning said that during his childhood his mother was the person he feared most in the whole world.

Although Willem worked long hours at his job six days a week and attended classes at the Academy in the evenings, he still found time to wander around the area of the Coolsingel and adjacent districts, where he observed a mix of pimps, sailors, businessmen, artists, poets, and musicians. He also watched the prostitutes in the red-light district, noticing how they would entice potential customers by briefly flashing their breasts. Many years later, Conrad Fried (brother of de Kooning's wife Elaine) gained the impression that the provocative flash of the prostitute "was the basis of de Kooning's later description of his art as a 'slipping glimpse' — an attempt to capture in paint those quick, oblique but illuminating moments that the eye registers almost subliminally" (Stevens and Swan, 2004, p. 32). Little is known about romances that Willem had as a teenager. His biographers mention seeing photographs of a charcoal on cardboard drawing of an early girlfriend which they describe as "beautifully detailed" and the "first image of a de Kooning woman" (Stevens and Swan, 2004, p. 36).

Willem's father remained distant throughout his son's childhood and adolescence. He did not even attend Marie's wedding. With his second wife, Leendert had four children, including twins, one of whom died. Apparently, he was as distant and selfish with his second family as he was with Marie and Willem. According to Wolfe (1996), "Leendert's second son, called Leo, described his father as closed and introverted, a man who did not express his feelings" (p. 394). Willem felt emotionally hurt by his father's lack of attention and became resentful in later years. In a letter that he sent to Marie decades later, he stated that their father "was a stranger again . . . he forgot that the children must have something from <u>both</u> . . . the father and the mother" (Stevens and Swan, 2004, p. 13; Wolfe, 1996, p. 36, Fn. 53). It seems probable, however, that Leendert had been deprived of a close relationship with his own father, since he had to share him with nine siblings. Moreover, he lacked a paternal grandfather, who had died when Leendert's father was age twelve, a loss that probably scarred his father emotionally. Consequently, Leendert failed to learn how to be a good father.

By mid-adolescence, Willem was becoming more assertive and seeking independence. He enjoyed reading adventure stories about American cowboys and Indians and became interested in American pop culture; he liked listening to jazz, watching Hollywood movies, and looking at photographs of girls in magazine advertisements. He was also fascinated by the American shield with the blue band on top and vertical stripes below, supported by a bald eagle. He thought it looked like a medieval shield, almost from the heraldic period of the Crusaders (Sylvester, 2001). These interests stirred his imagination and perhaps gave rise to his wish to eventually travel to America. Not long after his sixteenth birthday and the end of his third year at the Academy, Willem left his job and joined Marie and her family, who were living in Amsterdam; he was missing her greatly and needed her emotional support. However, he soon returned to Rotterdam and found freelance jobs in commercial art, all the while living sporadically at his mother's home. But when he was feeling down, he sometimes returned to stay with Marie. Sometimes he lived with the family of a friend he met at the Academy; according to Stevens and Swan (2004, p. 44), "they were a warm, generous, and unconventional family," an experience that de Kooning apparently considered "the happiest time of his life." He reenrolled in the Academy and was eventually hired as an assistant to Bernard Romein, a freelance designer whose main client was a large department store in Rotterdam. Willem's work involved making signs for this store, which was located on an elegant shopping street in the city. Although Romein was only ten years older than Willem, he was an excellent mentor, providing his young assistant with experiences that he had missed out on with his father. He gave Willem considerable creative freedom in his work and encouraged him to remain at the Academy; he also helped Willem develop intellectual interests and broaden his imagination by introducing him to the works of Piet Mondrian and Frank Lloyd Wright, to authors such as Dostoevsky and Walt Whitman, and to other modern ideas and styles. Romein even took Willem to the Rijksmuseum in Amsterdam and to various art exhibitions. Moreover, as de Kooning told Wolfe (1996, pp. 266–267) in an interview in 1985, Romein had a marvelous sense of humor, which made for an enjoyable workplace. In later years Willem acknowledged Romein as the person who had the most important influence on his early life (Stevens and Swan, 2004, p. 38). It was probably while he was reenrolled in the Academy that he drew a still life with conté crayon and charcoal on paper, which is titled *Bowl, Pitcher, and Jug* (dated ca. 1921) and is now in the Metropolitan Museum of Art in New York (Hess, 1968, 13–14; Zilczer, 2004, pp. 15–16).

During the early 1920s, de Kooning sometimes visited his father at his shop asking for money, but also to give him gifts of small drawings, for which he received only grudging praise. Leendert resented being asked for money even when his business was going well, but as Stevens and Swan (2004, p. 48) suggest, father and son may have pretended that the money was to pay for the drawings. According to Willem's half-brother from his father's second marriage, shortly after the family had glanced at the drawings, Leendert rolled them up and put them away in a cupboard (Wolfe, 1996, pp. 395–396). Willem remained estranged from his father, but occasionally accompanied him to check on the horses at the stables.

At age twenty, feeling restless and a need for adventure, Willem decided to test how long he could stay away from home by going to Brussels for six months or more; the test was connected with his wish to go to America. He went with two friends, and they worked initially at odd jobs trying to survive but were often without food. Eventually, Willem and one of the friends managed to get jobs as painter-decorators with a family decorating firm; accommodation and meals were provided by the family. The two young men stayed in Belgium for about six months and either before or after their time in Brussels, they visited Antwerp, where they would have seen numerous paintings by Rubens. During this time Willem made at least forty-one sketches, many of which have survived because they were kept by his employer's family. The young men's departure from Brussels came as a surprise to their employer, because it happened precipitously; and although Willem took the paint box and oil paints with him, he left behind a sketchbook and many drawings (Wolfe, 1996, pp. 466–467). Judith Wolfe was able to view many of the drawings, and she describes and comments on a large number of works that Willem made in Belgium and Holland during the two years before he left Europe.

Most of the drawings are done with pencil and conté crayon, and two are completed in watercolor.[3] Wolfe (1996) identifies two main styles, a curvilinear symbolism style and a cartoon-like illustration style. Only two pictures qualify as symbolic works—*Women and Tree*, which was made in Belgium in 1924, and *The Kiss*, which was drawn the following year after Willem had returned to Rotterdam. The numerous illustrative-style drawings depict scenes of everyday life in the city including folks on market day, women with flowers, and prostitutes with pimps, café scenes, men walking, an organ grinder, and a man with a walking stick. In addition, there are ten images of children or adolescents, including a boy with automobile, and children with balloons. One of the pencil and watercolor pictures presents a lower working-class family group of father, mother, pre-adolescent daughter, somewhat younger son, and infant child; the boys are looking downwards, and the expressionless faces of the parents and a dark background give the picture a somber mood. Although the ages of the children correspond roughly to those of the household in which de Kooning grew up, Wolfe points out that they do not bear a particular resemblance to any individuals; in fact, she says, they seem not to be portraits of actual people, but characters drawn from de Kooning's imagination. Wolfe suggests that this drawing has some similarity to family portraits by the Dutch artist Charley Toorop and to an illustration by Romein. Nonetheless, the daughter has black hair

---

3   Only a small number of the drawings are reproduced in books about de Kooning; and for copyright reasons, they cannot be viewed in the copy of Wolfe's dissertation available online through ProQuest.

like Willem's sister Marie, but her hair is scraggly across her brow, and she is depicted with a sinister, demonic gaze and "the curl of her lips verges on cruel" (Wolfe, 1996, p. 550). Could she represent Willem's sister with his angry feelings and intentions assigned to her?

There is a sinister quality as well in the two symbolic drawings. *The Kiss* (Figure 8), which is drawn in an Art Nouveau style, depicts only the heads of a man and a woman and the woman's hand on the man's shoulder. The scene is sensual but the woman's hand, which is placed tenderly upon the man's arm, ends in menacing long sharp fingernails. The long fingernails have been compared to the fingers in some of de Kooning's paintings of women from the 1940s; they may also anticipate the claw-like hands in *Woman I, II, and III*. I noticed that the fingers are similar in Pablo Picasso's well-known painting *Dora Maar*, which was completed in 1937, and therefore more than a decade after *The Kiss*, but well before de Kooning's Woman paintings. According to Wolfe (1996), Marie and her nine-year-old son Antonie were the models for *The Kiss*, which was simply a matter of practical convenience. The picture was kept in the family and is seen hanging on the wall in a snapshot from the 1920s that shows Willem, Marie, and Antonie. Wolfe examined this snapshot and comments that Marie's particular beauty, dark hair, and large eyes, often figure in Willem's drawings from this period. In 1982, Marie told the writer of an article for the *Holland Herald* magazine that the drawing was "a fantasy." Did she mean her own fantasy or her brother's fantasy?

**Figure 8**: *The Kiss*, 1925
Graphite on paper, 19 x 13 in (48.2 x 34.7 cm)
The Allan Stone Collection, New York

**Figure 9**: *Women and Tree*, ca. 1924
Conté crayon and pencil on paper, 13 ⅝ x 10 in (34.5 x 25.4 cm)
Private collection

In *Women and Tree* (Figure 9), three nude young women are slumped in somnolence, and seemingly bound into a pollarded willow tree that appears to imprison them.[4] An owl flying low on the horizon indicates that it is nighttime, but the presence of the owl has menacing overtones. The women's bodies are tense and appear vulnerable in a predatory world, as the owl is engaged in a low hunting glide, seeking prey to grab with its sharp talons (Wolfe, 1994, 1996). This drawing reminds me, as it did Judith Wolfe, of Francisco Goya's 1799 etching *The Sleep of Reason Produces Monsters*, in which an artist asleep amidst his drawing tools is surrounded by owls and swarming bats. Willem may have seen a print of this work in the Rijksmuseum when he was staying with his sister's family in Amsterdam. Owls have been given benign or malevolent symbolic meanings down through the ages, including representation of a foreboding that some evil is at hand, or as symbols of wisdom, knowledge, and carriers of messages from the spirit world. Goya had been drawing a series of nightmare fantasies that tormented him while he was seriously ill; in *The Sleep of Reason* one of the owls is handing a drawing tool to the sleeping artist, which Wolfenstein (1966) suggests is a message to Goya that he will master his nightmares by means of his art. Like *The Kiss*, the drawing *Women and Tree* conveys sensuality in the presence of an ominous threat; could the owl represent an internal predator, which Willem would have to contain by way of his art? The threatening owl swooping low toward the naked women alongside the phallic tree might suggest a sexual anxiety; could the owl represent the oedipal father or the witch

---

4   The title *Women and Tree* was assigned to this drawing by Wolfe (1996), as it was not inscribed with a title and had never been exhibited.

mother? Wolfe suggests that the drawing might have been influenced by Giovanni Segantini's 1894 painting *The Evil Mothers*, depicting a floating bare-breasted woman caught in the branches of a tree, which Willem may have seen in one of Bernard Romein's German art books.

When Willem returned to Rotterdam in late 1924 or early 1925, Marie and her family had already moved back from Amsterdam, but she was abandoned soon afterwards by her husband, who left on a ship for America. Unable to stay with Marie and Antonie, and having no money, Willem resorted to living with other impoverished individuals on a barge at the docks. Marie would sometimes leave packages of food for him (Stevens and Swan, 2004, p. 54). He hoped to fulfill his fantasy of emigrating to America and making a lot of money as an illustrator. With the assistance of a friend he eventually managed to become a stowaway on a British freighter. Because of the ship's imminent departure, he had to leave rather hastily and had no time to collect his possessions and say goodbye to Marie and other members of his family. He entered the United States in July 1926 without papers, speaking little English, and without his commercial portfolio to help him find work (B. Hess, 2012). He was aged twenty-two, and at that stage in his life the desire to be a painter had not yet emerged. Based on his training at the Academy and work experience in Rotterdam, he thought it was more logical to become a designer or a commercial artist (Sylvester, 2001).

De Kooning felt guilty about abandoning his sister when he left for America, but was deeply grateful that she had stood up for him against their mother when he was a child. It is puzzling, therefore, why he did not correspond with her until forty years after he left Holland. In that regard, his behavior was similar to that of Marie's husband, who never

108

wrote to her from America or sent money to help support their son. Why did de Kooning break contact with his sister? And why did he so abruptly leave the family that gave him work and accommodation that enabled him to survive in Brussels? Was he beginning a pattern of abandoning people who cared for him?

According to his biographers, de Kooning rarely spoke about his childhood; he remembered great loneliness but said that he was "not one to go down memory lane" (Stevens and Swan, 2004, p. 11). In fact, he admitted that he avoided thinking about his childhood in order to protect himself from his own feelings. Given the disruptions and quality of the family environment, he most likely experienced intense episodes of anxiety and loneliness during the first four or five years of his life, and physical and emotional abuse during his latency and adolescent years. It is now well established that adverse childhood experiences (such as prolonged separations from parents; witnessing parents demeaning or physically harming one another; threatening a child with a weapon; shoving, hitting, or kicking the child; and unresponsiveness to the child's distress) are associated with an increased risk for developing medical and psychiatric disorders in adulthood including mood and anxiety disorders and substance use disorders (Heim *et al.*, 2010; Lippard and Nemeroff, 2020). As I will describe in a later chapter, de Kooning suffered from panic attacks and depression from his early thirties onwards and soon became addicted to alcohol, which he initially began drinking with the hope that it would reduce anxiety and allow him to relax. It seems safe to assume that de Kooning's early childhood experiences rendered him vulnerable to developing anxiety and depressive symptoms during his adult life.

# CHAPTER 4

# The Interplay between Internal and External Worlds and the Compulsion to Repeat the Past

De Kooning's biographers believe that most critics made a mistake by overemphasizing the female figure in *Woman I* and isolating her for discussion. In their opinion, this painting "is the depiction of a relationship. It suggests two figures locked in a struggle. If the artist is not literally described, he is present nonetheless in the slashing and furious brushstrokes. The perspective is that of a child looking up at an adult. . . . There is no better suggestion in art of a tantrum, no truer rendering of the child who knows what he *wants*—and is desolate—as he hurls himself back and forth against an unyielding strength" (Stevens and Swan, 2004, p. 339). In a similar way, but without referring directly to a relationship, Thomas Hess described *Woman I* as "a noble battlefield" with the figure representing the Black Goddess (*i.e.*, the Terrible Goddess or the "bad" mother). Having watched de Kooning at work through the various stages in the development of this painting, Hess (1968) was attuned to the artist's inner turmoil and struggle and could easily state that "Facing this image and getting beyond it, perhaps, was one of the reasons it took [the artist] so many months to finish *Woman I . . ."* (pp. 75, 78). Can we think of this painting as representing an internal phantasy relationship that is projected and reconstituted on the canvas and has its origin in an actual relationship in childhood? Are the seven Woman paintings a misogynistic attack on the female as many of the early critics argued? Is the Woman strong and powerful enough to survive the attack? Or does she represent a powerful female who threatens the artist?

Stevens and Swan (2004) are very attuned to de Kooning's childhood trauma and to the ambivalent emotions he experienced toward his mother; in their view, the artist succeeded in conveying not only terror and hatred in *Woman I,* but also "so much physical longing" (p. 339). I fully agree with their interpretation; the notion of a relationship provides an entry point for exploring the possible influence of traumatic childhood experiences on de Kooning's adult life and on his compulsive need to paint women. But how might this influence come about? How do many important experiences from the past, especially from early childhood and not remembered consciously, continue to play a significant role in our current lives as adults?

In this chapter I suggest some answers to these questions by applying concepts from attachment theory and psychoanalytic object relations theory, both of which consider the interplay between a person's internal world and the external (real) world. This interplay takes place within the dimensions of time and space, which are indissolubly linked in the lives of all human beings. I also discuss psychoanalytic thinking about childhood trauma, including an important distinction between pre-conceptual trauma and conceptual trauma. I then turn to Freud's concept of the "compulsion to repeat" (also referred to as the "repetition compulsion"), which illustrates the timelessness of the unconscious, including how trauma collapses time and renders past, present, and future undifferentiated. Finally, I review the psychoanalytic concept of "object usage" and discuss the contribution of Teressa Broll (2005), who proposed how this concept might explain the negative reactions of many of the early critics to the Woman paintings. For the benefit of readers who are not very familiar with psychoanalysis, I have taken space to explain each of the concepts or theories before applying them to de Kooning. Perhaps my explanations will trigger some additional ideas among psychoanalysts and other readers who are already familiar with the concepts. Let us begin with the infant's first relationship, which is usually with the mother.

## The Quality of Maternal Care

The interplay between inner and outer worlds begins at the moment of birth, when the neonate leaves its secure home inside the mother's womb, breathes the air in the external world for the first time, and announces its safe arrival with a loud cry. The Austrian psychoanalyst Otto Rank (1924) believed that this abrupt separation from the mother and exposure to the highly stimulating external world has a traumatic impact on the infant. However, his focus on the early stage of infancy rather than on the Oedipus complex as the causal factor in neurosis, together with some other theoretical differences, alienated him from Freud. Yet it seems evident that how well infants are able to cope with birth trauma depends on the quality of the attachment to their mothers, both physically and emotionally. But following Freud, who had set aside his "seduction theory" and replaced it with a theory that the primary source of neurotic symptoms is inner conflict over incestuous and other wishes and fantasies, most psychoanalysts gave little attention to the impact of *real* experiences in childhood.[1] It was not until the late 1950s and the 1960s that several psychoanalysts in Britain began to investigate the quality of maternal care by observing mothers together with their infants. These analysts were neither rigidly Freudian in their approach, nor were they followers of Melanie Klein; they belonged to a diverse group of analysts who came to be known as the Independent Group. I will apply theoretical contributions from several members of this group, especially those of Donald Winnicott and John Bowlby, who were particularly interested in how external relationships influence infant and child development.

A pediatrician before he became a psychoanalyst, Winnicott (1960) made extensive observations of babies with their mothers. He conceptualized the infant's early environment as a "holding environment," encompassing both the physical holding, feeding, and dressing of the infant, and the mother's holding an image of the baby in her mind, so that she is aware of and attentive to the baby's physical and emotional needs. The physical aspects of holding include the experience of being held, touched, rocked, spoken to, and sung to in the arms of the mother. These early sensory experiences serve to partly regulate certain physiological systems in the infant and to initiate affect communication (Hofer, 2005). "Holding-the-baby-in-mind" requires a

---

1  Freud's trauma or "seduction" theory was based on his studies of hysterical symptoms in young women in the late 1800s (Breuer and Freud, 1893; Freud, 1894), which led him to initially propose that neurotic symptoms were caused by repressed memories of sexual abuse or molestation that *occurred during early childhood*. A few years later, after he had acquired more clinical experience, Freud concluded that the memories of abuse were the child's imaginary fantasies rather than events that actually occurred.

mental state of preoccupation by the mother in which she loses her own sense of separateness through an intense identification with the infant, yet simultaneously maintains a sufficient sense of her own distinct subjectivity to interpret her infant's experience and to respond to the infant's needs (Ogden, 1992). Obviously, no mother can be perfectly and continuously attuned to her baby, and some degree of infant distress is necessary for healthy development. The goal of the mother is simply to be "good enough" for her infant.

Since there is minimal biographical information about de Kooning's infancy, we can only speculate about the quality of the holding environment into which Willem was received upon his birth. In the late part of the nineteenth century and well into the twentieth century, many mothers in Europe and America were guided by so-called medical "experts" such as Luther Emmett Holt, who advised parents not to touch, kiss, or hold their babies much, to only interact and feed them according to a strict schedule governed by the clock, to not respond to their cries during the night, and to not play with them for the first four to six months (Giron, 2019; Holt, 1894). A similar regimented approach to infant care was recommended to mothers in New Zealand and several other countries by Dr. Truby King (Mander, 1996). We have no knowledge of whether Willem's mother Cornelia was guided by these principles. Did she cradle the baby in her arms and soothe him when he cried? How attuned was she to his emotional states? Could she imagine herself in the baby's place and know when he needed to be fed or have a wet diaper changed? Given that Willem's parents had already experienced the deaths of three infants, it seems likely that the ability of Cornelia to hold-the-baby-in-mind would have been compromised by anxiety that her baby son might also not survive the first year of his life. Moreover, given the atmosphere in the de Kooning's tiny apartment during the critical first two years of Willem's childhood, when his parents were shouting, arguing, and fighting with each other, it was probably extremely difficult for Cornelia to protect her infant from the distressing stimulation of angry voices. As the Parisian psychoanalyst Joyce McDougall said in an interview, "the way in which the mother relates to the father affects the baby even before its birth"; and "the way the mother is feeling, all her emotional states are transmitted to her baby through her voice, her skin, and her smell" (Molino, 1997, pp. 73, 82).

In 1920, Freud introduced the idea of a stimulus barrier (*Reizschutz*) as a kind of shield or precursor ego function that protects the mind from excessive external stimuli. Based on his observations of men suffering from the trauma of shellshock after WWI, he proposed that an experience is traumatic if this barrier is breached. Freud's Hungarian colleague Sándor Ferenczi argued that psychic trauma in childhood requires not only a breach in the stimulus barrier but also lack of support from the parents, in particular the mother, on whom the child depends. His ideas gradually led to the view that the primary stimulus barrier for the infant and young child is the mother (Peláez, 2009), a view consistent with Winnicott's belief.

Winnicott (1962) thought that if the external stimulation is too early or too intense, or the mother adds to excessive external stimulation, and if the stimulation is prolonged, the infant experiences an "unthinkable anxiety" and reacts in ways that fragment its developing sense of self. Wilfrid Bion (1962) similarly proposed that the baby experiences a "nameless dread" and fear of dying when the mother lacks the capacity to contain and transform the baby's unbearable emotional states into more bearable feelings. As I will discuss in more detail in the next chapter, Bion introduced the idea of the mother's functioning as a "container" for her infant's primitive emotions, which she renders meaningful to the infant by the way she responds and intervenes. It is through the feelings and thoughts that go through her mind in response to the infant's distress that she serves as the "thinking apparatus" of the infant. How effective a container was Cornelia for her baby? And what had been the quality of her own mother's containing function? Intense emotions that are evoked by an external or internal stimulus, and not modulated by an attuned and soothing caregiver, remain undifferentiated and may contribute to the development of anxiety or depressive disorders or other psychopathology at an older age. De Kooning developed anxiety and depressive symptoms as an adult and feared he was dying whenever he suffered panic attacks. These attacks likely signified the presence of undifferentiated emotions associated with trauma caused by excessive impingements and inadequate maternal responsiveness during early infancy.[2]

An important aspect of the relation between inner experience and outer experience during early development is the infant's perception of the mother's face. Through their mutual gaze, facial expressions, and vocalizations, mother and baby communicate with each other. During nursing at the breast, the baby looks intently at the mother's face, and what is reflected through her emotional expressions is an image of

---

2  It is important to emphasize that psychoanalysts do not blame the mother, but regard limitations in her mothering capacities as consequences of her own childhood trauma, which may itself be transmitted to her children (De Carli *et al.*, 2018; Salberg, 2015).

himself.[3] Winnicott (1967) regarded the mother's face as the precursor to the mirror and argued that this mirror function is important for establishing a sense of self. If the mother's face is unresponsive or reflects her own mood, the infant's developing self may suffer. As the child grows, he will continue to monitor the facial expressions of the parents in order to predict their mood and will also see himself in the attitudes of the parents. This internalization of himself provides an alternative way to interpret de Kooning's statement that some of the Woman paintings of the early 1950s may be self-portraits or depict "the woman in me." They may be derived partly from mnemic traces of the reflections of his mother's face that have become confused with his self-image. Winnicott (1967) made a similar comment about the artist Francis Bacon, who also repeatedly painted significantly distorted images of the human face. He suggested that Bacon "is seeing himself in his mother's face, but with some twist in him or her that maddens both him and us" (p. 114). Without knowing anything about the artist's private life, Winnicott thought that through these faces Bacon was "painfully striving towards being seen" (p. 114).

Winnicott (1971) proposed that, in addition to the external world and the concept of an internal world, we need to conceptualize a third area, which he called *potential space,* a space that we fill when we are enjoying playing, listening to music, viewing pictures in a gallery, or engaging in some other cultural activity. He conceptualized this space

---

3   In early infant research, René Spitz (1955) made the common observation that infants nursing at the breast gaze constantly at the mother's face and eyes. He concluded that the first visual percept is the *Gestalt* configuration of the human face rather than the breast, and that breast and face are experienced as one and indivisible. Perhaps in a playful way, de Kooning drew and painted breasts to resemble eyes in a small work titled *Woman,* 1950, which is in the MoMA. In another work titled *Woman,* 1953 (in the Hirshhorn Museum and Sculpture Garden, Smithsonian Institution), he created a face within the body by rendering the breasts as eyes and painting a mouth across the torso.

as originating during an early phase of infant development. While the infant initially experiences itself as merged with the mother, as it becomes aware of its separateness from her, and the mother is lowering the degree of her adaptation to the infant's needs, a (potential) physical and mental space opens between mother and infant. Yet, at the same time, using a *transitional object* (such as a soft cloth or stuffed toy animal, which stands for the mother) the infant maintains an illusion of being merged with the mother. Thus, as Winnicott proposes, potential space "both joins and separates" the infant and the mother. It is neither inner nor outer but is conceptualized by Winnicott as an intermediate area of experiencing that lies between the inner world ("inner psychic reality") and actual or external reality. And it is within potential space that the capacity for symbolization and creativity originates (Ogden, 1985).

The movement away from mother-infant unity through the development of potential space involves the infant's internalizing the holding and containing functions which the mother needs to have reliably provided. But engagement of the mother continues within the potential space, as it is the area in which she (and other caregivers) and the infant learn to play together. In a healthy environment, this play evokes pleasurable emotions for both mother and infant. However, some mothers interfere with the development of transitional objects or transitional phenomena (such as babblings, tunes, mannerisms, and nursery rhymes). By prohibiting every attempt on the infant's part to use a soft object for comfort or to suck on, or by continually offering herself to the infant as the only source of satisfaction, these mothers deny the infant an adequate illusion-disillusion experience and the psychic space in which to create a transitional object and form mental representations of experiences drawn from the external world (Taylor, 1987).

Though children eventually relinquish their transitional objects, Winnicott (1953, 1971) believed that the adaptive function which the transitional object has for the infant continues throughout life in the form of play, religion, daydreaming, interests, and artistic creativity, all of which can re-create a similar illusory state in which an individual can transcend his or her sense of separateness. It is not known whether de Kooning had a transitional object as an infant, and perhaps his sister Marie was the only one in the family who enjoyed playing with him when he was a baby; but as a child and adolescent, his interest in drawing, reading adventure stories, and watching reflections of the sky in the sea, would qualify as transitional phenomena. And, as an adult, he frequently whistled while working in his studio, a habit that bothered his wife Elaine when they worked at opposite corners of a small apartment that served for a while as a shared studio as well as their home.

## The Conceptual Model of Attachment Theory

In the same year that de Kooning began painting *Woman I*, British psychiatrist and psychoanalyst John Bowlby took a temporary appointment with the World Health Organization to conduct a study examining the effects of maternal deprivation on the mental health of children. He visited several countries in Europe, including The Netherlands, as well as the United States of America, had discussions with childcare and child guidance workers in those countries, and made an exhaustive review of the relevant world literature up to that time. His study resulted in the publication in 1951 of the monograph *Maternal Care and Mental Health,* in which he argued that psychological deprivation during infancy caused by prolonged separation from parents, or by the absence of a warm and loving relationship with a mother or mother substitute, can have deep and long-lasting adverse effects on the child's mental health. Bowlby was just three years younger than de Kooning, and although he had been born into an upper-middle-class family, he was not spared childhood trauma (S.W. Coates, 2004). The fourth of six children, he was raised by a nanny, his beloved and primary caregiver who left the family when he was almost four, which he described years later as a tragic loss. His mother held the view (perhaps influenced by Dr. Holt's book) that it was dangerous to spoil children; and so she failed to respond to bids for attention and affection. When they were living in their winter home in London, she saw the children for only one hour each day and usually read to them. Bowlby's father, a surgeon, was apparently a remote and inaccessible man who had been traumatized at age five by the loss of his own father, a war correspondent who had been captured and brutally tortured to death. John was sent to boarding school at the age of seven, which exposed him to more suffering from separation, loneliness, and deprivation of love and affection. As Susan Coates (2004) points out, Bowlby's repeated experiences of loss and trauma allowed him to easily identify with traumatized children and strongly influenced the theory he developed. Bowlby would have had considerable empathy for de Kooning.

Similar to de Kooning's determination to paint in whatever style he chose, Bowlby followed his own interests and convictions within the field of psychoanalysis, even though he was criticized harshly by his colleagues in the British Psychoanalytic Society. When he qualified as a psychoanalyst in 1937, the focus was on the internal phantasy world of the patient; it was assumed that anyone interested in the influence of events in the external world could not be interested in, or was running away from, the internal world. Bowlby reports that this contrast of internal with external never appealed to him. Furthermore, in his work with children and families, he was "daily confronted with the impact on children of the emotional problems from which their parents suffered" (Bowlby, 1988a, p. 48). The principal focus of his work became a study of the interaction of the external world with the internal world, namely, between the way a child is treated by his parents and the mental representations he has of them, and how these representations influence subsequent relationships. Based on systematic observations of children and their parents, rather than speculative reconstructions from the psychoanalyst's couch, he developed a theory of attachment, which provides a conceptual framework for evaluating the quality of early childhood relationships, and the quality of close relationships a person establishes throughout life.

Bowlby (1973) was influenced by observations in ethological studies that the offspring of different species form strong emotional bonds with the parent they have contact with early in life.[4] Recognizing that these early attachments serve basic survival functions, in particular protection from predators, he proposed an *innate attachment system*

---

4   Bowlby watched René Spitz's films of orphaned infants who failed to thrive, films of Harry Harlow's studies with infant monkeys separated from their mothers, and received guidance from the ethologist Robert Hinde. He was also influenced by psychoanalytic concepts proposed by Ferenczi, Fairbairn, and Suttie.

in humans, which he considered a primary motivator of behavior that is operative from "the cradle to the grave" (Bowlby, 1988a). He proposed that attachment behavior is activated under certain conditions, especially by pain, fatigue, and anything frightening, and when the mother is inaccessible. The conditions that terminate the behavior vary according to the intensity of the arousal and can range from the sight or sound of the mother, to touching or clinging to her, or sometimes a prolonged cuddle is needed. It was evident to Bowlby that attachment behavior is not confined to children but can also be observed in adolescents and adults whenever they are anxious or under stress.

Bowlby's ideas, coupled with findings from early studies on the effects of maternal deprivation, inspired extensive research over several decades that not only advanced attachment theory, but, as he had anticipated, also expanded his conceptual framework to accommodate many of the psychological phenomena to which Freud called "attention." Attachment theory thereby offers an alternative to the metapsychology of traditional psychoanalysis. Moreover, the attitude of most psychoanalysts toward attachment theory gradually changed as they shifted their emphasis from conflicts over sexual and aggressive drives and wishes to relational motives and interactional processes (Eagle, 2013).

Infants and children depend on their parents to be available and to comfort them when they are distressed, a need that continues well into adolescence. Bowlby (1988b) recognized that when the parents are available and sufficiently attentive and responsive, the infant becomes confident that it is safe to begin to explore the world around them knowing that there is someone to turn to if they encounter adverse or frightening situations. If the infant experiences a traumatic situation that activates attachment behavior, the parent provides solace and reassurance, which shelter the infant from being overwhelmed by distressing emotions. Such infants are described as having a pattern of *secure* attachment; they relate well to others and gradually acquire a capacity to mentally represent and regulate their affects and also a capacity to think about their own and others' mental states. Attachment researchers identify two other patterns of attachment, which they describe as *insecure* attachment. With parents who are consistently rejecting or dismissing when the infant seeks comfort and protection, the infant learns to not express emotions openly or seek support and develops an *avoidant* attachment to them. These infants engage in explorative behavior but try to cope with distressing emotions through their own efforts. Other parents are inconsistent in their caregiving, being sometimes responsive and sometimes rejecting when the infant seeks comfort from them. Uncertain what to expect, the infant develops a pattern of *anxious* attachment; these infants are prone to separation anxiety, tend to be clinging, and are anxious about exploring the world.

The different patterns of attachment to caregivers are internalized in early childhood to form what Bowlby termed *representational models* or *internal working models*. Because these models enable the child to predict behavior and select the strategy that will best preserve a link to their primary caregivers, the secure pattern and the two insecure patterns of attachment are considered *organized*. Attachment researchers also identified a fourth category of infant behavior in relation to caregivers, which they describe as *disorganized*. Upon reunion with their primary caregiver after a short separation, these infants appear fearful, conflicted, apprehensive, and disoriented. This odd behavior often appears only briefly, and it coexists with avoidant, anxious, or secure patterns of behavior. The disorganized pattern of behavior is thus considered a secondary classification, although some researchers describe it as a *fearful-avoidant* pattern of attachment. The disorganized behavior is thought to result from the activation of competing needs to approach and avoid the caregiver. In their daily interactions with their children, the caregiver seems frightened or behaves in frightening ways, which encourages the infant to avoid them. But this response is opposed by the infant's innate need to seek proximity to the attachment figure and relief from their fear, even though the caregiver is the source of the fear. Thus, there is a paradox of fearing the person they wish to approach for comfort when they are feeling distressed (Fonagy, 2001). Unlike securely attached infants and children, those with insecure patterns of attachment, and especially those with disorganized behavior, are unable to effectively contain and process distressing emotions associated with trauma, which become a permanent presence subject to the repetition compulsion, which I describe further on.

According to Bowlby (1988a, 1988b), an organized pattern of attachment does not develop until the second half of the first year. And during the first two or three years of infancy, patterns of attachment are open to change because they are responsive to different experiences with the mother and with other caregivers. Bowlby recognized that the child may form a pattern with the father that is different from the pattern with the mother, and he proposed coexisting multiple internal working models. Once patterns of attachment have been formed, they tend to persist especially if the way a parent treats the child tends to continue unchanged. By age five, "most children are using a sophisticated working model of mother or mother-substitute which includes knowledge of her interests, moods, and intentions, all of which the child can then take into account" (Bowlby, 1988b, p. 4). As the child grows older, internal working models of attachment become progressively more elaborated and differentiated and remain relatively stable from adolescence onward (Waters et al., 2000).

It might seem to the reader that I have deviated into a long and too detailed account of the conceptual framework of attachment theory, but it is a key to understanding how aspects of de Kooning's inner representational world developed during childhood, and for understanding his pattern of relating to women as an adult, which will become evident in Chapter 6. It may also help us understand why, "Throughout his life, he returned to the female figure as to eternally unfinished business" (Stevens and Swan, 2004, p. 228). Based on what is known about the artist's infancy and formative years, we can assume that he developed an insecure pattern of attachment, most likely an avoidant pattern in relation to his mother, since his sister was the only member of the family he could turn to for comfort when he was distressed. Because of the frequent arguing and fighting between his parents, and his mother's frightening behavior that continued long after separation from her husband, the infant Willem probably sometimes also manifested disorganized attachment behavior. We can assume that he wanted to be physically close to and feel loved by his mother but would have been fearful that she might unpredictably become angry and slap him or lock him in a closet. Yet, as he grew older and could be absent from the home, like other avoidantly attached children, Willem was able to engage in explorative behavior; he freely explored the city with other boys, especially the waterfront, where he enjoyed looking at the sea and watching the ships for hours. De Kooning later told the critic Harold Rosenberg: "There is something about being in touch with the sea that makes me feel good. That's where most of my paintings come from, even when I made them in New York" (Rosenberg, 1972; Yard, 2007, p.152).

Many people find comfort looking at the sea, which can be regarded as a symbol for the mother. As Viederman (1987) and McDougall (1989) point out, the sea, *la mer*, is a homonym for *la mère*, the mother. It appears that de Kooning depicted water or a representation of the sea in most of the Woman paintings, including at the lowest part of the canvas in *Woman I* and *Woman IV*, and as a blue rectangular shape in *Woman VI*; *Woman III* is standing in water. As Marlene Clark (2020) observes, "*Woman II* is surrounded, like Persephone, by swaths of a mesmerizing blue-green, reminiscent of the sea" (p. 101) (Figures 1, 4, 5, and 7).[5] These representations, together with the artist's comment that *Woman I* brought back a childhood memory of a woman sitting by a canal in Holland, support an interpretation that the images in the

---

5   Christopher Bollas (1997) thinks that "anyone who grows up by the sea forms a type of myth about the meanings of his or her childhood, that invariably incorporates the order between two entirely different worlds: the terrestrial world and the sea." (pp. 35-36). Having grown up near the sea myself, I agree with Bollas that the child "lives in an intimate relationship to that which gives life and takes life" (p. 36). I frequently heard of people's drowning when I was a child and adolescent in New Zealand, which instilled in me a fear of the sea, but I immensely enjoyed surfing in the waves or simply looking at the sea. For de Kooning, with his interest in American pop culture when he was an adolescent, the sea represented freedom from his suffocating family and the limitations of the Dutch culture. As an adult, he disliked being away for too long from the sea, yet he disliked swimming and feared drowning. The Woman paintings communicate this intimate relation between life and death. It seems relevant to mention the Belgian artist James Ensor, who grew up in Ostend on the North Sea coast and throughout his life sought solace and calm from the sea. However, he denied the cruelty and dangers of the sea. As David Werman (1989) describes, Ensor totally idealized the sea; it came to represent the consoling pre-oedipal mother, the sensual oedipal mother, and a muse that he turned to for reassurance in his work.

third series convey aspects of a fantasied "good" (alluring) mother. While playing on the canals and streets, however, Willem sometimes performed dangerous stunts, and once "dangled precariously from a high church wall, delighting in the other children's fear" (Stevens and Swan, 2004, p. 14). This dangerous behavior might have been a counterphobic response to the fear and helplessness induced by his frightening "bad" mother and to restore a sense of power.

It is not known how often de Kooning's father visited Willem during his formative years, but according to Stevens and Swan (2004), Leendert had little contact with his son even during the ten months Willem spent with him as a four-year-old. Willem would have been insecurely attached to this gruff and authoritarian father, whose absence contributed to the profound loneliness he felt growing up. Though the sensitivity and attunement of fathers contributes to attachment security, another important role of fathers is to provide praise and encouragement, and foster positive feelings in their children (Holmes, 2005). As mentioned in the previous chapter, Willem received minimal praise and encouragement from his father when he visited his shop during the early 1920s and gave him gifts of small drawings; according to Wolfe (1996), Leendert resented being asked for money. Reflecting on his experience in the letter he sent to his sister several decades later, de Kooning thought that their father "forgot" that children need something from the father as well as the mother (Stevens and Swan, 2004, p. 13). His wish for a connection with a masculine father is suggested by two powerful memories from childhood days which I mention in Chapter 2; he never forgot the sound of the stamping of the hooves of the horses or ponies who pulled his father's beer and lemonade wagons, and he had a strong memory of his father's "impressive, but forbiddingly high, starch collars—and wanted to get their feeling in his painting" (Stevens and Swan, 2004, p. 13). The father's unresponsiveness and lack of empathy were evident even when de Kooning was in his early forties and reached out to him in a letter he wrote while he was going through a dark period and feeling that he was failing as an artist. He told his father that he had an irresistible longing to see him again, and he tried to defend his desire to succeed as a painter. But rather than his father's acknowledging Willem's commitment to his work and bolstering his self-esteem, Leendert focused on the difficulty his son would have with selling his work. De Kooning could never feel loved and approved of by his father. Leendert's second son also experienced their father as closed and introverted, a man who did not express his feelings (Wolfe, 1996).

Consistent with Bowlby's (1988a) clinical approach, it is necessary to consider what led Cornelia and Leendert to adopt the style of parenting each had with Willem. Given their different temperaments and frequent arguing, they probably provided little emotional support to each other; and there is no record that relatives were available to counsel the couple during the early years of their marriage, or to assist Cornelia with shopping, laundry, babysitting, or looking after Marie while Leendert was at work. Leendert's mother participated in looking after Willem during the ten months he lived with his father, but the demands of Leendert's work gave him little time with his son. Cornelia and Leendert might have had unhappy childhoods themselves, because of inadequate mothering they received and fathers who were probably not very available. Once these factors are recognized, "the idea of blaming parents evaporates . . ." (Bowlby, 1988a, p. 142 ).

Bowlby (1988a) acknowledged that it would be easy for an unwary reader to assume that a term like "internal working model" belongs "within a psychology concerned only with cognition and one bereft of feeling and action" (p. 177). He emphasizes, however, that during early infancy emotional expression and its reception are the only means of communication that we have, and thus the internal working models are mental representations of the self, the other person (the object), and the affectively charged interaction between them.[6] Moreover, in addition to providing the experience of safety in the early family environment, as well as responsiveness to the infant's and child's distressing emotions, the attachment system plays an important role in the development of affects and the capacity to regulate affects. The secure and insecure patterns of attachment described by Bowlby and subsequent attachment researchers reflect different strategies used by the child to regulate affective arousal during interactions with, and separations from, the parents. Bowlby's theories of attachment and separation also cast new light on the problem of separation anxiety by considering it a direct response to the loss, or threat of loss of the mother, rather than a consequence of accumulated drive and need tensions. He linked anxiety disorders in adult life with the experience of long or repeated separations, or frequent threats of such, during childhood. Subsequent investigations of anxiety disorder patients found that those suffering panic attacks often reported a history of being separated from one or both parents for one month or longer during childhood (Breier, Charney, and Heninger, 1986; Raskin *et*

---

6   This conceptualization of internal working models approximates what Clark (2020) referred to as the Kernbergian triangle of self, object, and the affective interaction between them, which I mention in Chapter 2.

*al.*, 1982). Thus, the separations that Willem experienced in infancy, may well have contributed to the panic attacks and loneliness he experienced in his adult life.

## The Internal Object World

The formulations of attachment theory overlap with some aspects of object relations theory, which provides an alternative approach for conceptualizing de Kooning's inner representational world, as well as his adult relationships. Object relations theory is really a group of theories that were proposed during the middle decades of the last century by several psychoanalysts and psychotherapists in Britain including Ian Suttie, Ronald Fairbairn, Harry Guntrip, Melanie Klein, and Donald Winnicott. Most readers will know that psychoanalysts use the word "object" to refer to a person, and "object relationship" to refer to the actual relationship one has with another person. An "internal object" is the mental representation of another person; the term "part-object" refers to the mental representation of an aspect or part of a person and may be described as either good or bad depending on whether it represents an object that satisfies or an object that frustrates a person's libidinal or attachment needs. To reflect the infant's double experience of satisfaction and frustration with the nurturant mother, a part-object is often referred to as a good or bad breast. A "whole-object" is the term for the mental representation of a whole person, who is regarded as someone with similar rights, feelings, and needs as oneself, as opposed to someone who is perceived as being present primarily to satisfy one's needs. Thus, self and object representations can be split into good and bad self-representations and good and bad representations of the object. The internal object world involves dynamic interactions among internal objects, in which one part of the self may be identified with an internal good or bad part-object, and another part identified with a good or bad self-representation (Ogden, 1983). An internal object is often "projected" into the external world and identified as belonging to another person, a mechanism referred to as "projective identification." All of the objects in a person's inner world are conceptualized as unconscious *phantasies*. The more popular term *fantasy* refers to conscious derivatives of phantasies, such as daydreams.[7]

The concept of unconscious phantasy was introduced by Melanie Klein in the 1940s and elaborated by Susan Isaacs (1952) in a classic article on the nature and function of phantasy. As Thomas Ogden (1984) explains, Klein conceptualized phantasy as the psychic representation of instinct, which itself is a biological entity and therefore present from birth. The infant's early phantasies are based on bodily impulses and sensory experience, with most sensations being experienced through contact with the feeding mother—touching, sucking, swallowing, spewing, and biting, as well as kinesthetic and visceral experience and excitations induced by external stimuli. Early in development, these subsymbolic experiences are given mental form as primitive phantasies that are linked with images such as visual perceptions of shapes, and especially eyes and other aspects of the human face. As every parent has observed, the infant comes to know the outer world through its

---

7   As noted in Chapter 2, some psychoanalysts use the terms fantasy and phantasy interchangeably to include conscious and unconscious elements.

eyes and by taking everything into its mouth. Psychoanalysts refer to the taking in of sensations and perceptions as *introjection*; the expelling of something unpleasant from the external world and the discharge of inner tensions are referred to as *projection*. The infant's subjective experience and perception of the mother are assumed to take extreme forms of being "all good" or "all bad," such that there is a tendency to introject what is pleasurable and treat it as belonging to the self, and to project what is painful or unpleasurable and treat it as belonging to another person (the object). The mechanisms of introjection and projection are conceptualized as essential to early development of the ego and an inner life and cannot be divorced from object relations; they occur throughout life, albeit influenced by the expanding functions of the ego (Heimann, 1952).

Although psychoanalysts have long used the terms introjection and projection to describe transactions between the inner world and the external world, these terms are somewhat misleading because we do not "take in" other people when we interact with them; nor do we actually project something from ourselves "into" other people. Clarifying the meaning of introjection, Grotstein (2009) cites a neurocognitive scientist's theory that "when we encounter objects in the outer world, we . . . recreate them imagistically from the raw clay of our own inner resources." In this way, "the unconscious is a 'portrait artist' who uses the pigments of imagination and archetypal prefigured noumenal forms to construct images that finally come to be shaped by the perception of experiences with live models" (p. 148). Explaining projection, Grotstein proposes that the projecting person, in unconscious phantasy, projectively re-identifies aspects of him- or herself (good or bad) in his own *internal image* of the other person, with which its image is confused. That is, projection is into one's image of the other person rather than into the actual person. The projecting person may then in some ways coerce or attempt to make the other person conform to this image. Since projection always involves an object- or part-object relationship, it is more correctly conceptualized as projective identification. This is a complex explanation of a common phenomenon, but it will help us understand aspects of de Kooning's relationships with women, which I discuss in Chapter 6.

Similar to Bowlby's postulate of internal working models of the self and the attachment figure in interaction, object relations theorists propose that the internalization of early patterns of attachment result in mental representations of self and object, and representations of affectively charged interactions between self and object. Findings from empirical research partially support a conceptual overlap of the attachment and object relations paradigms.[8] For example, in a study with young adult participants, those involved in a committed (*i.e.*, secure) relationship tended to have complex, well-differentiated representations of self and others, a greater capacity to invest emotionally in others, and a better understanding of the intentions of others (Calabrese, Farber, and Weston, 2005). However, there are several important differences between the two theoretical paradigms. Bowlby thought that internal working models were based largely on actual events, rather than on the infant's phantasies. Contemporary psychoanalytic object relations theory also gives importance to early environmental experiences but does not regard mental representations

---

8   Geoff Goodman (2002) has provided a comprehensive discussion of attachment theory and object relations theory, including a review of empirical evidence supporting the conceptual relatedness of object representations and internal working models.

as veridical reflections of actual behaviors and interactions with caregivers. Instead, strong emphasis is given to the infant's phantasies and childhood wishes, which are believed to generate distortions in the child's perceptions and understanding of the caregiver's behavior, and thus to modify the mental representations of early dyadic relationships (Eagle, 1997; Fonagy, 2001; Goodman, 2002).

Bowlby (1973) proposed that "it is not uncommon for an individual to operate, simultaneously, with two (or more) working models of his attachment figure(s), and two (or more) working models of himself" (p. 205). One working model is usually dominant and conscious to the individual, while other working models may be operating unconsciously. Linking attachment theory to object relations theory, as conceptualized by Fairbairn, Clarke (2006) suggests that individuals with a secure attachment style are likely to have minimal splitting of internal objects, and to relate to others as whole objects. Those classified as avoidant or anxiously attached are likely to have different degrees of splitting of internal objects, the avoidant child being more used to feeling rejected by the mother and therefore influenced more strongly by a powerful internal "bad" object. The disorganized attachment pattern might be explained by the presence of two internal working models of equal power, but with significantly different expectations and responses; activation of both working models would send contradictory signals to the muscles and lead to apparently contradictory behaviors. Thus, to some extent, the anxious and avoidant dimensions of attachment behavior map onto the spectrum of paranoid-schizoid and depressive modes of mental functioning defined by Klein, secure attachment being associated with the depressive position and its higher-level defenses and cognitive ability, and disorganized attachment associated with the paranoid-schizoid position and primitive defenses. Steele and Steele (1998) believe that "the Kleinian description of the troubled and often chaotic internal world of the developing human infant is very likely to apply to the inner experience of the child with a disorganized attachment and a controlling pattern of relating in the pre-school and school-age years" (p. 140).

Though there are multiple internal object relations, I posit that de Kooning's inner world was dominated by a powerful, alluring, but frightening part-object (*i.e.*, a persecutory maternal figure that he both needed and feared), and a weak, helpless, needy self-representation. I suggest that when de Kooning told Selden Rodman (1957, p. 102) that perhaps he was painting "the woman in me," he was unconsciously referring to this powerful, internal part-object, and when he told Amei Wallach that the *Woman* looked like him, "Not the woman in me, but me" (Wallach, 1994, p. 9), he was unconsciously revealing an identification with this internal part-object. De Kooning also unwittingly revealed a link between this internal part-object and *Woman I*, when journalist Curtis Pepper was visiting the artist in 1983 and showed him a reproduction of *Woman I* in Harry Gaugh's (1983) book about his work. De Kooning expressed both fear and puzzlement; he said, "She even frightens me. Not so much to look at, as to think how she came out of me, how it happened" (Pepper, 1983, p. 88). As a helpless young boy without protection from his father, and lacking a close relationship with his stepfather, Willem likely perceived his mother as a "threatening giant." Indeed, when Willem's mother came from Holland to visit her son in New York in 1954, as she descended the gangway of the ocean liner, de Kooning quietly said, "She's only five feet tall, but to me she looms ten" (Lieber, 2000, p. 40). And in 1968, after visiting his elderly and then frail mother in a nursing home in Holland, de Kooning said, "That's the person I feared most in the whole world" (Stevens and Swan, 2004, p. 514). We can speculate that if Leendert had been more present and provided good fathering throughout his son's childhood and adolescence, de Kooning may have felt less of a compulsion to paint the female figure; an internal representation of a "good" father protects against the overwhelming presence of a powerful mother.

## Childhood Trauma and the Compulsion to Repeat

Although Bowlby's work redirected psychoanalysts to pay attention to early development and the psychological consequences of adverse experiences in childhood, he did not develop an adequate conceptual framework for how the mind responds to traumatic experiences at different ages. The framework I find most useful was proposed by Rafael Lopez-Corvo (2014, 2020), a psychoanalytic scholar from Venezuela, who practices also in Canada and the United States. Lopez-Corvo makes an important distinction between *pre-conceptual* trauma and *conceptual* trauma. According to his definitions, pre-conceptual trauma occurs in the early years of life, before the child's mind has developed the capacity to contain and metabolize the impact of traumatic events, and when there is an absence of an empathically responsive parent or other caregiver to contain and help the child manage the distressing emotions evoked by the events. Conceptual traumas occur at an older age, when the child's mind has the capacity to contain the fact of the trauma but fails to provide an adequate meaning.[9] Pre-conceptual traumas of various kinds and severity occur in the early life of every human being, and as Lopez-Corvo explains, they become entangled with all conceptual traumas, thereby intensifying the emotions evoked by subsequent traumatic situations. He proposes that the extent to which pre-conceptual trauma becomes a permanent presence that continuously repeats the past and affects a person throughout life depends largely on the quality of the early infant-caregiver relationship. For de Kooning, the biographical history I reviewed in Chapter 3 provides ample evidence that he suffered significant pre-conceptual trauma during his infancy years, which was compounded by conceptual trauma that he experienced during his childhood and adolescence. An exploration of the artist's childhood trauma and its impact on his adult life shows how trauma collapses time and brings past, present, and future together. Indeed, as Freud (1920) described, unconscious mental processes are not changed by the passage of time—the unconscious is timeless. This takes us back to Rosalind Krauss' (2015) suggestion that de Kooning's inability to get away from painting the woman has the ring of a repetition compulsion.

In psychoanalysis, *repetition compulsion* or the *compulsion to repeat* refers to the tendency to repeat or act out aspects of past experience

---

9   The distinction between pre-conceptual trauma and conceptual trauma is derived from Piaget's (1951) theory of cognitive and affective development, in which the formation of mental representations follows a sequence of incremental changes from an initial sensorimotor stage (up to age 2), to a preoperational stage (age 2 to 7), followed by a concrete operational stage (age 7 to 11), and finally to a formal operational stage (early adolescence through adulthood). Mental representations that are formed in the early preoperational period (ages 2 to 4) are referred to as *preconcepts*; emotions in this early preoperational period and in the preceding sensorimotor stage are experienced as sensations, perceptions, and impulses to action. As cognitive development proceeds, conceptual representations are formed that are organized on a more abstract, logical, and reality-oriented level (Frosch, 1995).

138

without awareness of the meaning of the present behavior and its connection to the past (Auchincloss and Samberg, 2012). The continual repetition sustains an illusion of timelessness (Weiss, 2020). This phenomenon was first described by Sigmund Freud in a 1914 article titled "Remembering, repeating, and working through" and it soon came to be regarded as a fundamental feature of human psychology and behavior. The tendency to repeat the past is especially evident with childhood trauma that has not been adequately contained and processed by the person's mind. The repetition of trauma causes further suffering to the person and often also to other people in the person's life. In his "seduction theory" of hysterical symptoms, Freud (1894; Breuer and Freud, 1893) referred to the memory of the trauma acting like a "parasite" or "foreign body" that produces recurring symptoms long after its entry. Lopez-Corvo (2014) similarly proposes that pre-conceptual traumas leave permanent impressions in the child's mind (analogous to the fossil footprints of a dinosaur), which are structured as "a narrative of conjoined presences of absences" (p. xxi). He suggests that these hidden presences function like highly toxic and emotionally organized "parasites" that inhibit the development of symbolization and logical thinking, alter the experience of time and space, and are projected everywhere, thereby determining most forms of psychopathology as well as affecting the individual's ways of behaving and thinking.

I can best illustrate the distinction between pre-conceptual and conceptual traumas and the influence of repetition-compulsion by briefly mentioning Milton Viederman's psychoanalytic articles about the Norwegian painter Edvard Munch and the Belgian painter René Magritte. Like the current study, Viederman's (1994) article about Munch focuses on the theme of the artist's relationship with his mother and the influence of early childhood trauma on his paintings and adult relationships with women. Munch's mother, who was raising five young children and struggling to cope with limited finances, as well as progressive illness and frequent separation from her husband due to his professional obligations, died from tuberculosis when Edvard was age five. The traumatic emotions associated with this loss were re-evoked at age fifteen by the death of Edvard's one-year-older sister, who had taken on a maternal function. Viederman does not use the term pre-conceptual to define the trauma, but the loss occurred at an early stage of cognitive development when a child's thinking is illogical and egocentric and generates fantasied meanings for traumatic events. Viederman suggests that, at the young age of five, Edvard felt in some way responsible for his mother's death and, in his immature mind, constructed an unconscious phantasy that his rage over the mother's limited availability to him during infancy had killed her. Viederman demonstrates the compulsive repetition of the trauma in a series of relationships that Munch had with women during his adult life. The relationships were stormy and conflicted, beginning with intensely passionate attachment but ending with separation, despair, and self-destructive behavior. Viederman also draws attention to a recurring curvilinear form in many of Munch's paintings, which is related to the contour of his mother and is consistent with the idea of traumatic repetition. Undiluted hatred emerges in some of Munch's later paintings, including scenes of murder as well as scenes of tenderness directed toward women. Viederman was careful to emphasize that the theme he explored was only one dimension of a complex life and creative work, and that his interpretations were speculative and leaned heavily on general theory about how a child's mind functions.

The study of Munch can be compared with Viederman's (1987) earlier psychoanalytic article about the Belgian painter René Magritte, whose mother committed suicide by drowning herself in a river when he was fourteen. At that age, Magritte had the cognitive capacity to think logically about the loss and to employ higher-level defenses to contain traumatic emotions. Viederman shows that, although the trauma had a profound effect on the form and style of the artist's paintings, in particular a play between reality and illusion, his creative work represented a mostly successful effort to contain and master the despair and helplessness evoked by the trauma. Some paintings reveal a breakthrough of primitive aggressive impulses and phantasies, but these were painted around the time Magritte's wife had a miscarriage and a lingering postpartum illness. Viederman suggests that the possibility of Magritte's losing his wife and the actual loss of a child likely aroused painful memories of the loss of his mother. Magritte had a long-lasting marriage, and although he had at least one affair and was estranged from his wife for nearly four years, they reconciled and remained together until his death (Molcard, 2019).

Like Edvard Munch, and all of us, de Kooning would not have been able to recall the pre-conceptual trauma and other experiences that occurred during the early years of childhood. This is because during the first few years of life, children rely primarily on their *procedural memory* systems, which underlie the learning of skills and habits, but also encode information that cannot be recalled. *Declarative memory* develops later and refers to information that can be consciously recalled, such as facts and events. These two memory systems are developmentally and anatomically distinct (Siegel, 1999; Yovell, 2000). According to Robert Clyman (1991), the declarative memory system "is not fully functional until around the age of five, when declarative memories are consolidated and stored in a form which permits later retrieval" (p. 355). Declarative memory (also referred to as "explicit" memory) involves the *hippocampus*, which is immature at birth and develops throughout early childhood. Procedural memory (also referred to as "implicit" memory) is largely mediated by the *amygdala*, which is functional soon after birth (Clyman, 1991; Siegel, 1999; Yovell, 2000). Thus, the amnesia we have for the first few years of our lives is not owing to repression, as Freud thought, but to immaturity of the hippocampus. The amygdala has rich neural connections within the limbic system and with other parts of the brain, and it mediates the behavioral and physiological responses to threatening stimuli. A different set of circuits is involved in generating the subjective feelings of fear and anxiety (LeDoux and Pine, 2016). Once the neural connections that mediate a traumatic association are made, they are not forgotten by the amygdala, which is readily activated by traumatic stimuli without requiring conscious recollection of the original threatening situation. In contrast, the hippocampus is easily forgetful, and its structure and functioning can be reduced in states of chronic stress due to damage caused by high levels of cortisol and other stress hormones (Siegel, 1999; Yovell, 2000). Given de Kooning's proneness to depression and panic attacks as an adult, and his history of childhood trauma, it is possible that his amygdalae were hyper-reactive, and perhaps the volume of his hippocampus was reduced at times (Teicher and Samson, 2013). Stevens and Swan (2004) have the impression that "Even as an adult, de Kooning was unconsciously on guard against the unexpected attack: Conrad Fried once innocently raised his hand, and de Kooning flinched as if he were about to be struck" (p. 339). Hyper-reactivity of the artist's amygdalae is suggested also by a statement he made in a letter to his sister Marie in 1967. Of their mother, he wrote (in English): "When I was around 38 or 40 years old I had become in a terrible state of anxiety. My heart would start beating wildly if I just thought about her" (quoted by Wolfe, 1996, p. 405). And, as I will illustrate in Chapter 6, he often behaved impulsively rather than rationally.

When Freud discovered that early childhood traumas are reproduced as actions rather than memories, he initially thought the aim was to achieve mastery over each trauma and its resolution. He later invoked the idea of a "death instinct" as an innate biological urge in all living organisms to restore a previous state of being. However, mastery is rarely achieved by compulsively repeating past trauma in the present, and the idea of a death drive is controversial and not part of mainstream psychoanalytic theorizing. Contemporary theorists conceptualize repetition compulsion as *communicating*, as well as defending against, traumatic experiences that cannot be consciously remembered (Chu, 1991; Levy, 2000). Psychiatrist James Chu (1991) notes, "the behaviors are communications about past realities which need to be understood" (p. 330); yet the person engaged in the behaviors is unaware of this communication and is protecting himself from painful and overwhelming emotions. As mentioned in Chapter 1, the critics Peter Schjeldahl and Richard Brody recognized that de Kooning's Woman paintings of the early 1950s communicate anguish and trauma, of which the artist was seemingly not conscious.

In my opinion, the artist's anguish is associated with pre-conceptual trauma experienced during the first few years of his life, when holding and containing functions of his parents were inadequate. Remember that emotions are the infant's first language, and if they are not adequately interpreted and responded to by the parents, they fail to be mentally represented and linked with words; inchoate emotions are therefore experienced as sensations, perceptions, and impulses to action. The anxiety that de Kooning often experienced as an adult can be considered a signal, a sense of anticipation that something from the past was about to re-occur in the present, which the artist had not yet identified, but "remembered" by an expectation of feelings of helplessness. As Perelberg (2018) explains, this is an experience in which the past, present, and future dimensions of time are brought together.

Clinicians report that almost any aspect of past traumas can be repeated—behaviors, affects, images, and sensations (Levy, 2000; van der Kolk, 1989). And, as Wilson and Malatesta (1989) explain, the repetitions that arise from experiences early in development "tend to contain and carry the actual experiential content of the early dyadic interaction between caregiver and the child, specifically the affectively-laden content" (p. 266). As I have already mentioned, because pre-conceptual traumas occur during preverbal and pre-symbolic development, they are encoded in the procedural (implicit) memory systems and stored in the amygdala and other subcortical brain structures. Thus, following Lopez-Corvo's model, the traumas that de Kooning experienced during the first four or five years of his life were encoded in his implicit memory system and were therefore not accessible to reflection and logical thinking by his conscious mind.

He would have been able to recall conceptual traumatic experiences that occurred after age five (such as being beaten or threatened by his mother), but prior to early adolescence, he was likely confused and puzzled as to why his mother treated him and his sister and half-brother so harshly and without good reason. The pre-conceptual trauma would also have intensified the experience of conceptual traumas, resulting in what Masud Khan (1963) referred to as "cumulative trauma." Influenced by some of Winnicott's work, Khan considered cumulative trauma a consequence of successive failures of the mother to act as a protective shield over the whole course of the child's development, from infancy to adolescence, especially in areas of experience where the child continues to need the mother to support his immature and unstable ego functions. De Kooning undoubtedly suffered cumulative trauma.

Freud (1914, 1920) proposed that unremembered early childhood experiences may be repeated not only as contemporary experiences within a person's adult relationships, but also in other activities without the person's knowing they are repeating something that belongs to the past. I propose that de Kooning's compulsive need to paint the female figure was driven in part by a continuing repetition of the procedurally encoded, disorganized pattern of attachment behavior that originated in infancy and remained as an unresolved pre-conceptual trauma. Some of the critics of the Woman paintings appear to have intuited that the images reflect an unresolved childhood conflict between the competing need to approach the mother for comfort and love and the need to avoid her for fear of further rejection. For example, as I indicated in Chapter 1, Crehan (1953) made the insightful comment that "He [de Kooning] can't paint without the Woman, yet he can't connect with her." This early observation is consistent with Bowlby's view that attachment is an innate need, and even when the infant or child has been traumatized and learned to fear the mother, they will still seek to remain attached to her. Carol Duncan (1989) recognized the artist's conflict between desire and fear when she commented that *Woman I* conveys complex and emotionally ambivalent meanings— "the fear of and flight from as well as a quest for the woman" (p. 178). And Robert Hughes (1997a) intuited "the simultaneous allure for and fear of woman implanted by Mama" (p. 478–479). The desire to approach is suggested by the Women's prominent breasts which appear bountiful and alluring; however, the simultaneous need to avoid the Women is conveyed by the nearby danger from the bared teeth and the claw-like hands. For example, as Stevens and Swan (2004) point out, the lower set of teeth in *Woman and Bicycle* forms "a necklace above her breasts, as if she were ready to snap should any pathetic boy wish to suckle" (p. 339). Although none of us remember suckling milk from our mother's breasts, Hustvedt (2016) comments that "our motor-sensory, emotional-perceptual learning begins long before our conscious memories" (p. 17). Hustvedt's comment is consistent with my discussion of the slow maturation of the hippocampus and what is known about the encoding of early experience in the procedural memory system.

As mentioned earlier, de Kooning confirmed the fear he had of his mother during childhood when he said that she was the person he had feared most in the whole world. I suggest that he unconsciously communicated this fear and also a desire for the alluring mother to viewers of the Woman paintings; but the conflict between approach and avoidance remained as an unresolved trauma in the artist. The allure is not that of a sexually desirable woman taken from a pinup calendar, nor a seductive mother as Marlene Clark (2020) proposes, but of a mother who could potentially gratify a desire for comfort, love, and security yet remains tantalizing and withholding.

## Aggression in the Woman Paintings

In his interpretation of the Woman paintings, Kuspit (1998) refers to de Kooning's lust for the Venuses and need of their love and tenderness; and he proposes that the artist hates woman as much as he desires her. He comes closest to acknowledging the artist's pre-conceptual trauma when he suggests that "De Kooning's painterliness is a manic defense against the depressing and destructive effect of the Magna Mater on the infantile, primitive psyche. . . . He spoils her out of paranoid envy, even as he luxuriates in her flesh, hanging on to her breasts for dear life, even as he acknowledges that they're not exactly a comforting resting place . . ." (Kuspit, 2011). With this description, Kuspit inadvertently captures the dilemma of the infant, who fears the very person he needs to be close to, resulting in a disorganized pattern of attachment. But despite recognizing the ambivalent meaning in the paintings, he fails to attribute hate to the thwarting of de Kooning's childhood desire for closeness to a comforting and loving maternal figure.[10]

---

10   The Scottish philosopher John Macmurray (1995) conceptualized love and fear as the two motivational forces in human beings; he regarded hate as derived from the thwarting of love. Is de Kooning hating woman as much as he desires her, as Kuspit proposes, or does he fear woman as much as he desires her, a fear based on the traumatic childhood experiences with his mother? Recall that when he was interviewed by David Sylvester in 1960, de Kooning said that when he looks at the Woman paintings now, "they look vociferous and ferocious . . ." (Sylvester, 2001, p. 51).

Kuspit seems to have adopted Freud's and Klein's views on aggression and the death instinct rather than those of Winnicott and Bowlby, who understood aggression as a reaction to unmet needs, and as a protest to the caregiver. As Grotstein (2009) writes, "Aggression and its spectrum [anger, hate, rage, violence, etc.] begin as a *protest* by the individual about an unfair or untenable situation that the object [*e.g.*, the mother or father] must redress. In other words, it is a cry for help because of the exposure of the individual's sense of helplessness and vulnerability" (p. 179). Given the lack of overt love and affection from both parents and the frequent beatings by his mother (Stevens and Swan, 2004, p.12), we can assume that Willem had to repress any expression of anger and hatred until he was old enough to engage in physical and verbal battles with his mother.

Another psychoanalytic concept that can help us understand aggression in the Woman paintings is the concept of "object usage." This concept was introduced into the psychoanalytic literature by Winnicott (1969a, 1969b) in the same year that the first volume of Bowlby's three-volume series *Attachment and Loss* was published. Winnicott rejected the idea of a death instinct and toward the end of his life developed a monistic theory in which he conceptualized aggression as part of a "life force" (a "combined love-strife" drive) (Erel, 2020). The aggressive component is first evinced in infancy, when the baby expresses its motility impulse with energetic thrusts of its limbs, sometimes hitting the mother in the face or breast, tugging at her hair, or writhing in her arms. Though this muscular activity seems

---

In the next chapter, I will outline how the "ferociousness" of the image could involve the artist's own projected aggressive impulses as well as the aggression he experienced from his mother.

ruthless and potentially destructive, at this early stage of development anger and hate do not exist and any destruction is incidental, as it is not yet possible for the infant to recognize the separate existence of the mother. Winnicott emphasized that it is important for the mother to not misinterpret the behavior as intentional aggression; she needs to survive the infant's aggression and not react with counter-aggression. Indeed, for the infant, the survival of the mother is experienced by a lack of retaliation. Whereas a primitive love impulse and the satisfaction of the infant's urges maintain the illusion of unity with the mother, the motility (aggressive) impulse helps place the mother outside of the self, and for the infant to distinguish "Me" from "Not-me." Winnicott united these two impulses into a single energy source which paradoxically contains both love and strife (Erel, 2020). This paradox is expressed in his statement about the infant: "While I am loving you, I am all the time destroying you in (unconscious) *fantasy*" (Winnicott, 1969a, p. 90). As Erel (2020) explains, it is a normal developmental process that allows the infant to advance from a subjective to an objective view of the mother. He describes pathological aggression (*e.g.*, hate, malice, violence, revenge, cruelty) as "the outcome of encounters with an environment, which did not enable the ongoing spontaneity of motility, and caused the life force to detach from the core self" (p. 275).

Although we lack information about the early relationship between Willem and his mother, given Cornelia's temperament, it seems likely that she often reacted negatively to her infant's aggressive gestures. This speculation is consistent with how she behaved during her son's latency years. We know from a conversation that Richard Shiff had with Elaine's brother Conrad Fried, that de Kooning "remembered

149

the mother of his childhood as stern and unwilling to let him do things in his own way or at his own pace" (Shiff, 2011, p. 297, Fn. 475). In Winnicott's opinion, a mother who does not give her infant the experience that she has survived his "destructiveness" (*i.e.*, primary aggression) impinges on the child's emotional development, with the risk of the child's developing a compliant, false self (Abram, 1996). Though Willem learned to be compliant as a child and developed a pattern of avoidant attachment, by mid-adolescence he fought back with his mother, and was sometimes impulsively aggressive in his adult life. And, as described in Chapter 1, he was determined to choose his own style of painting and not be directed by Clement Greenberg and other art critics.

In her dissertation discussing some psychoanalytic perspectives on de Kooning's art, Teressa Broll (2005) applies Winnicott's concept of "object usage" to the Woman paintings of the early 1950s and offers an interpretation with which I fully agree. She proposes that "What has been seen as aggression and misogynistic could also be viewed as an unconscious attempt at destruction in fantasy of a mother who can continue to survive" (p. 72). In developing this idea, Broll points out that the distortion and ambiguity of the figure, which began in the artist's drawings of the late 1940s, has the function of beginning "to separate the figure from objective reality relegating it now to the role of subjective object—that which is part fantasy and part reality" (p. 73). As de Kooning advanced to the third series of Woman paintings, the image had become a symbolic representation, which allowed him to mercilessly attack the figure in fantasy, not in reality. Broll writes:

Gradually, by the distancing from the reality of the image, he begins establishing the psychic freedom to engage in "object usage" — the space to destroy the mother safely in fantasy. The canvasses and women become increasingly bigger, eventually being almost greater than life-size. Now they have the presence to be taken on, freely fragmented, dislocated and reassembled. These women can withstand the attacks, they even grin back, display themselves and laugh with mock aggression. They refuse to be pitied remaining immovable on the canvas joking with the artist in this safe orbit. 'Maybe the grin — its rather like the Mesopotamian idols, they always stand up straight, looking to the sky with this smile, like they are the forces of nature you feel . . . '(de Kooning, 1963) — but they remain safely on the canvas like perfect, soon to become objective, mothers. Neither do they retaliate or go away, enabling de Kooning to endeavor to 'get beyond the image' to subjectivity and reality (p. 74).

Broll opines that "What de Kooning does is take what should remain *in fantasy*, and places it outside into the world of tangible reality *for the viewer*" (p. 75). She suggests that this is disconcerting to the viewer because it involves destruction of the maternal body — the source of life. This interpretation explains the alarming reactions of many of the spectators of these works and the responses of some of the early critics, for the paintings are "far too close to unconscious murder. De Kooning took something outside of the safety of unconscious fantasy into the realm of reality" (p. 75).[11] Like me, Broll emphasizes that de Kooning was not consciously aware of the aggression that went into the Woman paintings, which is most evident in the violent brushstrokes, and therefore did not anticipate the effect it may have on the viewer. But for the artist, *Woman I* is "strong enough to confront her attacker... [She] looks out at the viewer, undaunted by what may be happening to her. The glaring teeth are evident. There are still no hands, but she sits with her legs astride clearly facing her attacker. This is the strong surviving mother" (p. 76).[12]

The application of the concept of object usage allows me to reaffirm my argument that rather than expressing hate, as Fitzsimmons, Kuspit, and other critics thought, the Woman paintings of the early 1950s communicate an attempt by de Kooning to separate himself from a tie to an internal mother that he experienced as threatening and suffocating, rather than liberating. At the same time, he is trapped by his childhood need for consolation from the woman, which renders the image alluring, as he projects onto her aspects of a nurturing good mother. This is the "dynamic of attraction and repulsion" that Cateforis (1991) identified as operating on de Kooning as he painted these images, and which I conceptualize as the repetition of a disorganized pattern of attachment.[13]

---

11  Broll fails to employ the Kleinian distinction between conscious fantasy and unconscious phantasy.

12  As I mentioned in Chapter 2, *Woman I* has claw-like hands.

13  As described earlier in the chapter, a disorganized pattern of attachment is a secondary classification that coexists with a primary pattern of relating, which for de Kooning was most likely an avoidant pattern.

# CHAPTER 5

# The Canvas as Container

Although de Kooning was criticized for alternating between abstract and representational styles of painting and for his treatment of the female figure, he was much admired for his distinctive brushstroke and for his knowledge of paints and brushes. His academic training and background experience as a commercial artist in Europe and America—and his employment as a housepainter for a short time after arriving in America—gave him a broad knowledge of tools and materials with which other artists were not familiar. He sometimes used house painter's brushes and, according to Stevens and Swan (2004), he once recommended the sign-painter's liner brush to his friend Arshile Gorky; this greatly pleased Gorky, who quickly discovered that he could then paint thin lines, which he had been trying to do previously with his "fat Rubens brushes" (p. 105). De Kooning gave special attention to the canvas and its interaction with the paint. Although he most often used pre-primed canvases, he sometimes used a technique for preparing the canvas which involved first sizing and resizing it, then painting it with lead white paint, sanding it down until the surface became almost translucent, and finally roughening up the surface so he could draw more easily with charcoal (Stevens and Swan, 2004, p. 562). Painting almost every day, de Kooning worked slowly, often spending hours just looking at the canvas, but his brushstrokes were applied speedily and were an expression of his personal sensations and feelings. According to Thomas Hess (1968), the artist mixed his colors in salad bowls—"He starts out with a few basic tones, then 'breeds' them with one another until he has some eighty possibilities—all from the same source and of the same chemistry, so the skin of the painting can be 'all of one piece'" (p. 103). De Kooning liked to keep the paint "juicy," and the surface of the canvas wet and greasy, because keeping it wet and "alive" allowed him to work with the full image. He created this surface by mixing his paints with a medium of turpentine, stand oil, and damar (resin) varnish. He considered himself "the world's greatest mixer of paint" (Stevens and Swan, 2004, pp. 324, 562) (Figure 10). While working and at the end of the day (more often after the mid-1960s), de Kooning pressed newspaper onto the painting to slow the drying process, so that he could easily change the image or scrape it away.

De Kooning greatly admired the sensual technique of the Lithuanian-born artist Chaim Soutine, especially his highly tactile handling of paint. At age 73, he could still recall the impression he had of Soutine's large paintings that he saw at the Barnes Foundation in 1952; he thought they "had a glow that came from within the paintings—it was another kind of light" (quoted in Zilczer, 2016, p. 76). Zilczer believes that the fluid sensuality and materiality of paint that de Kooning observed in Soutine's work helped him resolve problems he was having with *Woman I*. She writes:

**Figure 10**: De Kooning at work in his studio, Springs, East Hampton, New York, 1967. Photograph by Ben van Meerendonk

In the months following their trip to Merion, de Kooning would obliterate all traces of cubist interior space and instead mold the seated figure to become one with the surrounding space. The conventional distinction between foreground and background disappears in the activated surface of the painting, and yet the figure of the woman looms as a massive presence. *Woman I* and the other five works in the series came to share a sculptural solidity that emanates from the palpable texture of paint applied to canvas (Zilczer, 2016, p. 84).

Some of de Kooning's paintings prior to the Woman paintings of the early 1950s evoke a sense of movement for the viewer as well as a tactile experience. For example, as work on his large painting *Excavation* progressed, "it appeared palpably alive, its surface a kind of 'skin' beneath which beat a pulse, the paint yielding to the brush as flesh does to the hand" (Stevens and Swan, 2004, p. 295).[1] And later in his career, when he was painting landscapes inspired by the watery landscape of Springs, Long Island, de Kooning built up the surface of the canvas with layers of overlapping colors so that the paint seemed to rise tumescent from the surface of the canvas. The pictures "were full of puckers, bubbles, ridges, and spatters" and captured the free play of water, light, and sky. "I get the paint right on the surface," he said to his friend Emilie Kilgore. "Nobody else can do that" (Stevens and Swan, 2004, pp. 561–562).

---

1   De Kooning thought there was a "fleshiness" about Soutine's paintings, and he declared in a talk and later in an interview that "Flesh was the reason why oil painting was invented" (de Kooning, 1951b; Sylvester, 1994).

As I described in Chapter 1, when de Kooning was painting *Woman I*, he repeatedly reworked or replaced the image, scraping away the figure and then beginning anew. Art critic Dore Ashton points out that de Kooning had acquired a reputation for this way of working as early as the 1940s, when there were "frequent allusions in his work to the drama of what had once been there on the canvas; little, half-erased signs of previous life, scraped off the surface but still existing in phantom-like areas between the immediate picture plane." In the paintings of seated figures between 1943 and 1946, "he juxtaposed forms clearly defined by his strong curving lines, with forms that were blurred almost to extinction. An arm or a shoulder would seem discrete from the rest of the composition until the eye chanced upon those mysterious whispered allusions—the forms that were at one and the same time erased and retained in a state of ambiguous suspension" (Ashton, 1972, p. 176). Like Thomas Hess, Ashton believed that it was inherent in de Kooning's temperament that the image be allusive and ambiguous.

Even when things were proceeding well, de Kooning might scrape down a painting at the end of a working day to ensure a fresh start the next day. According to Shiff (2011), when the artist resumed work on the canvas, he took hints from the traces of aesthetic thought that remained, but "This was neither an entirely new beginning nor a stage in the completion of a continuing composition; either of these possibilities would have appeared too definitive and formulaic to satisfy de Kooning's need for openness and insecurity" (p. 46). Shiff relates that the artist struggled against having habits of thinking and conclusive thoughts; for de Kooning, painting was a process to be lived and he had a way of experiencing many alternative "ends" in a picture. As mentioned in Chapter 2, some of the artist's friends thought his constant revising and inability to finish a painting were self-destructive and that he should see a psychoanalyst. De Kooning dismissed this advice, but we have a record of how one psychoanalyst experienced de Kooning's work in later years. In an interview with Italian analyst Anthony Molino in London during the winter of 1995, Christopher Bollas described his reaction when he saw an exhibition of de Kooning's work in New York:

> I think de Kooning's way of painting captures something about the nature of the unconscious; there's something about his expression of textures, of thought and ambition and endeavor, and about the way he erases ... the way he scrapes off certain lines, certain figurations that are then painted over ... but the erased lines are still there somewhere. Something about his vision, his vision and revision, really spoke to me. What he taught me, in a way similar to Freud's theory of deferred action, is that the unconscious is not just an envisioning, but a re-visioning; and therefore, while one is writing one's self, one also edits and cuts and pastes and reviews, again and again and again. I think this was a very profound 'discovery' on de Kooning's part. One has to put it that way. It's in Freud, but de Kooning actually, literally, illustrated the discovery. So in all I've been very affected by this, and seeing that exhibit has changed my whole way of thinking about life (Molino, 1997, p. 34).[2]

---

2  The concept of "deferred action" is the reactivation of an earlier experience that could not be assimilated at the time it originally occurred, or a retrospective understanding of something that occurred earlier. Freud thought that memory traces are rearranged or revised over time, such that

Bollas retained a positive view of de Kooning and his work, in particular what he considers the artist's understanding of the unconscious. Sixteen years after the interview with Molino, he wrote:

> De Kooning knew paints. He knew how to keep the paint on the canvas alive until the last possible moment, ready for its eradication and substitution with another color, another shape. For every vision there was a revision. And revisions of the revisions. The cumulative visual effect is of time and space suspended in a moment congealed into one representation. If this leads us to think of Freud's mystic writing pad as a metaphor of the unconscious, realized in these paintings as layer upon layer of the many strokes of the brush, it also suggests Freud's metaphor of life itself, the self as the city of Rome in all its stages — Etruscan, Empire, Medieval, Renaissance — visible in the same gaze and superimposed on one another: such is the story of any self. In the works of de Kooning one gazes upon an object that, in its revisional intensity, reflects the dense overdetermination of psychic life (Bollas, 2011, p. 196).

Though de Kooning may have intuitively understood a certain aspect of how the mind processes experience at an unconscious level, we have to wonder as well whether the constant scraping and revising of images was driven, at least in part, by a repetition-compulsion, *viz.*, a repetition of an early trauma that was encoded pre-conceptually

---

memories are registered in different versions (Auchincloss and Samberg, 2012, p. 53). In the French language this concept is referred to as the *après coup*.

and remained as an "unthought-known" (*i.e.*, something known but not yet thought), to use a concept introduced by Bollas (1987). As I indicated in Chapter 1, the *New Yorker* film critic Richard Brody (2011) seemed to sense this when he wrote "[it is] as if the artist were pulling each brushstroke from deep in his psyche, and *each were another layer or another trauma*, and, with each one, telling himself—and us—'You think that's it? There's still more,' and then, agonizingly, delivering it" (my italics). Brody was likely aware of de Kooning's childhood trauma when he wrote his review of the retrospective of the artist's work at the MoMA in 2011–2012. His interpretation of the paintings contrasts with the reaction of Sidney Geist and that of several other critics in the early 1950s, who did not recognize the communication of trauma in the Woman paintings and instead accused de Kooning of attacking the canvas violently with powerful, masculine brushstrokes. Even three decades after the exhibition at the Janis Gallery, Robert Rosenblum (1985) referred to "de Kooning's audacity in handling pink and red paint as if he were a wrestler or a rapist attacking resistant flesh" (p. 100). We might recall Cateforis' (1991) comment that for these critics, "the 'act' of painting becomes a sexual one, with the 'arena' of the canvas functioning as a substitute for the body of a woman" (p. 138).

After reading about de Kooning's childhood trauma and looking closely again at the Woman paintings, I thought that the canvas, with its defined borders, functioned not as the body of a woman but as a "container" for the artist's unmentalized emotions, in a way comparable to the container in Bion's (1962) model of the "container/contained." When I began exploring this idea, I discovered that I was not the first author to apply this concept to de Kooning's work. But let me first remind the reader of what psychoanalysts mean by the *container/contained*.

The concept of container/contained was formulated by British psychoanalyst Wilfrid Bion (1962, 1970) to conceptualize an important aspect of the early mother-infant relationship in which the mother receives and contains the infant's projected primitive emotions and responds in ways that inform her infant what it is feeling; she may also delay returning what she has sensed in the infant until an appropriate time. Through the mother's ability to contain the projections and to think about them, and thereby give them meaning, the infant has the experience of being understood (Auchincloss and Samberg, 2012, p. 25). This interaction occurs unconsciously and, as Grotstein (2007) proposes, constitutes "the *unconscious template for attachment phenomena*" (p. 155). Grotstein explains that the act of containment involves the transformative reconfiguration of the infant's raw, unprocessed proto-emotions and meaningless perceptions (which Bion referred to as *beta elements*) into emotions, images, unconscious phantasies, and primitive thoughts (*alpha elements*).[3] Through this ongoing interaction with the mother, the infant gradually introjects and identifies with her alpha function, thereby acquiring its own capacity to transform beta elements into alpha elements and usher in the beginning of an ability to think. Thus the container/contained relationship is considered a critical factor in the infant's development. If a mother is unable to adequately fulfill her containing function, she

---

3   Bion used the notation of *alpha* and *beta* to describe these elements in order to avoid terms with associations, and so that we are not misled into thinking we understand what they are. He coined the term *alpha function* to describe the process by which proto-emotions and proto-thoughts are transformed into primitive thoughts (Auchincloss and Samberg, 2012, p. 25).

may be affected negatively by her infant's projected proto-emotions and behave in a persecutory way, which reduces the infant's sense of safety and confidence in the relationship. Aspects of the developing child's primitive emotional states may fail to be linked with images and words, and, instead of being experienced subjectively as feelings that can be identified and talked about, are experienced in puzzling and confusing ways as bodily sensations and impulses to action; although "known," they are not at the level of thought, and are hence referred to as "unmentalized" experience or the "unthought-known." It has been suggested that some mothers may be overwhelmed by their own anxieties and re-project unwanted experiences into the infant. This can result in an obstructive, hyper-moralistic, attacking internal object in the child, which I will discuss further on. Grotstein (2007) points out that Bion's theory of the container function (including maternal reverie, alpha function, dreaming, and phantasizing) leads to the conclusion that "mental health, on the one hand, and psychopathology, on the other, are direct functions of the activity of the container, first external and then internal" (p. 163). We can speculate that a deficient container function in de Kooning's mother during her son's infancy contributed to the presence of undifferentiated traumatic emotions in the artist, which, as I suggested in Chapter 4, may partly account for the puzzling and deeply distressing psychological symptoms he experienced as an adult.

To conceptualize alpha function in a more scientific way, I will make a short digression to briefly describe a contemporary theory of emotion-processing that approximates Bion's theory and adds to our understanding of the creative process and how emotional experience is represented in the mind. Conceptualized by psychoanalyst and cognitive scientist Wilma Bucci (1997, 1998), this is a multiple-code theory in which emotion schemas comprise components from three modes, or systems, of representing and processing emotional experience—nonverbal subsymbolic, nonverbal symbolic, and verbal symbolic modes. These components develop on the basis of repeated interactions with caregivers and others from the beginning of life. The nonverbal modes develop first and include subsymbolic processes, which are patterns of sensory, visceral, and kinesthetic sensations and motor activity that are experienced during states of emotional arousal and constitute the core of the emotional schema. As these states are activated repeatedly and regularly in response to certain people and events, they are laid down in memory. The infant's repeated observations of the object or person associated with the emotion leads to the formation of images within the schemas, such as an image of the loving mother that is associated with a pleasurable feeling, and an image of a scary mother that is associated with distressing feelings. The images give symbolic interpersonal meaning to the subsymbolic processes comprising the core affective state. As the child develops language, verbal components are incorporated into the emotion schemas. According to Bucci, the verbal and nonverbal components within emotion schemas are connected, to varying degrees, by a "referential process"; the referential connections are most distant for subsymbolic representations, such as sensory experiences and patterns of autonomic arousal, which may require specific images within the nonverbal domain before they can be connected to language in the verbal domain. The linking does not transform one modality into another but allows for a transformation of the meanings represented in the nonverbal mode and for translation into logically organized speech. Moreover, it is the nature of emotion schemas that any element within the schema—a word, an image, an action, a sensation (such as a smell)—may activate any of the other elements. For example, when a negative emotion schema is activated by an image or words, the subsymbolic physiological core and the behavioral response associated with the schema will also be aroused. The arousal and behavioral response is immediate, such as the person's impulsively smashing or throwing a nearby object, or punching a fist through a wall, behaviors that de Kooning sometimes engaged in when he became frustrated in adult life. Thus, "In operating without explicit intention or direction, subsymbolic processes and representations may be experienced as, in a sense, 'outside of oneself,' outside of the domain of the self over which one seems to have intentional control" (Bucci, 1997, p. 174). Bucci indicates that as an "outside agent," subsymbolic processing may appear to act at times in malevolent ways, and at other times in benign ways. Unlike subsymbolic processing, images can be recalled or constructed intentionally, but they may also come into one's mind in an unbidden way. Subsymbolic processing enables the creative process to flow, whereas discrete images and sequences of images "provide an intrinsic basis for the organizing and symbolizing of subsymbolic experience, operating within the nonverbal system outside of language, and also provide the basis for connecting nonverbal experience to words" (p. 175).

Normal emotional development depends on the integration of the subsymbolic (sensory, visceral, and motor) elements in the emotion schemas together with images and words, resulting in a shift from the pre-conceptual world of sensation to a conceptual world of abstraction. This developmental process is influenced strongly by the parents' abilities to be attuned to, and to contain and regulate, the child's emotional states, and to gradually translate states of emotional arousal into nameable feelings that the child can think about and communicate to others (Fonagy *et al.*, 2002). There is an obvious parallel between Bucci's theory of emotion processing and Bion's (1962) description of the mother's alpha function by which she transforms (subsymbolic) *beta elements* experienced and projected by the infant into *alpha elements* that can be used for dreams and fantasies and for logical thinking and to express feelings. However, we should not be misled by Bion's use of the term "transform"; the subsymbolic component of emotions remains and is "transformed" only in the sense of being linked with images and words, thereby entering mental life and made meaningful. But clearly language is not the only mode for the construction of meaning. As Glover (2009) points out, the "corporeal" meaning of a picture (which I discuss further on) "operates independently of narrative and linguistic structures, and is grounded in unconscious phantasy" (p. 212).[4]

Bucci (1997) associates creative work with an interplay between subsymbolic processing systems and the systems that process imagery. She emphasizes that experiences that occurred early in life (including pre-conceptual traumas) and are represented only in subsymbolic form can emerge only when the subsymbolic system is given the freedom to do its work. This is especially so when the early experiences are too horrible to be stated in words and the images are unbearable. In the subsymbolic modes, the same images and thoughts cannot be

---

4  In a similar way, Bion (1967) argues that in any account of a psychoanalytic session, no matter how soon it is made afterwards, "memory should not be treated as anything more than a pictorialized communication of an emotional experience." He regards his own accounts of clinical cases as "verbal formulations of sensory images constructed to communicate in one form what is probably communicated in another" (pp. 1-2).

avoided, because the subsymbolic processors operate independently and in their own modalities and formats, without being directed, and in this way facilitate connection to the unutterable before the integrative processes of the symbolic systems take over and divert attention away. The artist may not be able to directly "utter" the unutterable, but the dreaded emotions will be expressed as symptoms and be present in some form by way of connections with images in the artist's work. Indeed, the artist may communicate experiences represented in the subsymbolic system to viewers before their emotional meaning is known to himself (if it ever is). De Kooning had the ability to work within the subsymbolic systems, and to create images on the canvas that communicate traumatic emotions that he could not allow himself to think about. That is, like the failure of his mother to contain, understand, and respond empathically to her son's emotional distress, he lacked an adequate container in his own mind to connect distressing emotions associated with his pre-conceptual trauma with verbal symbols. I am proposing, however, that the canvas sometimes serves as a container for his unmentalized emotions, and through the interactions with his paints and the scraping away and repeated revising of images, a partial alpha function takes place that results in a painting which, although it presents something quite new, brings something from the past into the *here and now* that is not likely to overwhelm the artist, and is waiting to be interpreted by an informed and perceptive viewer.[5] Thus, to borrow an idea from

---

5  Of course de Kooning's paintings could communicate not only "unmentalized" emotions associated with early trauma that could not be thought about, but also emotions the artist was consciously aware of and able to identify and think and talk about. Extending his reference to Freud's metaphor of the city of Rome, Bollas (2011) suggests that abstract expressionism may present us with "a history of the differing emotional experiences of the painter, congealed into

Perelberg (2013), we could say that the final picture offers the potential for a new beginning, as it "establishes, in the *après coup*, a link with *another time and another space* that is not the here and now and that opens to the very notion of a future" (p. 580).

In my search of the literature, I found that the British philosopher Richard Wollheim (1987) made a similar proposal to my idea of the canvas as container. He described de Kooning's paintings as a metaphorical "box or container" into which the artist projects objects of the senses other than sight, but including sensations of moving the limbs or muscles, all of which are experienced in a heavily regressive mode and incorporated into the paintings.[6] This idea stems from Wollheim's view that one way in which a painting gains meaning is when it becomes "a metaphor for the body, or . . . some part of the body, or for something assimilated to the body" (p. 305). He argued that this metaphorizing does not require the content of a painting to be figurative; it is achieved largely through the artist's engagement with the medium, and by the texture of the surface, which arouses emotions, sentiments, and phantasies related to the body. Aligned with Kleinian theory, he opined that unconscious phantasy is the psychic mechanism

---

one single image, one that materializes psychic life in the form of painting" (p. 197). Similar to my idea of the canvas' functioning as a container within which unmentalized emotions are partially symbolized and thereby acquire meaning, Bollas proposes that the transformation from the "unthought-known" to a painting, poem or musical composition "transubstantiates internal objects from the deep solitude of an internal world into an altered external actuality" (p. 201). Bollas emphasizes that the painting, poem, or musical composition is presentational, rather than representational; it has not existed before.

6   Whereas I link the canvas/container with Bion's concept of a mental space, Wollheim describes the container as being "like a body." However, he was strongly influenced by Kleinian theory, in particular the idea of unconscious phantasy, which Kleinian analysts conceive as the link between bodily experience and its mental (symbolic) representation (Glover, 2009). In an earlier essay, Wollheim (1974) proposed that conceptions of the mind itself are derived from an assumption of the mind-to-the-body, of mental activity to bodily functioning.

responsible for the transmission of meaning. Wollheim wrote: "The figurative aspect of *Woman I*, which undoubtedly exists, makes a negligible contribution to the metaphorical meaning of the picture, which is induced almost exclusively by what we might now . . . call the Venetian mode," by which he means the sensations the artist "tips into the picture" (p. 352). He observed that de Kooning found ways to incorporate sensations of activity and a variety of other sensations that are first experienced in infancy. As though he were describing subsymbolic emotional experience or the beta elements defined by Bion, and impressed by the effects produced by the differential drying of the paint especially in works in the late 1970s, Wollheim (1987) wrote:

> The sensations that de Kooning cultivates are, in more ways than one, the most fundamental in our repertoire. They are those sensations which gave us our first access to the external world, and they also, as they repeat themselves, bind us forever to the elementary forms of pleasure into which they initiated us. Both in the grounding of human knowledge and in the formation of human desire, they prove basic. De Kooning then, crams his pictures with infantile experiences of sucking, touching, biting, excreting, retaining, smearing, sniffing, swallowing, gurgling, stroking, wetting. These experiences, it will be noticed, extend across the sense modalities, sometimes fusing them, sometimes subdividing them: in almost all cases they combine sensations of sense with sensations of activity (pp. 348–349).

Consistent with Freud's ideas about traumatic excitations and the need for a stimulus barrier, Wollheim recognizes that these early sensations are heavily charged with excitation, and therefore pose a threat to the infant's fragile mind unless there is a parent to contain them. In addition, Wollheim emphasizes not only the perceptual response one has to the paintings but also the affective response, which "draws upon emotions, sentiments, and phantasies" (p. 306). He describes a duality of content in the paintings: The sensations and their archaic character are conveyed through the "lusciousness of the paint" and the "fat and gaudy substance" into which de Kooning works it up. But the viewer also experiences the drama created by the various ways in which the huge paint-marks engage with the edge of the supporting canvas, swerving to try to avoid collision with the edge, or, if there is collision, generating an undertow of paint as it curves back. Wollheim comments that "De Kooning's pictures assimilate themselves to enormous shallow saucers in which a great deal of primitive glory is held in delicate suspense as it slops around, but it is kept back by the rim" (p. 349); and he suggests that "it is through the insurgency of the paint that we come to recognize the regulatory role of the edge" (p. 350). He adds, "However, if it is true that the container-like effect of the picture is achieved only indirectly or obliquely through the protest that its contents make against it, nevertheless, once this effect has been achieved, it is through it that corporeality attaches to the picture as a whole, so that the picture can then come to metaphorize the body. It comes to metaphorize the body under the most archaic conception that exists of the body and its workings" (p. 350) (see Figures 11 and 12; another striking example is de Kooning's luscious and highly sensual painting *Untitled V*, 1977, which is in the collection of the Albright-Knox Art Gallery, Buffalo, NY, and reproduced in Zilczer, 2016, p. 87).

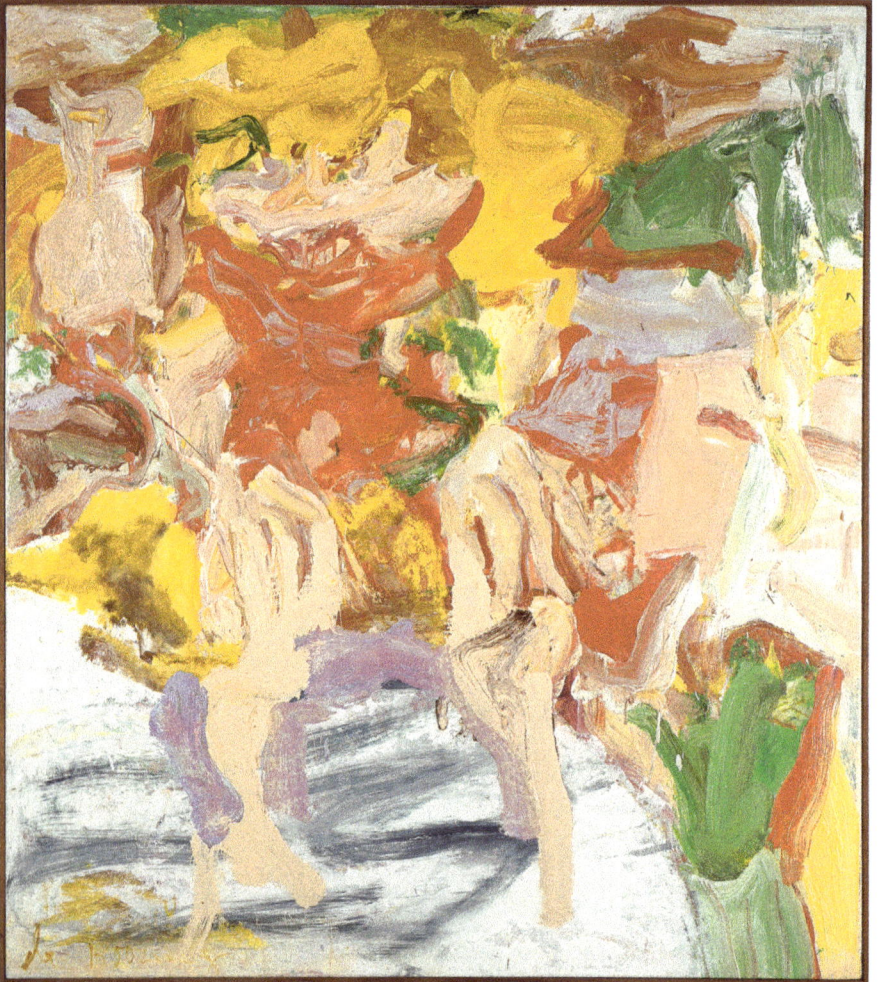

**Figure 11**: *Woman in the Water*, 1972
Oil on canvas, 59 ½ x 54 in (151.2 x 137.2 cm)
Collection Siegfried and Jutta Weishaupt, Germany

**Figure 12:** ...*Whose Name Was Writ in Water*, 1975
Oil on canvas, 76 ¾ x 87 ¾ in (195 x 223 cm)
The Solomon R. Guggenheim Museum, New York

Art historian Donald Kuspit (2011) briefly comments on an impaired container function in relation to de Kooning. He writes: "De Kooning's whiplash brushstrokes, however geometrically contained some of them are, suggest that the mother's containing, transformative reverie has failed, that is, he never completely internalized it." Using Bion's term, he comments that "beta sensations and feelings abound in de Kooning's paintings—including the so-called pastoral paintings, with their supposed idealization of Mother Nature—suggesting that he

171

never made it into the depressive position . . . "[7] Kuspit opines that de Kooning never got the maternal reverie and love he expected from the woman images he created, because they were not capable of giving it. He writes, "[the artist] seems to have painted the wrong woman, again and again, however much he thought his painting would turn her into the right woman." Although he obviously recognizes the repetition compulsion in de Kooning's work, unlike Wollheim and me, Kuspit fails to conceptualize the canvas as serving a container function. He might possibly disagree with Wollheim's view that "representation is by no means to be equated with figuration" (Glover, 2009, p. 206), and that "the most uniformly successful paintings of de Kooning's seem to be his semi-figurative paintings: paintings . . . in which representational content hovers between figurative and the non-figurative" (Wollheim, 1987, p. 352). Kuspit (1994) argues:

> [De Kooning's] paint is hemmed in by its representational purpose, by its instrumental role in his conscious reflection on the body, by his inherited wish to render the body, if in a new way. The paint must fit the body, its procrustean bed. When it doesn't, it seems wasted. De Kooning is a libertine, but not a painterly one: he wants to plumb female flesh, leave his painterly fingerprints in it, rather than paint for the sake of painting. . . De Kooning can never forget what he is painting.

---

7   Bion would more often use the term "proto-emotions" rather than "feelings," since emotions play out in the theater of the body, whereas feelings are represented symbolically and play out in the theater of the mind (Damasio, 2003). The depressive position of mental functioning was conceptualized by Melanie Klein and implies recognition that the good and bad objects are one and the same (*i.e.*, the infant's awareness of the mother as a whole object, who can be both gratifying and frustrating and has a life of her own).

Kuspit (1994) further opines that "de Kooning has a problem with the body, especially the female body. It causes him anxiety. This is why his gestures always adumbrate the body or its parts." He applies a distinction that psychoanalyst Michael Balint (1955) made between *ocnophilia* (clinging to the object for security) and *philobatism* (which allows independence from the object, relying on one's own resources); he writes, "however 'philobatic' de Kooning tries to be, especially in his landscapes, he remains anxiously 'ocnophilic' in his handling of both painting and the figure."[8] Kuspit believes that "[de Kooning's] paintings invite us to interpret them rather than merge with them" (p. 75). In my opinion, it is not a matter of either interpreting or merging with the paintings—both may occur. In psychoanalytic therapy, analysts rely on their reverie to capture unconscious communications, from which they gain increasing understanding of the patient and intuit what might need to be interpreted and when the patient might best be receptive to the interpretation. In a similar way, Wollheim (1987) argues that pictorial meaning is grounded in "some mental condition of the artist" that is somehow able to "induce in the mind of the spectator a related, an appropriately related, mental condition" (p. 357). It is an affective experience in the spectator that is set in motion by perception. As mentioned earlier, Wollheim argues that "the psychic mechanism that is responsible for the transmission of meaning [of a picture] is that of unconscious phantasy" (Glover, 2009, p. 201).

---

8   As I suggested in Chapter 4, this dilemma between approaching and avoiding the caregiver may be associated with a disorganized pattern of attachment.

Like an analyst with a patient, Wollheim (1987) seeks a personal encounter with the artist. He found that "it often took the first hour or so in front of a painting for stray associations or motivated misperceptions to settle down, and it was then, and only then, with the same amount of time or more to spend looking at it, that the picture could be relied upon to disclose itself as it was" (p. 8). As Glover (2009) concludes, "Wollheim values the quality of *otherness* in art, the capacity of the painting to reveal itself slowly, to speak for itself, as if it were a person with a rich inner life" (p. 211). Bollas (2011) describes having this kind of experience whenever he sees a de Kooning painting. He says the artwork evokes in him an experience that exists in and through the medium of paint: "It brings something out in me, or to put it in the vernacular: it 'speaks to me' " (p. 202). Bollas acknowledges that he would have difficulty putting what the painting "says" or what he "hears" into words, but he has grasped the communication from the artist.

The concept of the container has also been applied to poetry by Annie Reiner, a poet and psychoanalyst, who examines the struggles that poets and psychoanalysts have to express through language something from an infinite unknowable realm of the unconscious mind. She writes: "The nonlinear, nonverbal music and rhythm of a poem provide a container for the words, a vehicle by which the words are driven. These create physical as well as emotional sensations that can serve as a bridge between psyche and soma" (Reiner, 2008, p. 599). Applying Bucci's multiple-code theory, the nonverbal aspects of poetry reflect the subsymbolic mode of emotion processing, operating without being directed or blocked by the organizational processes of the symbolic modes.

Reiner (2008) further suggests that a poem "is a sort of waking dream, a marriage of conscious and unconscious mental processes that provides an alternate route to the unconscious" (p. 601). And, like a dream, a poem transforms aspects of the author's emotional experience into a story, image or symbol. In this way, Reiner makes an analogy between poetry and Bion's idea of beta elements ('raw experiences') being transformed into alpha elements (the primitive elements of thought) that are used in dreams, myths, and stories and can be mentally digested and stored in the mind as memories. As indicated earlier, I think that some of de Kooning's images of women similarly involve the transformation of beta elements into alpha elements. But unlike poetry, which links the sensory mode with both imagistic and word representations, paintings can only speak the language of emotion and sensations through imagery, shapes, and colors. De Kooning certainly accomplished this in his 1948 black and white picture titled *Painting*. When asked about this picture at a roundtable meeting at the MoMA, the critic Clement Greenberg said, "The emotion in that picture reminds me of all emotion. It is like a Beethoven quartet where you can't specify what the emotion is but are profoundly stirred nevertheless" (Davenport and Sargeant, 1948, p. 62; quoted in Krauss, 2015, p. 45).

In applying the container/contained concept to de Kooning's work, I am not suggesting that his images of women simply represent dream-like scenes. In abstract expressionist paintings, as psychoanalyst and painter Steven Poser (2008) explains, unconscious mental content is not depicted, but is projected by the artist into the pictorial space to be enacted on the surface of the canvas. In his view, which is similar to that of Wollheim, de Kooning's engagement with the unconscious involved the projection or discharge of a wide range of primitive emotions, instinctual impulses, sensory impressions, and mnemic traces onto the canvas (I would include unconscious phantasies). The final image of a woman "came into being" as a result of the artist's feeling into space for the figure and fighting his way to it with "stabs, slashes, gropes, and repeated scrapings-out" and through his "virtuoso ability to impart movement, feeling, and life in the handling of paint" (Poser, 2008, p. 136). That is, the paintings are not representations of preformed images of women, but like "the dream that comes to the dreamer unbidden" or a poem that "writes itself," they emerged from the creative process (Reiner, 2008, p. 608). Indeed, de Kooning indicated that he never knew how an image should look on paper or canvas until it appeared (Shiff, 2011, p. 20). However, as Reiner points out, a poem differs from a dream; and so also does a painting. Unlike the dreamer, the artist is awake and challenged with the dual task of containing the projected elements in the pictorial space and within the boundaries of the canvas, and using his or her creative skills to transform these elements into a meaningful image. Although I am repeating myself, this involves activating referential connections between subsymbolic and nonverbal symbolic processing systems and is similar to the mother's using her containing capacity and alpha function to transform the infant's or young child's distress into something with meaning. This experience was deficient in de Kooning's childhood and left him prone to panic attacks, fears of dying, and other dreaded emotional states associated with pre-conceptual trauma. Reiner (2008) makes the point that when there is deprivation of this containing/container experience in a child's primary relationship, "the child is left to 'drown' in his unmentalized feelings, flooded by raw sensation and his own emotional overload" (p. 606).

Leo Steinberg, in his thoughtful review of de Kooning's Woman paintings in *Arts* magazine in 1955, fully appreciated that the images are "born" from within the canvas. He wrote:

> We saw not things here but events—a darting, glancing, evading, overlapping, and colliding; a grammar of forms where all nouns were held in abeyance; systems of turbulence whose rate of motion was so flickering fast that the concretion of a 'thing' became unthinkable. And yet it has occurred—as the fetus occurs in the swarming of amassed cells. The agitated worlds of de Kooning's abstract canvasses were scenes of germination. And within these worlds—the fastest and most urgent ever put on canvas—de Kooning has descried a familiar shape, a form that even Adam would have recognized as from ancient knowledge (Steinberg, 1955, p. 46; 1972, p. 262).

Reiner (2008) points out also that poets often don't know the meaning of what they are saying "until ego capacities can be brought to bear on the fruits of more intuitive inspiration. However, the meaning may later on once again prove elusive. . . . Nonetheless, the poem retains its meaning in the music . . ." (p. 601). This applies also to abstract expressionist paintings. De Kooning did not give titles to many of his paintings, and when he did, he often chose titles that are quite literal or arbitrary (Shiff, 2011, p. 58). Except for *Woman and Bicycle*, the images in the Woman paintings of the early 1950s are simply numbered *Woman I* to *Woman VI*; several other paintings are simply titled *Woman*. Of course, de Kooning was well aware that the meaning of a painting is not found in the title, but is discerned by the viewer and may differ from person to person. And given my proposal that the painting of the images was influenced by unconscious processes and pre-conceptual trauma, the meaning of the Woman paintings would have been unknown to the artist himself. Like dreams, the paintings need an interpreter to complete the transformational process, a task that can be assumed by the viewer.

As mentioned in Chapter 2, de Kooning told an artist friend that he had a great interest in dreams (Pearlstein, 1989); but we do not know how well he recalled his dreams or attempted to find meaning in them. Upon awakening from a dream, we are often able to recall only a fragment or single image, as the remaining content has slipped deeper into our unconscious mind. Yet even a tiny fragment of a dream provides a "glimpse" into the unconscious and can convey a hidden meaning and lead to a new and different kind of conversation.[9]

In a recorded interview in 1959, de Kooning talked about slipping, glimpsing, and tiny things. At one point in the rambling conversation, he said:

When I'm falling, I am doing all right. And when I am slipping, I say, 'Hey, this is very interesting.' It is when I am standing upright that bothers me. I'm not doing so good. I'm stiff, you know ... As a matter of fact, I'm really slipping most of the time into that glimpse. That is a wonderful sensation, I realize

---

9  For example, a patient told me that the only thing he could recall from a dream the previous night was an image of the actress Elizabeth Taylor. He had no associations to this fragment and had not even wondered why the dream involved a woman with the same last name as mine. He rarely reported dreams, but the "glimpse" of Elizabeth Taylor as a character in his dream provided a new opportunity for exploring the transference relationship and the rigid defenses that limited access to his inner world.

right now, to slip into this glimpse, I'm like a slipping glimpser. (Quoted by Shiff, 2011, p. 234).

Having read this quotation in *The Collected Writings of Willem de Kooning* (de Kooning, 1963/1988, pp. 176-177), Reiner (2008) suggests that the experience of slipping and glimpsing denotes "a sense of relinquishing control as an inherent part of creativity. It is accompanied by a frightening feeling of letting go of what is known . . . Having dared to let go in this way, the writer may feel that the poem (or novel, essay, etc.) to be 'writing itself' as if an entity external to the self were responsible for the work. It seems more accurate to say that one has connected with an unfamiliar or split-off capacity to experience the vast unknowable unknown" (p. 607). Reiner acknowledges that this experience is often defined as "contact with the Muse." I am sure she would agree that her description of the experience applies not only to writers but to visual artists as well.

Given the traumatic emotions and probable nature of de Kooning's internal object world, he was certainly courageous in allowing his mind to be open to potentially overwhelming primitive images and emotions. This risk had been noted previously by Wollheim. Referring to the sensations captured in some of de Kooning's paintings from the 1970s, he opined: "They remind us that, in their earliest occurrence, these experiences invariably posed a threat. Heavily charged with excitation, they threatened to overwhelm the fragile barriers of the mind that contained them, and to swamp the immature, precarious self" (Wollheim, 1987, p. 349). Whereas the container function of an attuned and attentive mother protects her infant from being overwhelmed, the canvas can serve a similar function for the artist

179

who risks activation of unmentalized emotions associated with pre-conceptual trauma.

Art theorist Anton Ehrenzweig, who had a deep knowledge of British psychoanalytic theory, wrote about the organizing role of the unconscious in creative activity more than sixty years ago. In an article titled *The Hidden Order of Art* (which was published several years before his posthumously published book with the same title), he opined that, despite the danger of abandoning purposeful thinking and conscious control, the creative mind of the artist is able to engage with "the diffuse imagery of the unconscious and its dream-like stare" and have it "perform highly technical tasks that assist in building up the complex order of art." Furthermore, "The artist has learned from hundredfold experience that he can afford to allow conscious control to lapse; then, as if from nowhere, sometimes by what seems a miraculous accident, new ideas will emerge and bring the longed-for solution of a problem" (Ehrenzweig, 1961, p. 123). As though he were anticipating Bucci's description of the interplay of subsymbolic and symbolic processing systems in creativity, Ehrenzweig argued that there is "constant interaction between different levels of mental functioning—focused or unfocused—which co-operate in their specific way in performing the common task of building up the work of art" (p. 123).

Ehrenzweig also commented on the relation between the artist's interests in the functional properties of the material in which he works and an exploration of his own self. He noted that "if action painting appears to the painters and some critics mainly as an exploration of the medium, of its dripping, splashing, scratching properties, *i.e.*, of objective facts in the outside world," others describe action painting as "an art of inner necessity, a direct projection of unconscious form processes." In his opinion, "both descriptions are true . . . and refer to different aspects of one and the same psychological process. While the artist struggles with his medium, unknown to himself, he wrestles with his own unconscious" (p. 126).

There is some overlap of Ehrenzweig's and Bucci's understanding of the creative process with a theory of creativity proposed by psychoanalyst Ernst Kris at the same time de Kooning was painting *Woman I*. Kris (1952) conceptualized the creative process as comprised of two phases—first, an *inspirational phase* during which the artist is passively receptive to *id* impulses and their derivatives; and second, an *elaboration phase* which requires the artist to concentrate and actively use cognitive processes to purposely organize and transform what had been received passively into a communicable form. As Knafo (2002) explains, these phases may follow one another in rapid or slow succession or be interwoven with one other. The receptivity required in the inspirational phase involves experiencing sensations and inchoate emotions represented in the subsymbolic system. Working in the subsymbolic system, however, can feel as though one is working "in the dark," because the search for inspiration is "without clear direction and without categories and dimensions having been defined" (Bucci, 1997, p. 22). Yet, even when the person turns attention away from the search, the subsymbolic processer continues to work outside of awareness. Bucci regards processing in the subsymbolic mode as "the essential core of creative work, the basis for the mysterious and longed for visit of the 'muse,' and the basis for the illumination [that is hoped for in both psychoanalytic therapy and creative work]" (p. 240). De Kooning once said "I'm in my element when I'm a little bit out of this world" (quoted in Elderfield, 2011e, p. 453).[10]

In his essay on creativity and psychoanalysis, Bollas (2011) proposes that when painters, music composers, or writers are working creatively, "they transfer psychic reality to another realm." He writes: "An artist does not easily enter this altered state of unconsciousness. They[sic] feel the boundary between ordinary psychic life and the artistic workspace, as one that is always difficult to cross and sometimes unbearably so. Even as they become accustomed to entering this other realm they are acutely aware of leaving themselves behind, thrown into a different form of life" (p. 200). Yet, as Hanna Segal (1991) comments, "the artist never quite leaves reality. He has an acute awareness of his internal realities, the inner reality he seeks to express; but a grasp of inner reality always goes with the ability to differentiate what is internal and what is external and therefore also a sense of external reality—a basic difference between creativity and delusion" (p. 96).

Like most artists, de Kooning was attentive to inner experience as much as he was to perceptions and events in the real world. He

---

10    According to a recent review by artist and author George Sakkal (2015, 2021), there are now findings from neuroscientific studies that support the role of the cognitive-unconscious in artistic creativity and for creative actions originating outside of conscious awareness. Sakkal (2015) writes: "... as Cézanne assumed, the unconscious is the generator, the source, of creative vision. A conscious conceptualization of an idea is an illusion. The formation of the idea is dependent on the brain's unconscious, internal, visual construction of the image—which is passed on to the conscious, making it appear that the conscious [mind] is responsible for its creation" (p. 469). Commenting on the amazing capacity of the unconscious mind, Sakkal notes that it contains not only repressed emotions, but also all the emotions and associated experiences of a lifetime that are stored in memory in the billions of neurons and their synaptic connections that combine to form interactive networks. Drawing on this vast storehouse, and working in conjunction with the retina, the unconscious provides the artist with ideas and solutions that lead to the emergence of creative images.

appreciated the interplay between the internal [inside] and external [outside] worlds, as well as the potential discomfort of being in either space. In February 1951, he gave a talk in a symposium on "What Abstract Art Means to Me" organized by the MoMA. Commenting on artists such as Boccioni, Kandinsky, and Mondrian, he said: "The point that all had in common was to be both inside and outside at the same time.... Spiritually, I am wherever my spirit allows me to be, and that is not necessarily in the future.... I do not think of inside or outside or art in general—as a situation of comfort" (de Kooning, 1951a). And in the interview with Sylvester (2001) in 1960, he said "... but I think one could spend one's life having this desire to be in and outside at the same time" (p. 48).

Whereas Reiner (2008) associated de Kooning's remarks about getting a glimpse of another world with his unconscious mental life, we have to note that the artist also referred to fleeting perceptions in the external world. He told Sylvester that emotion must be there in his paintings, but he related the emotion to a concrete experience such as a "fleeting glimpse" of something that left a strong impression. And in Robert Snyder's 1968 film *A Glimpse of de Kooning*, the artist says:

When I was painting those figures, I got a feeling like I came into a room someplace—and I was introduced to someone— just for a fleeting second, like a glimpse—I saw somebody sitting on a chair—I had a glimpse of this thing—you know, this happening. And I got interested in painting that—it's like [a] frozen glimpse ... I watch out of the window, and it happens over there. Or I can sit in this chair—sit and think, and I have a glimpse of something. That's the beginning, and

I find myself staying with it—not so much with this particular glimpse—[but] with the emotion of it . . . Each new glimpse is determined by many, many glimpses before. It's this glimpse which inspires you—like an occurrence. And I notice those are always my moments of having an idea that maybe I could start a picture (quoted in Shiff, 2011, p. 232).[11]

From this statement, Shiff concludes that "de Kooning's picture begins with an unforeseen 'happening . . . an occurrence' and is as much 'an emotion' as it is a scene" (p. 232). He suggests that when de Kooning referred to himself as a "slipping glimpser," he was not only describing how he experiences things (quickly, spontaneously, obliquely, while off-balance), but also how he performs as an artist. In addition to emotion and unconscious phantasy (which are internal) and "tiny" images encountered like a flash (external perceptions), there are stable conscious influences on de Kooning's paintings. Cateforis (1994), for example, includes the artist's awareness of earlier art, the "vulgar" imagery of American popular culture, and the sights and sounds of lower Manhattan. In his opinion, however, the work was always allusive, and never illustrative. "And the ultimate meaning of each work remained, for the artist and for the viewer, elusive" (p. 1). But that is the nature of the *unconscious* mind and, as Reiner (2008) indicates, if the "news" from the unconscious is not heard, it will not let one rest. The compulsion to repeat is interrupted only when the person comes to understand the meaning of the behavior

---

11   This statement was audio-recorded in the summer of 1959 and later used by Robert Snyder in his 1968 film *A Glimpse of de Kooning*. Shiff quotes a transcription by Brenda Richardson from the soundtrack of this film.

and repeatedly works through that meaning, as was emphasized by Freud (1914); and this process is essential for psychoanalytic therapy to have a successful outcome. De Kooning sometimes said, "You have to change to stay the same" or variants of this, especially during the 1980s. Shiff (2011) suggests that the artist's line may be a corruption of the well-known aphorism, "The more things change, the more they stay the same," which appeared in the writings of Alphonse Karr in the satirical journal *Les Guêpes* (The Wasps) in the mid-1800s. De Kooning was unwittingly describing the repetition compulsion, in which the same early trauma is repeated in different forms.

Readers might wonder how de Kooning was able to work creatively if he was struggling with the consequences of cumulative trauma, especially when pre-conceptual traumas are likely to become entangled with, and intensify the emotions elicited by, subsequent traumatic events in a person's adult life. As stated in the previous chapter, pre-conceptual traumas of various kinds and severity occur in the early life of every human being. According to Lopez-Corvo's (2014) theoretical model, these pre-conceptual traumas split the mind into "traumatized" and "non-traumatized" states that interact following different dynamic principles. In the non-traumatized state, a person uses the capacity to think logically, has a high frustration tolerance, discriminates between the inner world and external reality, and successfully modulates emotional experiences. In the traumatized state, the person thinks in a concrete black-and-white way, has low frustration tolerance, uses projection and other primitive ego-defense mechanisms, experiences confusing emotions, and tends to equate aspects of his/her internal world with objective reality. The traumatized state is always present, existing alongside the non-traumatized state, waiting for opportunities to sneak out and be re-enacted in some form in the *here and now*, in a current relationship or between parts of the self. In a healthy individual, the traumatized state of the personality is adequately contained by the non-traumatized state, thereby allowing the person to form mature interpersonal relationships, be content with him- or herself, and to enjoy life and realize creativity. Biographical material, which I review in Chapter 6, suggests that de Kooning's mind was often taken over by a traumatized state, in which he experienced confusing emotions, particularly panic attacks and fits of despondency; he also expressed rage impulsively, rather than reflecting on angry feelings; and he unthinkingly assaulted his mind and body by bingeing on alcohol. De Kooning would have been unable to work creatively when his mind was taken over by this traumatized state, which essentially broke through any protective barrier and, through the repetition compulsion and the collapse of time, brought situations of helplessness from infancy and early childhood into the present.

## Ugliness and Beauty

As I mentioned in Chapter 1, several early critics of the Woman paintings perceived either the images or the slashes of paint as ugly. Alexander Eliot (1953), for example, described the *Women* as "mighty ugly," and Hubert Crehan (1953) wrote, "the color is raw when it isn't ugly." Even de Kooning himself said to an interviewer, "For me, I found them comical, but with a little pathos because they are so ugly" (Hunter, 1975, p. 70). And although Kuspit (2011) admires de Kooning's earlier paintings of women, and an exquisite, tender pencil portrait of his wife Elaine (see Figure 13 in chapter 6), which he notes are influenced by classical art and are beautiful and convey love, he considers the Woman paintings of the early 1950s (as well as later images) "ugly and repulsive" and "full of murderous hatred," as the women's bodies are "sadistically slashed, hacked, and finally torn to pieces . . ." In a footnote to his article published in *Artnet Magazine*, he argues that like Picasso, de Kooning "could not live with or without a woman." In his opinion:

> They messed around with her body, conveying their ambivalent attitude to her. It seems that for them fucking her was never as completely satisfying as making art, which is why they mucked around with her—and fucked her over—in their art. . . . Woman was supposed to be unequivocally, completely beautiful and good. Slowly and surely, because she was disappointingly neither—because she was a bad girl underneath her good looks—de Kooning vengefully turned her body into painterly shit (Kuspit, 2011, Fn. 11).

I suspect that Bollas would disagree strongly with Kuspit's opinion. In his essay on creativity and psychoanalysis, he writes:

> Many critics, looking at Picasso's or de Kooning's paintings of a woman, argue that she is being destroyed in a misogynistic attack on the female. These criticisms miss the context of this breaking-up. It usually occurs just before the fragmentation of the sublime other into a bizarre refiguration or a shattered object, often abstracted into a thick movement of color and

shape. I suggest that what we see here mirrors what Freud and Winnicott wrote about the breaking-up of the figurative. Breaking the woman becomes the breaking of the mother's body, momentarily losing the need for configuration but employing her as a project for the realization of self. She is now the process of painting, an immanent presence, de-objectified and reformed as the guardian intelligence of the form of painting (Bollas, 2011, p. 205).

The issue of ugliness and beauty in art was addressed by the British psychoanalyst Hanna Segal (1952, 1991), who considered ugliness a most important and essential component of a satisfying aesthetic experience. Adopting some ideas introduced initially by Melanie Klein, Segal proposed that the creative act involves a need to repair the object from the imagined damage caused in infancy by phantasies of greedy, sadistic attacks that tear the loved object into fragments. In her view, an original and successful work of art involves a balance of ugly and beautiful elements that reflect both the destructive forces and their transformation. There is certainly destructiveness in the content of the Woman paintings, but many critics and viewers might question whether the destruction is compensated for, and repaired by, the formal and aesthetic aspects of the paintings, thereby allowing for ugliness and beauty to coexist. Swiss psychoanalyst Adela Abella (2010) argues that Segal's theorization may not apply to contemporary art which "deliberately renounces wrapping its content with formal beauty" (p. 1172). Indeed, during the post-war years, as Thomas Hess (1968) indicated, New York artists changed the basic hypothesis of art by making "a shift from aesthetics to ethics; the picture was no longer supposed to be Beautiful, but True—an accurate representation or equivalence of the artist's interior sensation and experience. If this meant that a painting had to look vulgar, battered, and clumsy—so much the better" (p. 45). Abella (2010) suggests that contemporary art provides the artist a "container" and socially acceptable setting for expressing primitive, destructive, and perverse phantasies that rarely find an outlet in everyday life. Her view is consistent with earlier proposals of Bose (2005) and Laub and Podell (1995) that visual art may serve to represent and communicate traumatic experiences, as well as associated emotions that have defied mental representation and involve a struggle between knowing and not knowing. Similar to Lopez-Corvo (2014), Laub and Podell (1995) conceptualize the core of psychic trauma as an *absence* owing to "the real failure of the empathic dyad" at the time of traumatization (p. 992). Bose (2005) proposes that "When trauma occurs in a family setting rather than in a larger social situation like the Holocaust, a persecutory introject [experienced as a 'toxic presence'] may result instead of an inner void" (p. 67). He suggests that the artist creates in the artistic work a *concrete presence*, which provides poignant symbolization and can function as an integrating or sustaining object for the artist. Thus, de Kooning's *Woman* images could be considered affectively charged "memories" of his pre-conceptual trauma, which he unconsciously communicates to viewers, who, not surprisingly, find them disturbing.

In Chapter 4, I indicated that Klein and her followers place considerable emphasis on unconscious phantasies, which are assumed to emerge from earliest infancy before the acquisition of verbal language and are conceptualized as the mental representations of instincts, forming the initial narrative transformations of inner and outer sense-impressions or stimuli (including visual and auditory perceptions) (Grotstein, 2009).[12] Grotstein proposes three layers of phantasy life, the deepest being the continuous mythic stream within us that is archetypal—the collective unconscious. The second level is that of personal unconscious phantasy—the dialogue of internal part-object relations. The third level of phantasy is that of our perceptions of actual persons, the fantasies we have about them. We can speculate (as I did in the previous chapter) that the Woman paintings reflect aspects of de Kooning's unconscious phantasy life, especially phantasies associated with his pre-conceptual trauma. Because of the absence of containment of distressing emotions by an empathic parent during the artist's infancy, the painful loneliness and helplessness associated with his pre-conceptual trauma would have generated an intense longing for an idealized "breast-mother," as well as fear of retaliation owing to the infant's oral-sadistic impulses and phantasies induced by frustration. The projection of these aggressive impulses into Willem's image of his mother, fused with her own inherent aggression, would make her appear even more threatening and create the kind of monstrous internal object I referred to earlier, and which Grotstein (1997) describes as a *chimera* or alien "third form." I suggest that de Kooning unconsciously "discovered" and made manifest this monstrous internal object in the Woman paintings, and that these seven images represent an amalgam of phantasies of the idealized "breast-mother" and the ugly, threatening, monstrous mother in

---

12  We could link the concept of unconscious phantasy with Bucci's (1997) description of subsymbolic and nonverbal symbolic modes of processing emotion.

varying proportions.[13] The images represent the "absence" of the essential breast-mother that has become a "permanent presence" (the dinosaur's footprints) (Bion, 1965; Lopez-Corvo, 2020)—a "traumatic" internal object that repeatedly tantalizes the artist and is projected into his pictorial space. In this regard, my formulation is consistent with Grotstein's (2009) proposal that an infant who cannot tolerate frustration "forms an image of the 'no-breast' as a concrete object that persecutes the infant in mother's absence" (p. 126). At the same time, as Estella Lauter (1976) described so well, the images are infused with the archetypal mythic stream of the deepest layer of unconscious phantasy life.

## Fragmentation and Reconstruction

As described in earlier chapters, de Kooning's approach to creating *Woman I* involved the cubist method of fragmenting and dislocating the anatomy of the figure and then using collage to reassemble it. Clement Greenberg (1955) commented on this approach when he wrote that the "savage dissections" of the female form were carried out with methods that were patently Cubist. And noting that *Woman VI* is largely made up of segments, Marlene Clark (2020) commented that "the figure here is as close to Cubism as one can get without being overtly Cubist . . . (p. 208). However, Greenberg and Clark say little about the

---

13  Steven Poser (2008) opines that, for abstract expressionists like de Kooning, Pollock, and Rothko, painting was "a process of discovery, both of the self and the object" as they engaged with their unconscious. He contrasts their work with the progressive repudiation of unconscious processes in the making of pop, minimal, and conceptual art (p. 135).

reconstruction and transformation that follow the fragmentation of the figure. They overlook the Kleinian view, mentioned earlier and best expounded by Segal (1952, 1991), that the aesthetic experience is a particular combination of what has been called ugly and what could be called beautiful (p. 90). "In cubist art," Segal (1991) writes, "the 'ugly' is in the breaking up of form itself—the beautiful in its reconstruction in a new form" (p. 91).

The idea of fragmentation followed by reconstruction was extended by Adrian Stokes, an art historian, critic, painter, and poet, who had a lengthy personal analysis with Melanie Klein. Like Segal, Stokes regarded successful art as restoration of the "good" mother. He formulated two approaches to art—carving and modeling—which he applied initially to sculpture and later to drawing and painting. In sculpture, carving is cutting away and releasing what already exists in the stone; modelling is building up with a plastic material (such as clay) that has no rights of its own, and is thus a freer activity than carving (Glover, 2009; Stokes, 1934; Williams, 2014). A kind of painting in which the carving aim is realized is one in which the canvas is endowed with vitality, attacked in a certain kind of way, and carried on "long enough to give the image a chance to form of itself, emerging rather than being imposed" (Williams, 2015, p. 7). Modeling would include the manipulation of paint to create different levels of thickness, bubbling, puckering, etc. (Glover, 2009).

Stokes correlated modeling with Klein's concept of the paranoid-schizoid position (in which relations with part-objects dominate) and carving with the depressive position (in which relations with whole-objects are ascendant). He came to regard carving and modeling as complementary processes, as he realized that they were never found

192

in isolation. Whereas the modeling mode invites the viewer to merge with the image (while at the same time it finds a place for splitting and attacking the object), the carving mode celebrates the self-sufficiency of the whole object ("but there is also a place for depression due to the painful recognition of the otherness of objects") (Glover, 2009, p. 96). Glover points out that Stokes came to realize that, by mid-life, "the artist seeks a point at which he can sustain simultaneously an *ideal* object merged with the self, and an object perceived as *independent*, as in the depressive position" (p. 76). This view is consistent with Bion's notion that there is an ongoing oscillation between paranoid-schizoid fragmentation and depressive position reintegration, and that projective identification is a form of communication.

Applying Stokes' ideas to the Woman paintings, I suggest that de Kooning was engaged at different times in either carving or modeling but was sometimes carving and modeling at the same time. In creating *Woman I*, the aggressive element of carving was evident in the artist's method of sanding and scoring the canvas, marking it with charcoal, placing thick layers of paint on the surface, and then repeatedly scraping away the image and starting anew, until an image emerged that seemed to communicate an emotional aspect of his internal world. Aggressive carving fragmented the object, whereas carving and modeling (occurring separately and together) reconstructed the object in a form that does not exist in the real world, but corresponds to an object from de Kooning's psychic reality. The fragmentation and reconstruction safely took place within the container provided by the canvas and its edges.

In my view, the reconstructed object represented by the images in the Woman paintings cannot be interpreted within the Kleinian conception that authentic creativity results in *reparation* of the object that was damaged by destructive impulses during infancy. My proposal that *Woman I* may be perceived as an amalgam of idealized and threatening part-objects that exist as phantasies in the artist's inner world implies a type of integration. This acts as a representation and communication of early trauma, rather than an acceptance by de Kooning of his destructiveness and of an internal object that he can comfortably live with. The French psychoanalyst Chasseguet-Smirgel (1984b) agrees with the Kleinian view that creative activity may be rooted in a desire to repair the object, but she argues that for some artists, especially those who suffered trauma during infancy, the pursued goal may be reparation of the self. She believes that, for these traumatized artists, "the creative act derives its deepest impulse from the desire to mitigate, *by one's own means*, the deficiencies left or caused by others" (p. 405).[14] Moreover, she argues that the two categories of reparation are radically opposed—rather than restoring the object, repairing one's self requires destruction of the object in one's unconscious. There is some similarity between her notion of reparation of the self and Winnicott's concept of object usage, which, as I discussed in Chapter 4, involves destroying the mother in phantasy to achieve realization of a separate self. And as noted earlier, Bollas (2011) refers to Winnicott and suggests that the breaking-up of the woman in de Kooning's paintings "becomes the breaking of the mother's body" and employing the fragments "as a project for the realization of self" (p. 205).

---

14   Chasseguet-Smirgel (1984b) and Joyce McDougall (1980) suggest that drug addiction may also be viewed as an attempt at self-healing with drug-takers giving themselves a supposed "good breast" without the intervention of another person.

De Kooning pursued drawing and painting with passion. It was "a way of living," and, as he gained recognition as a major artist, his work no doubt provided gratification and enhanced his self-esteem. But how do we account for his inability to resolve his childhood trauma through creative activity? If, as Segal (1991) assumes, an artist is working through his infantile depressive position, which involves acceptance of mother's independent existence, "then he too has not only to recreate something in his inner world corresponding to the recreation of his internal objects and world, [but] he also has to externalize it to give it life in the external world" (p. 96). With this theory, Segal seems to presuppose that the artist has experienced a reasonably healthy childhood environment (what Winnicott would refer to as "good-enough" mothering), and that the need to repair the object which fuels the creative impulse stems from guilt over sadistic and destructive attacks on the "breast-mother." But what about artists like de Kooning who have experienced significant childhood trauma? Could de Kooning's compulsion to paint the female figure be considered an attempt to search for a lost and unattainable ideal maternal object, as well as to restore split-off aspects of himself?

In his book *Personal Relations Theory*, Graham Clarke (2006) refers to an unpublished paper by Ken Wright (1995) who noted that after Segal considered Stokes' ideas, she recognized that "the creative process . . . includes 'the attempt to create and merge with an ideal, maternal object' . . ." As Clarke points out, this phantasy object "belongs to an earlier stage of development than the depressive position" (p. 101). Segal did not adequately allow for a paranoid-schizoid element in the final product created by the artist, but I have included the idea of a search for a lost and unattainable ideal as a part-object component of the images in de Kooning's Woman paintings, each image's being an amalgam of idealized and threatening internal phantasy objects. And, as mentioned in Chapter 1, art historian Robert Hughes (1997a) recognized the *desire* for woman (as well as the fear) implanted by the artist's mother.

Sophie Richman (2014), an American psychoanalyst who writes about creative transformations of trauma, considers the altered state of "dissociation", an essential aspect of creativity. She proposes that, in this altered state, traumatized artists strive to represent externally some aspects of their trauma that has remained unsymbolized; a painting, for example, provides a visual image of what cannot be communicated in any other way. In a review of Richman's book *Mended by the Muse*, Jody Messler Davies (2016) describes the process as "a kind of intermediate form of symbolization and formulation that communicates at the same time that it elides the complete formulation and verbal expression that would otherwise overwhelm" (p. 231). This description is consistent with my earlier discussion of Bucci's model of emotion processing. However, to explain the healing that creative work may have, Richman proposes that the artist creates an imaginary muse who bears witness, affirms, and validates the emotional trauma that is being represented in the artwork. This formulation is not based on restoration of the object. In her book review, Davies (2016) conceptualizes the imaginary muse as a previously established internalized good object that is externalized and held in the artist's mind as an imaginary witnessing other. But she raises an important question: what happens to artists who cannot retrieve an intact good object, because they were victims of parental abuse and did not have a good-object experience to internalize? Davies suggests that the part-object that is "'conjured' to witness creative and artistic production can quickly become obliterating and annihilating rather than approving" (p. 234). She further suggests that there may be "an internal war between [the artist's] good object muse and the internalized bad objects who have the power to attack and destroy the work [the artist] strives to create" (p. 234).

> I do believe . . . that childhood trauma which occurs at the hands of one's parents creates a particular kind of dissociation—a fragmentation of the internal object world in which good and bad parental representations are split off from one another and move in and out of the foreground of psychic life alternately and in different intrapsychic and interpersonal contexts. Such individuals live in a perpetual cycle of creation and destruction, and therefore healing through creativity is elusive. It is only in the context of a therapeutic relationship that welcomes both the loving and hating objects within into the transference/countertransference enactments that integration and modulation of these cycles can occur (Davies, 2016, p. 235).

De Kooning was without a witnessing good-object muse or a therapeutic relationship that could provide him with a good-object experience and help him to reflect and find meaning in the images. Perhaps it was partly an internalized bad object that made him harshly critical of his work and led him to abandon the painting of *Woman I* until Meyer Schapiro (representing a good object) provided reassurance that it was almost ready to be exhibited. As we will see in the next chapter, it was not until he was in his mid-sixties that de Kooning established a relationship with a woman whom he idealized and experienced as a good object muse.

# CHAPTER 6

# De Kooning's Relationships with Women and his Self-destructive Alcoholism

D e Kooning's inability to escape from the female figure in his art was accompanied by a compulsion to enter a series of relationships with women and to have difficulty separating from them. Stevens and Swan (2004) describe as many as seven long-term relationships, and at least five short-term affairs, as well as numerous casual flings. From the information provided in their biography of the artist, I was able to identify several patterns of relating that illustrate de Kooning's insecure attachment style, as well as repeated re-enactments of the traumatic relationship he had with his mother. As I explained in Chapter 4, such re-enactments should not be considered veridical reflections of actual childhood relationships but involve instead the externalization of interactions between internal objects or part-objects. These are constituted from early relationship experiences that have been distorted and modified by the child's wishes, conflicts, and phantasies. Based on de Kooning's childhood history, I suggested earlier that his internal object world included a self-representation of a needy, helpless child and an object representation of a powerful and threatening, yet alluring, female figure. This formulation is consistent with Stevens and Swan's (2004, p. 339) suggestion that *Woman I* depicts a disturbing relationship between a child and an adult. From the perspective of attachment theory, we can expect de Kooning to manifest avoidant-dismissive behavior in his romantic relationships, as well as some contradictory behavior alternating between wanting closeness to his partner and being aloof and wanting to be alone. Typical of adults with elements of disorganized attachment, he would be prone to high levels of anger, impulsivity, and general negative emotionality. His tendency to withdraw, and a limited ability to empathize, would make it difficult for his partner to serve as a secure base (Paetzold, Rholes, and Kohn, 2015).[1]

To understand de Kooning's compulsion to repeat pre-conceptual and conceptual traumas within his adult relationships, I propose that at varying times he unconsciously projected into his mental image of his female partner *either* the object representation *or* the self-representation, which he then confused with his actual partner, while he identified with the complementary internal representation. He would then in various ways coerce or attempt to make the woman conform to this image. Thus, in situations in which the emotional memory of the early trauma was activated, de Kooning became either victim or perpetrator of the trauma as it was re-enacted in various scenarios with his female partner. Through his unconscious identification with the perpetrator, one could suggest that he got revenge for the trauma inflicted on him by his mother. Some of the women who entered a relationship with

---

1   A study with a sample of adults from the general population found that disorganized attachment mediates the important relationship between early childhood traumatic experiences and later externalizing behaviors in adult romantic relationships. The externalizing behaviors assessed in this study were angry feelings toward partners and aggression and violence toward partners, such as threatening or hitting a partner (Rholes, Paetzold, and Kohn, 2016).

the artist were receptive to assuming the identity projected on to them, because of traumas stemming from their own troubled childhoods. A change toward a less conflicted way of relating becomes evident in de Kooning's last two long-term relationships.

Womanizing and boozing were part of the culture for de Kooning and his friends, and for numerous other artists who frequented the Cedar Tavern in downtown Manhattan. As recalled by ninety-year-old artist Audrey Flack in an interview for the *New Yorker* in 2021, "You just knew what was going to happen there.... The Ab Ex women were worse than the men. Worse in the sense they had to outdrink the men. They bought into the behavior. The sex! It was crazy. I was no angel. But the women pay the price" (Allen, 2021, p. 15). From a psychoanalytic object relations perspective, I propose that de Kooning's alcoholism and other self-destructive behaviors were influenced not solely by his social milieu, but can also be considered a consequence of early trauma's being repeatedly enacted between parts of himself, with the addictive substance sought as a good "mother-breast," despite its consequences. At times, especially when he was drinking, he released an explosive infantile rage. Notwithstanding de Kooning's persistent conflict around attachment and separation, we can assume that when he was able to work creatively and interact in healthy ways with his female partners, the traumatized state of his personality was adequately contained by the non-traumatized state (Lopez-Corvo, 2014). His lovers, however, may have quickly learned that he could switch suddenly into states of anger or despondency and sometimes make life difficult for them.

In the following short descriptions of each of de Kooning's long-term relationships, readers will quickly notice the influence of the repetition compulsion. Some may wonder why the artist and several of his female partners were not more self-reflective and able to decide to end their maladaptive ways of relating. I am suggesting that the compulsion to repeat was determined in part by their own internal working models, which were encoded in procedural memory systems. The internal working models of both de Kooning and his partners would have provided expectations about relationships; and changing their way of relating would have been difficult because, as Eagle (1997) points out, people assimilate new experiences and relationships into their pre-existing working models. We can assume also that the behaviors and cues that de Kooning and his female partner/s displayed in their interactions with each other often elicited the kinds of responses that tended to confirm their own internal working models.

De Kooning's first two long-term relationships illustrate a pattern of relating in which the women enacted the victim role and he took the role of perpetrator. His first girlfriend in America was Virginia (Nini) Diaz, who worked as a tightrope walker in vaudeville. They met in late 1927 and lived together for approximately six years. Stevens and Swan (2004, p. 74) suggest that Nini was in many ways a perfect match for de Kooning, as she shared with him a traditional European notion about the roles of the sexes. She cooked and cleaned for him, satisfied his desire for a sexy American girl, and even sold some of his drawings to earn money. But despite Nini's loving attentiveness, de Kooning was unfaithful to her, and when she became pregnant in 1930, they decided against getting married and raising a child because there was too much poverty. Moreover, Nini had come to realize that de Kooning was very much a loner and too interested in other women to make a suitable husband. She underwent three abortions during her years with de Kooning and after the third one she bled for a year and became anemic and infertile. She deeply resented de Kooning's seeing other women; on one occasion when she expressed her anger by destroying one of his paintings, de Kooning became enraged and smashed his fist through a sheetrock wall. On another occasion, when Nini told him that many people considered his drawings "too far ahead of the times," de Kooning began shouting, banging things around, and throwing some of the furniture. This outburst surprised Nini, since she had observed him to often be highly self-critical of his work, destroying much of it (Stevens and Swan, 2004, pp. 75–79, 116). The outburst of aggression could not be attributed to alcohol, as de Kooning rarely drank in those days.

De Kooning's second long-term relationship began in March 1934, when he met Juliet Browner, a dancer and model, who was prettier than Nini and more experienced sexually. When Nini returned from a tour, she had no choice but to move out of the apartment, as Juliet was moving in (Stevens and Swan, 2004, p. 117). But despite de Kooning's ruthless behavior toward Nini at the start of the affair with Juliet, she accepted his invitation to join them in Woodstock for the summer; her and Juliet soon became close friends. After they returned to New York, Nini continued to suffer terribly from the breakup with de Kooning, and he was unable to completely end the relationship. When Juliet was out of town, he sometimes visited and slept with Nini. And when his mother came from Holland for a visit in 1935, he found a larger apartment for Nini and moved in with her to maintain a façade that they were a happily married couple. Clearly, de Kooning not only selfishly used Nini to meet his needs, but also tantalized her with the possibility of being reunited; and he failed to protect her from the risks

203

associated with an abortion. The relationship with Juliet followed a similar pattern, in which de Kooning seemed unable to integrate his sexual desire with a loving attachment. Whenever Juliet expressed her desire for a future together, de Kooning tormented her by saying he would rather marry Nini (Stevens and Swan, 2004, p. 116). By 1938, he was tired of Juliet but felt unable to break off the relationship. Juliet finally left him and took a trip to California; there she met the Dadaist and surrealist painter and photographer Man Ray and married him a few years later.

De Kooning's repeated unfaithfulness and his failure to commit to a relationship with either Nini or Juliet were understandably distressing to these young women. They must also have been confused by the contradiction between his distancing himself and maintaining a close connection, which is characteristic of disorganized attachment behavior. By maintaining insecure attachment relationships with the women, de Kooning seemed to unconsciously repeat his own pre-conceptual traumatic experience; but now the women were projectively identified with the needy infant and he was identified with the emotionally unavailable and sometimes cruel or absent mother. And, like his mother, he lacked the capacity to show genuine concern for his partner's emotional needs and to think about how they experienced his contradictory behavior. Moreover, although Juliet occasionally modeled for de Kooning, he never made her his muse, which suggests that he was unable to link her with an internal good maternal object. The failure was clearly on the part of de Kooning, because after leaving him Juliet was able to form a loving and secure attachment to Man Ray. She modeled for him and became his muse; he liked to have her nearby and to feel her presence while he worked. Juliet died at age

79 and was buried alongside her husband, who had died fifteen years earlier. Her epitaph reads "together again" (Flint, 1991).

While still living with Juliet, de Kooning began experiencing episodes of depression and feelings of loneliness, as well as heart palpitations and other anxiety symptoms (Stevens and Swan, 2004, p. 141). At times he feared he was having a heart attack. He also had difficulty getting started in the mornings and was often blocked in his work. The caffeine in the coffee, which de Kooning had a habit of drinking all day, may have contributed to his anxiety and kept him up late at nights. But he was probably suffering from a mood disorder and panic attacks, which, as I mentioned in Chapter 3, are often linked with a history of childhood maltreatment (Lippard and Nemeroff, 2020). To get relief from his symptoms, he frequently walked the dark streets of Manhattan late at night, usually alone but sometimes in the company of a friend. Although I agree with Stevens and Swan (2004) that a lack of money, and not yet having a solo exhibition, must have contributed to the artist's depression, it seems likely that his symptoms stemmed also from deeply repressed emotions associated with pre-conceptual and conceptual traumas. One can easily imagine that when de Kooning was a young boy, his mother consistently ignored or disavowed his subjective feelings, thereby discrediting the validity of the distress, anger, or fear she evoked in him. It seems likely also that during the first year or two of his life, de Kooning's mother failed to quickly repair disruptions that typically occur in the normal interactions between caregivers and infants. Consequently, Willem was probably prone to a predominance of negative over positive affect experiences. Referring to his need to defend himself against these negative feelings, de Kooning once said, "I lived with a sort of curtain which protected me from thinking too much about it" (Stevens and Swan, p. 507). Reluctant to think about his childhood, de Kooning probably failed to connect his symptoms with traumatic childhood experiences, and consequently could not make sense of the symptoms. And typical of avoidantly attached people, he was also probably unable to seek reassurance and empathy from Juliet. But why did his symptoms emerge at this stage in his life?

Not long after Juliet had gone, de Kooning met 20-year-old Elaine Fried, an attractive and lively art student, whom he began to pursue after she visited his studio in late 1938. It has been said that Elaine was the first woman he fell in love with, and although she was eager to gain his affection, she played hard to get (Stevens and Swan, 2004, p. 162). In contrast to the relationships with Nini and Juliet, de Kooning's childhood trauma was re-enacted with Elaine in the role of perpetrator and de Kooning in the role of victim. Initially the relationship went well. Elaine began taking art lessons from him, and in contrast to Nini and Juliet, she accompanied him in the evenings when he joined his friends for late-night discussions. She greatly admired de Kooning's work, often telling him that he was a genius and the greatest artist she had ever met. His biographers point out that her praise and love seemed to awaken a new spirit in de Kooning that began to course through his art in 1939. Whereas many of his previous paintings were of men and conveyed the gray mood of the Depression, many of his paintings now took on a sense of confidence and lyricism, with rich and powerful colors, not only as he engaged with the female figure, but also in some of the images of men that he continued to create (Stevens and Swan, 2004, pp. 165–167). America's entry into World War II, however, brought further financial hardship, and with few buyers of his work, de Kooning was often nearly destitute. Though Willem and Elaine were now living together, they frequently had difficulty paying the rent and there was often not enough money for both food and cigarettes, or for food and paints (Curtis, 2017). Enamored with Elaine, Willem was unable to deny her anything; whatever little spare money they had, she spent on clothes. De Kooning continued to paint but would destroy most of his work by painting over it. Harshly self-critical, he would become depressed and furious even though others thought highly of his paintings. On one occasion, he destroyed a painting of a big red bull because he thought it looked too much like a Joan Miró painting; Elaine had considered the painting a masterpiece (Curtis, 2017; Gabriel, 2018). Stevens and Swan (2004) were told that "throughout the early forties, de Kooning would paint and repaint portraits of women to the point of obsession" (p. 179). By 1943, he had developed a "reputation for working slowly, scraping out, starting all over again, and never really finishing a painting" (p. 189). There was an exception in 1940–1941, when he drew a beautiful portrait of Elaine that expressed his tender feelings for her; this pencil on paper drawing shows remarkable detail and use of shading, and the hands are perfectly drawn despite de Kooning's often saying that he had difficulty drawing hands and feet (Figure 13). He also painted a portrait of Elaine in 1942 which, to me, appears to be influenced by some of Modigliani's portraits of women (*e.g.*, Modigliani's 1917 painting of Madame Kisling). In the evenings they often read detective stories, and Elaine would read aloud from the writings of the philosopher Søren Kierkegaard; she was developing her own career as an artist but remained a strong promoter of de Kooning's work. She made several pencil sketches of de Kooning early in their courtship and gradually became a highly skilled portrait artist, with the ability to quickly capture a person's posture (Curtis, 2017). Years later, Elaine said that "Willem de Kooning provided her with the best teaching she ever had and the skills he taught her became a foundation for her confidence as a portrait painter" (Hall, 1993, p. 30).

**Figure 13:** *Portrait of Elaine*, 1940–1941
Pencil on paper, 12 ¼ x 11 ⅞ in (31.1 x 30.2 cm)
The Allan Stone Collection, New York

In 1943, having been together for four years, de Kooning and Elaine decided to get married. Elaine had undergone three abortions. Although Willem said he wanted a child, Elaine did not—she realized she could not be an artist as well as a mother, because mothering was a full-time job. However, as Curtis (2017) suggests, Elaine may have been conflicted about becoming a mother. There was one time when she thought she was pregnant and decided not to end it; after watching her body change for several months, she saw a doctor and was deeply disappointed to be told that she had a false pregnancy (*pseudocyesis*) (Curtis, 2017; Gabriel, 2018). She later needed a hysterectomy, making it impossible then to have a child of her own. According to Stevens and Swan (2004, pp. 213, 237–238), Elaine (in contrast to Nini) rejected the role of housewife; she did not cook or clean the apartment or attend to her husband's other needs. Visitors found the bathroom unclean, and noticed that the bedsheets were gray and grimy. Being fourteen years younger than de Kooning, Elaine was restive and often went out at night to go dancing or partying. They were also temperamentally different, Elaine craving attention, de Kooning a loner who enjoyed the solitude of his studio. De Kooning told Elaine that he had thought she would give up painting once they were married, to which Elaine replied that she was a painter when they met, wanted to paint as much as he did, and was willing to starve along with him. Yet she freely spent what little money they had and filled their closet with clothes she bought. De Kooning once said to Elaine, "You have a very nice life for a young man," and on another occasion he said, "What we need is a wife" (Curtis, 2017, pp. 27, 29). Elaine's brother Conrad tried to nudge her into performing more wifely duties, but was unsuccessful; she was not willing to adopt the accepted mold of an artist's wife (Gabriel, 2018, pp. 183–184). When photographer friend Rudy Burckhardt returned to New York in 1944 after service in the army, he noticed that Willem and Elaine's marriage had already begun to fray. To him, they "never seemed compatible. They were just different types" (Hall, 1993, p. 49).

In the fall of 1945, Elaine accepted an invitation to crew a male friend's sailboat to Provincetown and was away for several months. Upon her return, the couple were evicted from the loft that de Kooning had renovated, and they had to move to a tiny unheated apartment in Greenwich Village where it was difficult for both to work (Stevens and Swan, 2004, p. 214). De Kooning was heartbroken over the loss of the loft, and the conflict and tension between the couple increased. Elaine was annoyed by her husband's whistling themes from classical music while he worked, and when his painting was not going well, he "stormed around the studio, knocking over chairs, throwing brushes, cursing, and kicking" (Gabriel, 2018, p. 183). De Kooning eventually rented a studio and began to spend most of his time working there alone. His emotional support was no longer from Elaine, but from other artists whose studios were nearby. One artist with whom he developed a close friendship was Franz Kline, whose wife was mentally ill.

The deteriorating state of the marriage was painful for de Kooning, especially as he came to realize that Elaine was not the traditional kind of wife that he had expected; she cared more for herself and her public appearance than for his welfare. He assumed she had been unfaithful when she went on the extended sailing trip, even though Elaine claimed that the relationship with the friend was platonic. And during a party they had given at their loft soon after their wedding, he had found her in bed with his friend Robert Jonas. Unaware of the powerful influence of pre-conceptual trauma and the repetition compulsion on his choice of wife, de Kooning was destined to experience further suffering in his marriage. In 1946 he became ill with strep throat and required hospitalization (Stevens and Swan, 2004, p. 237). Elaine did not take care of him or even visit him in the hospital. Some friends brought food for him, but on one occasion when a female artist friend left a cooked duck for Willem, Elaine came home at 3:00 A.M. that night and ate the meal herself (Curtis, 2017). De Kooning deeply resented her for neglecting him, and for her indifference to the distress he felt when he suffered heart palpitations and sometimes feared he was dying. During one vicious argument between them over household chores, he smashed his fist through a plywood wall. As his love for Elaine waned, de Kooning withdrew from her sexually and sought satisfaction from casual flings. Elaine, believing she was entitled to play the field like a man, also had several brief affairs. Nonetheless, for public consumption, the couple maintained the pretense of a harmonious marriage (Stevens and Swan, 2004, pp. 239–241).

Despite Elaine's having an affair with her husband's art dealer Charlie Egan in the fall of 1948, her relationship with de Kooning survived. Unlike Nini and Juliet, she was not prepared to leave. Stevens and Swan (2004, p. 275) report that Elaine wanted to be seen as attached to an important man, even though she was creating her own powerful identity in the arts, especially as a portrait painter and art critic.[2] And as with the earlier long-term relationships, de Kooning was unwilling to end the marriage, even though he and Elaine no longer had a life

---

2   In late 1962, Elaine was commissioned by the White House to paint a portrait of President John F. Kennedy.

together. Reflecting the endurance of an attachment bond even in a negative relationship, de Kooning once admitted, "I'm psychologically attached to her" (Stevens and Swan, 2004, p. 275). Being married also protected him from any other woman who might "trap" him into marriage. In the late 1940s, however, especially when de Kooning was drinking, the explosive rage he harbored was sometimes expressed openly toward Elaine. According to Stevens and Swan, in the 1950s the artist hit Elaine at parties more than once, and possibly also in private arguments. His biographers also note a certain resemblance of Elaine's face with the face of a woman de Kooning painted in 1948; the woman has sharp teeth, flaring nostrils, and prominent eyes, features that would characterize the images in the Woman paintings of the early 1950s. And although many interpretations of *Woman I* have been suggested, Stevens and Swan (2004) argue that "she could not also fail to be, in some part, a reflection of Elaine's marriage to Bill" (p. 344).[3] They acknowledge, however, that the aggression directed at Elaine could be considered a legacy of the artist's childhood beatings. Indeed, from an object relations perspective, the roles learned as a boy could easily reverse, so that de Kooning would behave in ways like those of the mother, who struck him during his childhood. I consider de Kooning's frequent harsh self-criticism and destruction of his creative work also part of the legacy; the dynamic of the powerful mother's attacking the helpless son was enacted between parts of himself, resulting in annihilation of his work. One way in which this may occur

---

3   When friends speculated that either Elaine or de Kooning's mother had been the imaginary model for *Woman I*, Elaine declared "That ferocious woman didn't come from living with me; it began when he was 3 years old. That was no pink, nice old lady. She could walk through a brick wall" (in Pepper, 1983 and quoted in Shiff, 2011, p. 226).

is when the object component of the internal object relation experiences envious feelings toward the self-component (Ogden, 1983).

According to Gabriel (2018, p. 262), de Kooning was wounded by Elaine's affair with Egan and responded by establishing a relationship with a twenty-eight-year-old woman named Mary Abbott, who had recently separated from her husband. She was from a well-placed family and had been taking art classes. Stevens and Swan (2004, pp. 321–322) describe Mary as reserved and sensible, and unlike Elaine, she did not badger de Kooning or ask anything of him. They became lovers and continued a casual affair until the mid-fifties. Mary apparently sensed the unresolved anger in de Kooning, but she found him "magnetic" and thought he genuinely liked women. It was a warm and comfortable relationship, and they maintained a friendship for several decades long after Mary had remarried. Mary's warm and understanding personality and the on-again, off-again nature of their affair seemed to have protected against intrusion of the pathologic relationship dynamic associated with de Kooning's childhood trauma.

In 1950, as de Kooning painted and repainted what would become *Woman I*, his heart palpitations worsened, and he feared he was dying. Following advice from an artist-scientist friend, he began consuming alcohol to calm down. He soon found that whiskey helped ease the discomfort in his chest when his heart started racing, and it also helped him get started in the mornings. However, using alcohol as a medicinal began a pattern of drinking that eventually resulted in the artist's becoming addicted.[4] Elaine also became a heavy drinker, and despite

---

4   Gabriel (2018) notes that it was around 1949 that "alcohol replaced coffee as the drink of choice for artists," and according to Elaine, everything became more fun under its influence, "but also more destructive" (p. 262).

her attachment to de Kooning, in the late 1940s and early 1950s she had affairs with his two main critical champions, Harold Rosenberg and Thomas Hess. Although the marriage was collapsing, Elaine remained a strong promoter of her husband's work, which she truly admired. She helped him prepare for the exhibition of the Woman paintings at the Janis Gallery, and there was continuing affection for one another, even though Elaine has a somewhat wary expression in a photograph of the couple in 1953 (Figure 14). According to Hall (1993), "Grace Hartigan, a painter and long-time friend of the de Koonings, surmised that 'Elaine helped put Bill on the map. But then, Elaine herself would have had no place on a map, no career, without Bill. He was the genius. She was the manager of the genius. But she was a genius at the job' " (p. 5).

De Kooning loved having quick infatuations and often had several girlfriends, including in the spring of 1954, when he had a brief affair with a talented sculptor named Marisol Escobar. Marisol observed that "There was something about him that was like a little boy" (Stevens and Swan, 2004, p. 369), but she also sensed a pressure building within him, something that was constantly troubling him. I suspect that she was sensing the traumatic emotional pain that the artist had defended against since his childhood.

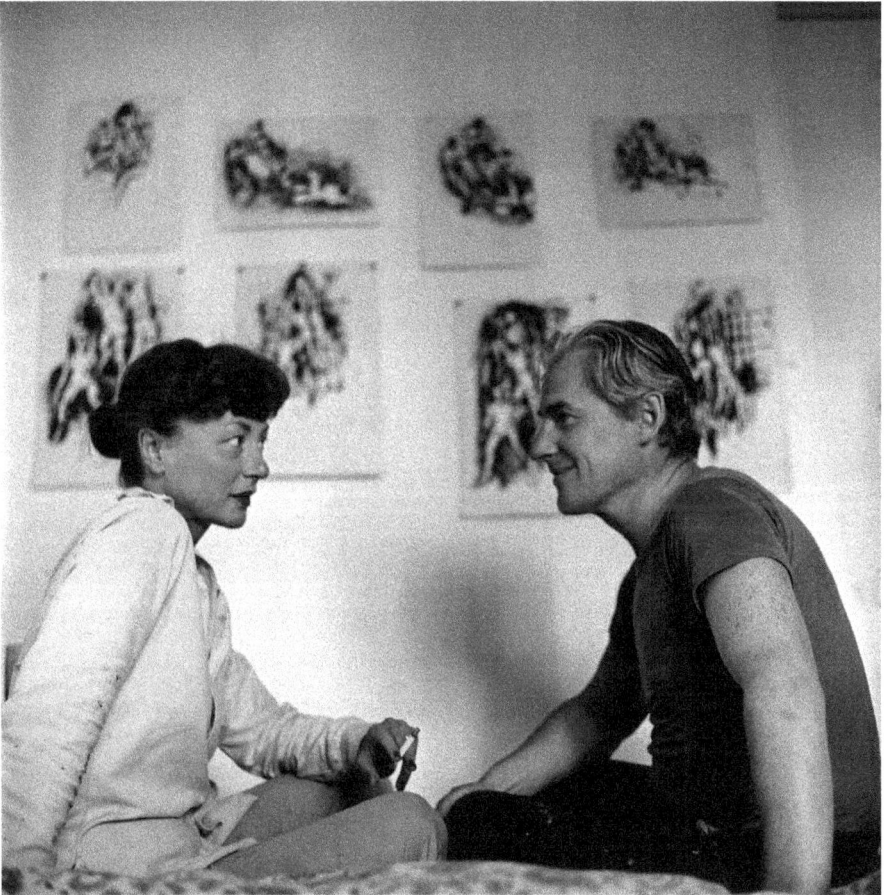

**Figure 14:** Willem and Elaine de Kooning, 1953
Private collection. Photograph by Tony Vaccaro

Stevens and Swan (2004, p. 347) report that two years before the affair with Marisol, de Kooning met Joan Ward, a successful young commercial artist. According to Gabriel (2018, p. 452), Joan was similar to Elaine in body type and coloring, but Joan had her heart set on snagging the leading role with the artist. As with other young women, de Kooning was smitten with Joan, but had no interest in an enduring relationship. Joan, however, fell deeply in love with him. Like Nini and

Juliet, she was cast in the victim role, but suffered for a longer period than any of the other women. In 1953, she reluctantly had an abortion; she was slow to recover from the experience and became depressed for at least a year. De Kooning apparently showed little empathy for her plight and continued to see other women. However, their affair was rekindled in August 1954, which Elaine much later said "is when her marriage to Bill reached its end" (Gabriel, 2018, p. 542). Because de Kooning's mother had visited that summer and extended her stay after they returned from Long Island to Manhattan, Bill and Elaine maintained the pretense of a traditional marriage. But that evaporated after Cornelia departed, and in 1955 Elaine moved into her own studio. She told an interviewer: "I'm doing what I damn please, and he's doing what he pleases" (quoted in Gabriel, 2018, p. 560).

When Joan became pregnant again, she was unwilling to have another abortion; she gave birth to de Kooning's daughter Johanna Liesbeth (Lisa) in January 1956. De Kooning fell in love with the baby, but he was not prepared to modify his lifestyle to accommodate Joan and Lisa (Stevens and Swan, 2004, p. 383–384). And while Elaine feared that he would divorce her and marry the mother of his child, de Kooning remained legally married, which protected him from committing himself to another woman. Moreover, as Gabriel (2018) writes, he was "in his very strange and estranged way still bound to Elaine" (pp. 593–594). Elaine's nephew Clay opined: "They never physically or emotionally left each other" (quoted in Gabriel, 2018, p. 594). De Kooning was now binge-drinking, and under pressure to create strong new art. That summer, while staying with Joan and the baby at Martha's Vineyard, he left to attend Pollock's funeral, where he met Ruth Kligman, who had been Pollock's mistress and was the only survivor of the car crash in which Pollock and a female friend of Ruth's were killed. The following year, de Kooning and Ruth began an affair. Gabriel (2018, p. 598) describes Ruth as an intelligent woman who looked like the actress Elizabeth Taylor and relied on her beauty to get ahead. When she moved to Manhattan from New Jersey in her mid-twenties, she hoped to become the mistress of an important man. Gabriel reports that Pollock had been the first name on a list of artists that Audrey Flack had suggested to Ruth; de Kooning's was the second name.

The relationship between de Kooning and Ruth lasted almost three years and was characterized by frequent quarrels, in which Ruth, who had endured her own troubled childhood, was all too ready to participate. It was as though they both enacted the role of perpetrator, sometimes screaming at each other, much like the quarrels between de Kooning and his mother during his mid- and late adolescence. It seems to me that neither he nor Ruth could employ the non-traumatized adult part of their personality to stop the anxious, angry, traumatized child part from responding to the cues and re-enacting scenarios from the past. This pattern of relating had been witnessed during the artist's 77-year-old mother's visit in 1954. Although Cornelia was proud of her son's eminence and financial success, she was highly critical and dismissive of his current work. Harping on her son's drinking, she triggered arguments that quickly led to their screaming at each other, even to de Kooning's mother hurling a hot cup of coffee at his head after he threw an alcoholic drink into her face (Stevens and Swan, 2004, p. 377).[5] De Kooning apparently began quarrels with women when

---

5  During Cornelia's visit that year, her controlling and domineering behavior became very obvious to Elaine. Years later, Elaine told author and journalist Curtis Pepper (1983) that Franz Kline and Jackson Pollock had similar mothers to Willem—"short, stout ladies. You can just see them on the prows of ships, breaking gigantic ice floes. Nothing turns them back." Elaine also told Lee Hall (1993) that the effect of these domineering mothers on the sons was "a rebelliousness, a kind

he felt trapped in a relationship and wanted to be alone. But he still needed to feel attached to a woman; when he and Ruth were apart, he either invited Elaine to stay with him or he stayed with Joan and Lisa. In 1959, de Kooning and Ruth spent five months in Rome, where they continued to quarrel even though they stayed in separate lodgings. Appalled by the back-and-forth affair de Kooning was having with Ruth, Joan "moved with Lisa to San Francisco, hoping to make a new life for herself as an illustrator" (Stevens and Swan, 2004, p. 424).[6]

After returning from Italy, de Kooning missed seeing Lisa so much that he pressured Joan to return to New York. They reluctantly returned in the early part of 1961, and that summer de Kooning bought a house for them in Springs, Long Island, which was close to the town where he spent his summers. Though he loved being a father, de Kooning was not able to tolerate domestic life for long and in the early sixties he had affairs with two other women. By late 1962, he was completely addicted to alcohol. Stevens and Swan (2004, p. 430) report that during long drinking binges, de Kooning was verbally abusive and could appear potentially violent, sometimes hitting his lovers, often provoking a woman to strike first. He would rant and rave about how much he hated his mother and Elaine, and he sometimes disappeared for days, wandering through dangerous parts of the city and sleeping in the gutters. The alcohol obviously

---

of resistance, and their attitude toward women. These were nondrinking mothers, straightlaced, hard and with ramrod backs" (p. 7).

6   After the relationship with de Kooning ended, Ruth Kligman became an abstract painter herself and had friendships with Jasper Johns, Andy Warhol, and Franz Kline. Between 1964 and 1971, she was married to a Spanish painter; and in 1974, she wrote a *Memoir* of her love affair with Jackson Pollock. After Kline died in 1962, he left his apartment to Ruth. She lived there until her own death at age 80 (Kennedy, 2010).

weakened de Kooning's defenses and released the traumatized part of his personality. Psychoanalyst Lance Dodes (1990), who has extensive experience treating individuals with substance dependence, opines that the release of narcissistic rage when drunk is a response to feelings of helplessness and powerlessness that may be traced to childhood trauma.

Stevens and Swan (2004, p. 431) propose that it was de Kooning's success as an artist, rather than years of failure, that turned him into an alcoholic. They argue that all his life he identified with bums and other marginal people. However, alcoholism also affected many of his fellow artists including Jackson Pollock, Franz Kline, and Mark Rothko. Moreover, as I noted earlier, like many addicts, de Kooning began using alcohol to manage intolerable affects, in particular intense anxiety and depression. From the perspective of contemporary psychiatry, his frequent and prolonged binges, and his tendency to relapse, were likely driven by dysphoria and the negative affect associated with withdrawal, which addicts attempt to reduce, terminate, or prevent by continuing to use the addictive substance (Koob, Powell, and White, 2020).

In March 1963, when he was age 59, de Kooning resumed living with Joan and Lisa in the house in Springs. Stevens and Swan (2004, pp. 448–454) indicate that he was not in love with Joan but appreciated the comforts of a clean and tidy house and a cooked breakfast. He believed that his daughter must have a father, and after working in a small garage studio all day, he returned in the evenings to draw and watch TV. As before, de Kooning soon experienced Joan as constricting and judgmental, and felt increasingly trapped. That summer the arguing between them became louder, some neighbors noticed bruises on

Joan's arms, and Lisa would become frightened when her father threw furniture. De Kooning began a prolonged episode of binge drinking and one night attended a party where he met 26-year-old Susan Brockman; she became his next long-term girlfriend. Joan found the situation unbearable and moved back to Manhattan; she maintained only distant contact with de Kooning for the next several years.

As described by Stevens and Swan (2004, p. 452), Susan was the antithesis of Joan, sensitive and tolerant, and unlike Ruth she was not tempestuous, nor was she demanding like Joan. Her insightfulness allowed her to recognize the link between de Kooning's addiction and his despair, and that the drinking binge had been an excuse for him to leave Joan and Lisa. Throughout de Kooning's frequent rages, including when he threw furniture and crockery, Susan remained calm and gentle, refusing to quarrel with him and ignoring cues pressuring her to re-enact traumatic scenarios from the artist's childhood. De Kooning did not hit Susan, but there were occasions when she had to call his doctor because of his excessive drinking and accompanying mood swings, and then drive him to be admitted to the Southampton hospital to dry out (Stevens and Swan, 2004, pp. 455-456). Based on what Mary Abbott told them, Stevens and Swan (2004, pp. 478-479) conclude that after the couple had been living together for almost two years, de Kooning became increasingly concerned about Susan and about her future, "much as a father might be." She was much younger and he realized that "he was interfering with her life." De Kooning went on a bender and disappeared, which Susan believed was his way of ending their relationship just as he "had gone on a bender in order to leave Joan . . ." (pp. 478–479). While it appears that de Kooning lacked sufficient courage to speak directly with Susan about the need to separate, this relationship differs from his previous long-term relationships in that he was not only in love with Susan, but he also showed genuine concern by appreciating the negative impact on her future if she remained with him.

After Susan left, de Kooning tried to persuade Joan to return to Springs; understandably, she was not willing to have a quick reconciliation. He spent the next two years alone during which he began seeing a psychiatrist (Dr. Wayne Barker) in a futile attempt to wean himself off alcohol. Stevens and Swan (2004) do not describe the frequency or nature of the psychiatric treatment; it seems from the minimal information in the biography that the visits were not regular, but occurred whenever de Kooning was admitted to the Southampton Hospital for a drying-out period. Influenced by the compulsion to endlessly repeat the past, the artist soon developed a new group of drinking buddies and resumed going on binges and behaving abusively when he was drunk. He also started a relationship with a woman named Molly Barnes who had become obsessed with the artist and devised a way to get introduced to him (Stevens and Swan, 2004, p. 483). Once again, de Kooning enjoyed having a woman in his life, but avoided becoming too close emotionally. Molly remained a peripheral friend until at least the late 1970s.

Continuing to miss his daughter, de Kooning convinced Joan to return to Springs in 1967, but nothing changed; neither the drinking nor the rages abated. Yet despite awful fights and several chairs in the kitchen's being smashed, neither of them was prepared to call it quits. Joan nursed the artist after the many times when he got drunk, but she was sad and lonely and cried a lot at nights (Stevens and Swan, 2004, p. 504). After a short trip to Paris and London in early

1968, de Kooning resumed painting images of women; the figures were now less sexually aggressive and confrontational, as he now depicted their bodies flowing into the landscape. As mentioned in Chapter 2, de Kooning told Thomas Hess in 1953 that "The landscape is in the Woman, and there is Woman in the landscapes" (Hess, 1968, p. 100). And in 1954–1955, he painted *Woman as a Landscape* in which the woman is hard to discern amidst the lush strokes of color representing the landscape (Yard, 2007); he had trouble with this painting and considered it unfinished (Hess, 1968, p. 102). But he now had ample space to work in his large studio/house in Springs, East Hampton, which he designed and had built during the early 1960s. The studio/house reminded him of a ship and kept alive a memory of his voyage from Rotterdam to America. In September 1968 de Kooning made his first visit back to Holland to attend a retrospective of his work at the Stedelijk Museum in Amsterdam. Joan's hopes were raised when de Kooning took her and Lisa with him, although, according to his biographers, he did so out of concern that his alcoholism could lead to problems on the trip if he traveled alone. He had been apprehensive about meeting his sister Marie, because of guilt over abandoning her when he abruptly left Holland in 1926. However, they had a happy reunion, and he also visited his 91-year-old mother in a nursing home. Stevens and Swan (2004, p. 509) mention a letter de Kooning wrote to Marie a year earlier, in which he said that he could not find love in his heart for either of his parents and had never forgiven his mother.[7] He apparently showed no emotion when his mother died soon after he

---

7   This is the letter mentioned in Chapter 4 in which de Kooning told his sister about his state of anxiety when he was around 38 or 40, and that just thinking about their mother in those days could trigger his heart to start beating wildly (Wolfe, 1996, p. 405).

returned to Springs. But, as I mentioned in Chapter 1, while he was in Holland and had seen a picture of a Mexican goddess to whom hearts were being sacrificed, de Kooning said to a Dutch journalist: "Maybe it also has something to do with my mother . . ." (Bibeb, 1968, p. 3). We are left wondering who the Mexican goddess might have represented for de Kooning and whether he was thinking of a connection between his mother and the Woman paintings.

Two years later, de Kooning travelled to Italy to attend a festival in Rome. His biographers tell us that Joan and Lisa felt painfully let down because rather than being invited on another family trip, he invited Susan, with whom he had maintained a distant friendship. Susan and de Kooning got along well, but given their difference in age, they realized they could never renew a romantic relationship (Stevens and Swan, 2004, p. 527). Once de Kooning was back in Springs and staying at his studio, he began visiting Joan and Lisa again. Joan was feeling deeply hurt, and whenever she dropped by the studio, she encountered Molly Barnes or some other woman. According to Stevens and Swan (2004), Joan "sometimes felt that [de Kooning] had no regard whatsoever for her feelings" (p. 532). The repeated separations and abandonments Joan was subjected to over the years are reminiscent of the traumatic separations and loneliness de Kooning experienced during the first five years of his life. Each of them was programmed by their internal working model to compulsively repeat some version of the past.

In August 1970, aged sixty-six, de Kooning met Emilie Kilgore, his last long-term relationship. Emilie was a married woman in her thirties who lived in Houston but spent most holidays in East

Hampton. De Kooning fell in love with her, and like the early phase of his relationship with Elaine, this relationship influenced his creativity. Flattered by his attention, Emilie responded to a man she considered a great artist (Figure 15). As described by Stevens and Swan (2004, p. 560), the relationship went well because Emilie was in Houston for much of the year, which meant no demands were placed on de Kooning, and the periods of separation invoked a deep yearning in the artist that increased his idealization of Emilie. During their periods apart, which Emilie realized actually strengthened their relationship, de Kooning sent love letters to her. His biographers got a sense of the content of some of these letters when Emilie read excerpts to them during interviews with her in July 2003 (Stevens and Swan, 2004, pp. 541, 551, 560, 680). They report that de Kooning seemed to tell Emilie "in many different ways that he was being reborn in her love. She was 'the angel' who 'made me over'" (p. 541). And as his passion deepened, they indicate that he called her "Santa Emilia," and expressed his attachment to her—"You're with me all the time even when you're not with me" (p. 551). Most afternoons, "as he bicycled through the countryside, he instinctively identified her with the watery landscape around him" (p. 560).[8] He communicated that he felt Emilie and he were not separated because he experienced her inside himself (p. 560).

---

8   According to Stevens and Swan (2004, p. 554), "Santa Emilia" became the artist's pet name for Emilie after they observed a sculptured angel on top of the baroque church of Santa Maria del Giglio, while they were in Venice in June 1972.

**Figure 15:** Willem de Kooning and Emilie Kilgore in his studio, Springs, East Hampton, New York, 1975.
Photograph by Nancy Crampton

The content of the letters, as it is reported by Stevens and Swan, suggests to me that de Kooning was developing a deepening sense of "oneness" with Emilie, an experience that is sometimes described by individuals who are passionately in love. Writing about healthy loving relationships between adults, Otto Kernberg (1976) proposes that their joyful and meaningful sexual relating can involve "a capacity for transcendence, for entering and becoming one with another person in a psychological as well as physical sense," which reconfirms the couple's emotional closeness and is "linked to the activation of the ultimately biological roots of human attachment" (p. 223). In the early 1970s, this state of being in love, perhaps together with the watery landscape of Springs, seemed to inspire an upwelling of images and a sudden burst of productivity in the artist. The works from this period suggest that a link had finally been established with a good internal object (an "inspirational muse") that unconsciously influenced de Kooning, as he now worked more consistently in a non-traumatized state of mind associated with what psychoanalysts refer to as the "depressive position" in which the object is recognized as a whole, rather than split into good and bad part-objects (Richman, 2014; Taylor, 2019). As Zilczer (2014) points out, ". . . he now focused on the intangible atmospherics of water and light," and "submerged figurative imagery within the aqueous maelstroms that now formed luminous abstract landscapes" (p. 199). This process of immersion is evident in such works as *Woman in the Water, 1972* (Figure 11), which contrasts markedly with *Woman I* completed two decades earlier.

In 1975, in merely six months, de Kooning completed twenty sumptuous abstract paintings that "contained none of the anger or bitterness that sometimes animated his earlier work" (Stevens and

Swan, 2004, p. 561). According to artist Joan Levy, he said: "They just poured out of me like water" (p. 563). He was seventy-one when he painted the seascape ...*Whose Name was Writ in Water* (Figure 12), with the title adapted from the poet John Keats' epitaph (Zilczer, 2014, p. 211). I suspect Stevens and Swan (2004) intuited the artist's connection with a benign internal maternal object when they wrote: "In his new paintings, the figure [Woman], finally, seemed to find a home in the sea" (p. 563). As noted earlier, the sea is a symbol of the mother. The canvas now seemed to function extremely well as "a holding, containing, and validating environment" (Knafo, 2002, p. 42), allowing de Kooning to move back and forth between subsymbolic and nonverbal symbolic systems within a "potential play space" and to represent bodily sensations and primitive emotions without endlessly scraping paint away and constantly revising to find the image.[9]

Richard Wollheim (1987), who is known for original work on the mind and emotions in painting, seemed to understand de Kooning's search for a link with the good mother. As I mentioned in the previous chapter, he observed (especially in the paintings of the 1970s) that de Kooning found ways to incorporate sensations of activity and a variety of other sensations that are first experienced in infancy. And, consistent with Freud's ideas about traumatic excitations and the need for a stimulus barrier, Wollheim recognized that these early sensations are heavily charged with excitation, and therefore pose a threat to the infant's fragile mind unless there is a parent to contain them. I

---

9  Of course scraping paint away with a taper's knife and repeatedly revising was a technique that de Kooning used routinely in his work; but at times early in his career it seemed to become an endless search for perfection, resulting in prolonged delays in completing a painting, and sometimes in destruction of his own work, even though it was much admired by others.

noted how his description of the container-like effect of the 1970s paintings, with their huge paint-marks engaging with the edge of the canvas, resembles Bion's concept of the container/contained and how it functions in early infancy. To add to this, I suggest that the comfort and physical intimacy de Kooning experienced with Emilie, coupled with his idealization of her as a "good mother," may have allowed him to safely re-experience early sense impressions and raw emotions without being overwhelmed by them, and to link them with the shapes and patterns and colors that emerged on the canvas.

Not all art critics would agree with Wollheim's impressions and my interpretations of de Kooning's paintings of the 1970s. Kuspit (1998), for example, argues that de Kooning remained creative for a long time only because of his obsession with woman, and that the landscape paintings mark the beginning of a retreat to pure painting. In his opinion, the earlier paintings reflect de Kooning's "struggle to possess yet not be possessed" by woman. "But when she is codified as cosmic landscape, she loses the disgusting attractiveness that made her alluring in the first place" (p. 287). Kuspit concludes that once the woman disappears from the paintings, "All that is left is the sterile act of painting" (p. 288). However, Kuspit fails to appreciate that the content of these paintings suggests that de Kooning had established a connection with a good internal object which occurred in parallel with the loving and sensual relationship he had with Emilie, and most likely with an unconscious infantile phantasy of being close to the body of his mother. This change within the artist is recognized by Carolyn Lanchner (2011), a former curator of painting and sculpture at the MoMA. Lanchner draws attention to a picture in the museum's collection which was painted in 1977 — *Untitled XIX* (Figure 16). She describes this "dazzling" picture as "one of the many that de Kooning prolifically produced in the last half of the 1970s. In these canvases, the artist's ongoing conflict between a bedeviling urge to paint the figure and another willing him toward landscape is subsumed in a joyful painterliness that integrates the two" (p. 34). Noting that the late-1970s abstractions are often compared to the late work of Claude Monet, Lanchner believes that they "attain a degree of coalescence between sensation and *matière* that is about as close as mortal painting can get" (p. 36).

We have to wonder what it was that de Kooning was searching for when he became discontented with each long-term or short-term relationship with a woman and replaced her with a new partner. Was he unconsciously seeking a particular kind of relationship that would repair a defect that he experienced within himself? He seemed to find something with Emilie that had a transformative effect on his self-experience. The deep subjective rapport he felt with her released a burst of creative work. Absent was the destructiveness toward his paintings that was present in earlier years. Elaine told writer Curtis Pepper (1983) that she used to weep in earlier years when she saw her husband "start to scrape off a work that looked great." She said on one occasion "he got so mad he jumped up and down on a painting and threw it in the garbage can." While I have suggested that the relationship with Emilie facilitated the establishment of a stronger link with a good internal object, an additional explanation might be that de Kooning experienced her as a "transformational object." This concept was introduced by Bollas (1978) to refer to the infant's early experience of the mother not as an identifiable other, but as a *process* that continually transforms the infant's internal and external environment.

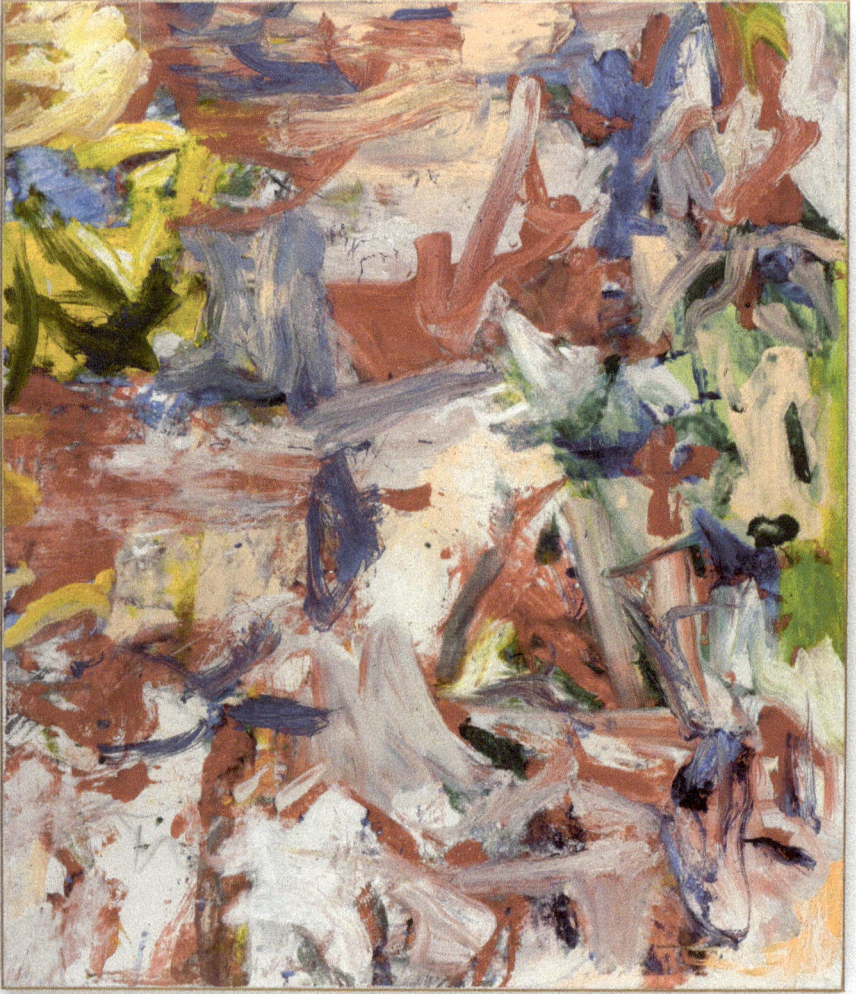

**Figure 16:** *Untitled XIX*, 1977
Oil on canvas, 79 ¾ x 70 in (202.6 x 177.8 cm)
The Museum of Modern Art, New York

That is, within the "holding environment" described by Winnicott, the infant "feels himself to be the recipient of enviro-somatic caring, identified with metamorphoses of the self." And while the mother

230

"constantly alters the infant's environment to meet his needs . . . the infant's own emergent ego capacities — of perception, motility, integration — also transform his world" (pp. 97–98). Bollas suggests that we all retain pre-verbal memory traces of the experience with the environmental mother, and that we search for this transformational experience in a variety of different ways in our adult lives. It might be through a religious experience or be an aesthetic moment, such as feeling a deep rapport with a poem, a painting, a symphony, or contemplating a landscape. As I mentioned, de Kooning identified Emilie with the watery landscape as he bicycled around the countryside. Moreover, because Emilie was not drawn into enacting a role projected onto her from de Kooning's pathologic internal relationship, the couple related to each other in a way different from de Kooning's previous long-term relationships, except for the relationships with Mary and Susan.

De Kooning's drinking binges were less frequent in the early 1970s. However, the positive relationship with Emilie and a probable link with a good internal object were not sufficient to break the pattern of compulsive drinking. As McDougall (1985, p. 67) formulated for substance-dependent patients, de Kooning for many years may have projected the good "mother-breast" onto alcohol, which became a bad persecuting mother-breast once it was consumed. During the latter half of the 1970s, he was hospitalized several times for alcoholism and did serious damage to his liver and pancreas. He also became addicted to Valium, which was prescribed when he was being weaned from alcohol (Stevens and Swan, 2004, p. 569). As usual, Joan was there to take care of him as he recuperated from binges, but eventually she could no longer cope with the situation. De Kooning was becoming increasingly depressed and having some difficulty with short-term memory, but he at least seemed to recognize the self-destructiveness of his alcoholism. Inscribed in one of his sketchbooks from the late 1970s is a quotation from an unknown source: "When an alcoholic takes a drink it is an act of violence against himself" (Zilczer, 2014, p. 256).[10] As he became increasingly unwell, de Kooning did not see much of Emilie.

Stevens and Swan (2004, p. 570) report that in the summer of 1977, an intervention was made by de Kooning's lawyer; he warned the artist that, because of his alcoholism, he could possibly need institutional care in the future and urged him to turn to Elaine for help. Even though de Kooning and Elaine had been apart for two decades, she was still deeply attached to her husband. She had bought a house in Springs not far from de Kooning's studio, and during the early 1970s had been gradually coming back into his life (Stevens and Swan, 2004, p. 567). She even introduced him to a man who got him attending AA meetings again. After the lawyer made a deal with Elaine to give up her rights to control de Kooning's estate in exchange for financial security, she agreed to take on the task of controlling her husband's drinking and monitoring his health every day (Stevens and Swan, pp. 581–582). By the late fall of 1978, however, she could no longer prevent de Kooning's serial binges. Elaine's brother Conrad moved into the studio to assist her, but he too had a difficult time coping with the artist's verbal and physical abuse. The drinking finally stopped at the end of 1979, but de Kooning had been deeply depressed throughout

---

10   This quotation is consistent with my view that de Kooning's addiction to alcohol involved the enactment of a pathologic internal relationship between parts of himself.

the year and his output of paintings was greatly reduced. His mental faculties were declining, and he wrote his last letter to Emilie, which he was unable to complete (Stevens and Swan, 2004, pp. 585–586).

The rivalry between Elaine and Joan seemed to subside a little over the years. When Elaine first came to live near Springs, Joan did not welcome her warmly, but in 1983, then aged fifty-five, she told Curtis Pepper that she now got along fine with Elaine, and that she liked her. She said that there were times when Bill had behaved cruelly to Elaine, but that was now all forgotten. However, Joan said nothing about Bill's abusiveness toward herself. In fact, Pepper (1983) reports that she had her own explanation for de Kooning's emotional turmoil. "It's lonely up there where he is," she said. "As an artist, as a creative mind, you're always faced with having to go beyond yourself. It's always there, the past work haunting you, the public and the critics on top of you. If you understand that, you can understand the drinking and the women. It's the other side of that loneliness." Joan had developed a drinking problem herself by the mid-1970s, which may have been associated with trying to cope with her own loneliness.

Would de Kooning's relationships with women have been any different if he had overcome his skepticism of psychoanalysis and entered treatment? This question is difficult to answer. He would likely have transferred onto the analyst the role of the withholding, persecuting mother; or he may have adopted that role himself and reacted in dismissive and demeaning ways toward the analyst, much like the pattern he enacted in some of his long-term relationships with women and between parts of himself. These roles would probably reverse at different times in the analysis. Like Susan and Emilie, it would have been important for the analyst to not respond angrily or to feel personally rejected. By taking a detailed history of de Kooning's childhood and family relationships before proceeding with treatment, the analyst would presumably have had some preliminary thoughts about the early trauma and, as the analysis progressed, paid attention to the artist's compulsion to repeat the traumatic past within the therapeutic relationship. Interpretations of the transference might have helped de Kooning gain some insight into the extent to which the childhood experiences with his parents, especially his mother, were unconsciously being repeated and had generated powerful emotions that were deeply buried and contributed to his depression, panic attacks, and feelings of loneliness. Given de Kooning's reluctance to think about his childhood, the analyst would have needed to consider the artist's anxiety about being flooded with intolerable affect, and his inclination to turn to alcohol or sexual encounters to manage the emotional pain. If de Kooning experienced the analyst as warm and supportive, he might have associated him with Bernard Romein and developed a positive paternal transference, within which he could explore the resentment he felt toward his own father, and eventually come to an understanding of how his father's emotional detachment was probably a consequence of his own childhood trauma.

If de Kooning had entered psychoanalysis or psychotherapy, the outcome would have been influenced strongly by the experience and theoretical orientation of the therapist. As mentioned earlier, he did see a psychiatrist in the late 1960s and early 1970s, but it is highly unlikely that he received any psychoanalytic psychotherapy. Based on my own training, while I worked a few hours a week in an addiction outpatient clinic in New York in 1970–1971, I suspect that the psychiatric treatment de Kooning received was merely supportive counseling, and encouragement to take Antabuse and to attend AA meetings.[11] Although Jackson Pollock gained some benefit from therapy sessions he had with Jungian analysts between 1939 and 1942, he was not helped by therapy in the mid-1950s when he was addicted to alcohol and behaving abusively to his artist wife Lee Krasner. In 1955, Clement Greenberg referred him to his own psychotherapist, Ralph Klein, who was a clinical psychologist in his early thirties; this inexperienced therapist lacked the skills to manage Pollock's self-destructive and psychopathic behavior (Gabriel, 2018, p. 581). In contrast, Robert Natkin, an abstract and color field painter, twenty-five years younger than de Kooning, benefited greatly from psychoanalytic psychotherapy with a Freudian psychoanalyst; he began therapy in the late-1950s and continued for almost nine years. British art critic Peter Fuller (1980, 1981) reports that Natkin had a similar childhood history to that of de Kooning and observes evidence of the impact of childhood trauma in some of Natkin's early paintings. Psychotherapy not only helped Natkin contain the trauma and transform his internal world, but to also overcome certain struggles he had with his creative work and to maintain a stable relationship with his wife.

Before closing this chapter, I will comment briefly about de Kooning's relationships with men. For the most part, these relationships were stable and rewarding, perhaps partly attributable to positive experiences he had with men during his adolescence. It was extremely fortunate for Willem, when, at the impressionable age

---

11   During the difficult period when Conrad and Elaine were trying to control de Kooning's drinking, Elaine would sometimes add Antabuse to his health drinks or eggs at breakfast. But by the time the medication took effect, he had often already consumed a large amount of alcohol. As a result, he would not only become very ill, but even lose consciousness (Stevens and Swan, 2004, p. 584).

of twelve, he was hired as an apprentice at the Giddings decorating firm in Rotterdam. The two brothers who ran the firm recognized his talent and took a paternal interest in him. The male teachers at the Academy also inspired him, and the excellent mentorship he received from Bernard Romein had a major impact, as de Kooning himself acknowledged. I think we can assume that these experiences with men who shared their knowledge with Willem, and respected and encouraged him, generated an internal working model that differed from the model based on de Kooning's boyhood experiences with his father, and was different also from the model that affected his romantic relationships with women. The friends de Kooning made in New York in the early 1930s included John Graham, Stuart Davis, and Arshile Gorky, who de Kooning affectionately referred to as "The Three Musketeers." As Stevens and Swan (2004, p. 93) describe, these three artists were essentially older brothers to de Kooning; they helped give him direction and demonstrated, through their own work, that it was possible to be a modern painter in America. Many years later, de Kooning told Harold Rosenberg that he had been lucky when he came to America and met these other painters; he described them as "the three smartest guys on the scene . . . They knew that I had my own eyes, but I wasn't always looking in the right direction. I was certainly in need of a helping hand at times" (Rosenberg, 1972; Yard, 2007, p. 141).

Gorky, an Armenian, took a dominant role in the relationship with de Kooning, who looked up to him as an older brother, but there were times when de Kooning had to tolerate Gorky's selfish and envious behavior. And disappointingly for the younger artist, Gorky dropped him in 1941 after marrying a woman with money. Yet de Kooning

236

greatly admired Gorky's work and always acknowledged his debt to him. He was deeply distressed and withdrew for several days when he learned in the summer of 1948 that Gorky had committed suicide after cancer surgery and serious injuries from a car accident had drastically changed the quality of his life (Stevens and Swan, 2004, pp. 261–262).

One other important relationship that was adversely affected by the personality of the other man was de Kooning's friendship with Jackson Pollock. Though they admired each other's creative work, there was considerable rivalry between the two men (Smee, 2017). Pollock could behave in obnoxious and extremely aggressive ways with many people, especially when he was drinking. On one occasion he provoked de Kooning into punching him in the mouth. The closest male friendship de Kooning developed was with Franz Kline, who he met in the early 1940s. Unlike Gorky, Kline was a pleasant, easy-going person, who respected de Kooning and was without pretensions. They met often at the Cedar Tavern, where they enjoyed chatting over drinks. But like de Kooning and Pollock, Kline drank to excess. By the early sixties he had suffered several heart attacks, and in 1962 he died in the hospital. Stevens and Swan (2004, p. 437) describe Kline's death as a profound loss for de Kooning, partly because it reminded him of the risks to his own life if he continued to drink heavily, but also because he was left without emotional support. The loss of his friend put him in the depths of despair, and after the funeral he began drinking heavily and disappeared for several days. He knew no other way to grieve.

# Epilogue

Despite de Kooning's mood disorder, self-destructive drinking, and unconscious compulsion to repeat pre-conceptual and conceptual traumas, he had an unusually long career and outlived most of his contemporary American artists. The alcohol addiction ravaged his body and almost killed him, but his interest in painting prevailed and helped keep him alive. Indeed, de Kooning once said, "I don't paint for a living. I paint to live" (Wallach, 1994). Morris Eagle (1981) proposes that interests (such as painting and writing) are best understood as object-relational phenomena that provide psychological functions similar to those served by relationships with other human beings. Knafo (2012) similarly suggests that "art works function as a type of object relationship" (p. 58). Thus, although de Kooning prioritized art over his relationships with people, painting was an object relationship that sustained him and gave him an identity and feeling of self-worth, beginning in mid-adolescence when his talent was first recognized and fostered, and continuing into old age. Some of the women who had long-term relationships with the artist described him as a "loner," not fully realizing that they were competing with the relationship he most valued, namely, the relationship he had with his art. Even his daughter

Lisa reported that although de Kooning loved her very much, he was not a good father, as his painting always came first (Stevens and Swan, 2004, p. 450).

I have mentioned several times that painting can have important "holding" and "containing" functions, especially for traumatized artists like de Kooning. Thus, consistent with Knafo's (2012) and Richman's (2014) view that art can transform and change an artist's inner world, de Kooning's work evolved over the course of his career in ways that suggest he was connecting with an internal good object. As he told art critic David Shirey in the late 1960s, his paintings of women had become less aggressive and were now "very friendly and pastoral, like [his] landscapes" (Shirey, 1967, p. 80). A decade later, in a review of an exhibition of de Kooning's later works at the Guggenheim Museum, Shirey (1978) commented on a change in mood in the paintings. Whereas the paintings in the early 1950s "were characterized by their fierce savagery," Shirey found an absence of tension in the later works and thought that the color had become "warmer, more tactile and accessible." "The bitch goddesses," he wrote, "have become sensual valentines as pliant as Rubens' Venuses and as harmless as kewpie dolls." However, the psychological transformation that occurred during de Kooning's relationship with Emilie, and, to a lesser extent with Susan, was incomplete. We are left wondering whether de Kooning might have gained mastery over his childhood trauma, or at least the ability to contain it more adequately, if he had undertaken psychoanalytic treatment.

In the spring of 1981, de Kooning's productivity began to increase as he turned in a new direction with his final series of paintings, which have been described as "lyrical abstractions" or "ribbon paintings"

(Elderfield, 2011e; B. Hess, 2012). In this late period of his work, which lasted throughout the 1980s, de Kooning abandoned Cubist "fitting-in" of pictorial elements, lost his enthusiasm for Picasso, and rediscovered his early interest in Matisse (Elderfield, 2011e, p. 450). His continuing admiration for Gorky's art was strengthened by a visit to a major Gorky retrospective exhibition in the Guggenheim Museum, which reminded him of Gorky's reverence for the past. He was very aware of his own mortality and was determined to forge ahead with the aim of achieving a lasting legacy (Zilczer, 2014, pp. 232–233). As he was weaned from Valium and no longer drinking alcohol, his mental health improved for a period of time. He enjoyed visits from Lisa and Emilie, and despite the gradual progression of Alzheimer's-like dementia, he completed more than one hundred and sixty paintings between 1983 and 1985 (Stevens and Swan, 2004, pp. 602, 612). Art critics have expressed various opinions as to the quality of these later works, some doubting whether it is possible to create good art in the midst of dementia. Carlos Espinel (2007), a physician at the Georgetown University School of Medicine, examined paintings created both before and during the artist's dementia; he used a combined observational and cognitive analytical method, which he had developed to investigate certain brain functions. Espinel concluded that de Kooning's procedural memory system was preserved, as well as his ability to remember remote events (which is referred to as *long-term declarative episodic memory*). He also thought that the artist's short-term (working) memory was preserved, but this seems doubtful, given observations reported by de Kooning's studio assistants. However, Espinel identified a deficit of *long-term declarative semantic memory*, which is the ability to recall recent facts and to retain

241

and use new knowledge. As he had done throughout his working life, de Kooning referred to some of his earlier works to get ideas, and then started a new work with an initial drawing on the canvas. In the early 1980s, he used charcoal and large sheets of vellum (tracing paper) to copy and transfer a drawing to the new canvas (Elderfield, 2011e, p. 453). He eventually had to stop this practice, because increasing back pain made it difficult for him to draw bent over. His assistants then began projecting images of previous drawings on to the canvas, and de Kooning would then trace in the lines of each projected drawing with charcoal (Stevens and Swan, 2004, pp. 591, 592, 614). Espinel suggests that this method activated the artist's brain and compensated for his deficit in declarative semantic memory. De Kooning would sketch the image and color the sketch, but then add new lines and use a palette or taper's knife to create new spaces; the final image did not resemble the initial sketch, which led Espinel to conclude that the final images were original in form, color, and expression.

Given the nature of procedural memory, it is not surprising that de Kooning still had the ability to skillfully draw and paint lines and shapes to create playful images, albeit with a limited palette. However, the reduction of the artist's palette does not necessarily imply a deficit; it may have been a deliberate decision by de Kooning, and perhaps, as Zilczer (2014) suggests, "resulted from his renewed emphasis on graphic line" (p. 236). Moreover, by the mid-1980s, de Kooning's assistants were responsible for preparing the colors; they therefore had a certain influence on the range of colors used by the artist (B. Hess, p. 90), until Elaine de Kooning suggested they begin "to introduce a range of green, orange and violet hues to de Kooning's formerly limited palette of primary colors" (Zilczer, 2014, p. 238). Elderfield

(2011e) reports further changes later in the decade. In 1987, the aging artist began "experimenting, in some works, with bizarre color combinations. In other works, though, perhaps in reaction, his range of colors narrowed . . ." (p. 477). And "in 1988, canvases appeared with a vivid range of clashing colors" (p. 481). De Kooning's physical and mental health further deteriorated in 1989.

In the early 1980s, spaces appeared increasingly in the paintings, which de Kooning allowed "to circulate between and prise apart the prismatic colored lines and shapes of his compositions" (Elderfield, 2011e, p. 468). The spaces, however, are not empty; either de Kooning or his assistants filled the spaces with white paint (and rarely one even color of white), and the artist allowed it to mix with other colors already on the canvas to produce areas of tinted subtlety (Elderfield, 2011e, p. 460). But with this departing subjectivity, some critics thought de Kooning may have been depicting his own disappearance in some of these paintings (Elderfield, 2011d, p. 43). Robert Hughes (1997b) described the ribbon paintings as "among the saddest things ever made by a once major artist" (p. 87) (quoted in Zilczer, 2014, p. 247); and Kuspit (1998) considered the later paintings devoid of meaning, and simply of technical interest, in the history of art. On the other hand, curator Gary Garrels (1995) opined that "These paintings of the 1980s are among the most beautiful, sensual, and exuberant abstract works by any modern painter" (p. 33). And, whereas Kuspit argued that the later paintings no longer reveal inner content, others observe that many of the patterns derive from the curvilinear female body; the paintings invite the viewer's participation to perceive body parts, including the motif of breast and nipple, which Elderfield (2011e) draws attention to in at least two of the lyrical abstractions.

Zilczer (2014) astutely notes that the irony of the criticism of the late works "is that the once controversial earlier productions, notably the series of 'Woman' paintings, was now accepted as the unquestioned benchmark against which the painter's subsequent achievements had to be measured" (pp. 247, 253).

Elaine had been a heavy smoker most of her life, and in 1984 was diagnosed with lung cancer. She had surgery to remove the affected lung, but refused chemotherapy, preferring to take her chances. In 1987, the cancer recurred with metastases in her bones that caused excruciating pain (Gabriel, 2018, p. 704). Elaine died two years later without de Kooning's realizing he had outlived her. By late 1992, he no longer recognized Emilie. He died from pneumonia in March 1997, one month short of age ninety-three. The funeral was held at Saint Luke's Episcopal Church in East Hampton and was attended by about 300 people, including Joan and Lisa, Ruth, Susan, Molly, and Emilie (Stevens and Swan, 2004, p. 629). Lisa did a great deal to preserve her father's legacy, but, like her parents, she struggled with alcohol and had a turbulent life. She studied at a school of arts in France, became a sculptor, married a French-Canadian landscaper, and had three daughters, but she divorced her husband in 2002. Tragically, she died in 2012 at age fifty-six, apparently from a fall at home. Her mother, Joan Ward, died in 2005 at age seventy-eight.

In this book I have offered a psychoanalytic exploration of de Kooning's Woman paintings of the early 1950s as well as important aspects of his life. My perspective differs from earlier Jungian and Freudian perspectives presented by non-clinicians, including several art critics and art historians. I apply the conceptual frameworks of attachment theory and British object-relations theory, and also Freud's concept of the repetition compulsion. However, paintings can have multiple meanings, and all perspectives on de Kooning and his work, whether psychoanalytic or otherwise, are determined by the theoretical ideas that influence how each of us observes the paintings and interprets whatever biographical information about the artist is available to us. The passage of time may also influence the meanings that are given to paintings. I noted, for example, that as more became known about de Kooning's adverse childhood experiences, several critics began to perceive the communication of emotional trauma in the Woman paintings. And in Marlene Clark's (2020) opinion, the "unorthodox" meanings that she perceives in these paintings could not have been revealed by de Kooning in the 1950s, for fear that they might lead to questions about his sexual orientation. But in contrast to Clark's perspective, my view is that an essential meaning of the paintings remains hidden, because it was unknown to de Kooning himself: it originated in an earlier time and space (namely during infancy and early childhood), although it was being repeated continually throughout his adult life. I suggest also that, similar to Rosine Perelberg's (2013, p. 569) description of psychoanalysis as *a journey toward the unknown*, we can regard the Woman paintings partly as an attempt by de Kooning to find knowledge about himself (the "unthought-known") and to repair his traumatized self. Lee Hall (1993) described abstract expressionism as "[pitting] the lonely and searching individual against the unknown (possibly unknowable) first forces of the universe, casting the painter in the role of voyager and seeker after truth" (p. 4). Psychoanalysts would understand Hall's phrase "first forces of the universe" as a metaphor for the infant's early sensory and primitive emotional experiences (positive and negative) within the holding environment provided by the mother. The first few months and years of life are a tumultuous time, mitigated only by the containing functions provided by sensitively attuned parents and other caregivers. The temperaments and stressful lives of de Kooning's parents would have limited their capacity to provide an adequate containing function for their son.

I began my exploration of the Woman paintings and de Kooning's relationships with women after reading Stevens and Swan's biography of de Kooning and Judith Wolfe's doctoral dissertation, whose collective research findings made me, for the first time, aware of the artist's childhood trauma and led me to a fresh way of thinking about his controversial paintings. With only limited information reported by de Kooning himself, however, the interpretations I have proposed are speculative. I am one of those viewers whom David Cateforis was referring to in 1991 when he predicted that the Woman paintings of the early 1950s would provide "new questions for new viewers" for decades to come, and that "the voyage of interpretation [would] continue" (p. 325). Three decades later, at age 91, artist Jasper Johns, whose work led the American public away from abstract expressionism to a more concrete form and style, said: "I don't know that art can be understood in any final way, but a search for understanding tends to open one's eyes rather than close them" (Luscombe, 2021). I hope that the exploration and perspective I have offered in this book will further encourage readers to open their minds and their eyes and think about de Kooning's Woman paintings, as well as his addiction and relationships with women, in ways that they had not previously considered.

# REFERENCES

Abella, A. (2010). Contemporary art and Hanna Segal's thinking on aesthetics. *International Journal of Psychoanalysis* 91:163–181.

_____ (2016). Psychoanalysis and the arts: The slippery ground of applied psychoanalysis. *Psychoanalytic Quarterly* 85(1):89–119.

Abram, J. (1996). *The Language of Winnicott. A Dictionary of Winnicott's Use of Words*. London: Karnac Books.

Allen, E. (2021, September 6). Ars Longa. *New Yorker*, pp. 15–16.

Ashton, D. (1955, December). Art. *Arts and Architecture*, 27. Cited in D.C. Cateforis, Willem de Kooning's "Women" of the 1950s: A critical history of their reception and interpretation. Doctoral dissertation submitted to the Department of Art History, Stanford University, 1991, pp. 154–155.

_____ (1972). *The Life and Times of the New York School*. Bath, UK: Adams and Dart.

Auchincloss, E.L., and Samberg, E. (2012). *Psychoanalytic Terms and Concepts*. New Haven, CT: Yale University Press.

Bak, R.C. (1968). The phallic woman—the ubiquitous fantasy in the perversions. *Psychoanalytic Study of the Child* 23:15–36.

Balint, M. (1955). Friendly expanses—horrid empty spaces. *International Journal of Psycho-analysis* 36:225–241.

Balsam, R.H. (2018). "Castration anxiety" revisited: Especially "female castration anxiety." *Psychoanalytic Inquiry* 38(1):11–22.

Barber, F. (1999). The politics of feminist spectatorship and the disruptive body. De Kooning's *Woman I* reconsidered. In A. Jones and A. Stephenson (Eds.), *Performing the Body, Performing the Text*, pp. 119–128. London: Routledge.

_____ (2004). Abstract expressionism and masculinity. In P. Wood (Ed.), *Varieties of Modernism* (pp. 146–186). New Haven: The Open University with Yale University Press.

Beres, D. (1959). The contribution of psychoanalysis to the biography of the artist. A commentary on methodology. *International Journal of Psychoanalysis* 40:26–37.

Berger, J. (1972). *Ways of Seeing*. London and Harmondsworth, Middlesex: British Broadcasting Corporation and Penguin Books.

Bibeb, D. (1968, October 5). Willem de Kooning: I find everything must have a mouth and I put a mouth wherever I please. *Vrij Nederland*, p. 3. Cited in J. Zilczer, *A Way of Living: The Art of Willem De Kooning*. New York: Phaidon Press, p. 129.

Bion, W.R. (1962). *Learning from Experience*. London: Heinemann.

_____ (1965). *Transformations*. In *Seven Servants. Four Works by Wilfrid R. Bion*. New York: Jason Aronson, 1977.

_____ (1967). *Second Thoughts*. London:Heinemann. Reprinted by Karnac, 1984.

_____ (1970). *Attention and Interpretation*. London: Tavistock Publications.

Blass, R.B. (2020). Introduction to "Can we think psychoanalytically about transgenderism?" *International Journal of Psychoanalysis* 101(5):1014–1018.

Blum, H.P. (2013). Picasso's prolonged adolescence: Blue period and blind figures. *Psychoanalytic Review* 100 (2):267–287.

Bollas, C. (1978) The transformational object. *International Journal of Psychoanalysis* 60:97–107.

_____ (1987). *The Shadow of the Object: Psychoanalysis of the Unthought Known*. London: Free Association Books.

_____ (2011). Creativity and psychoanalysis. In Bollas, C., *The Christopher Bollas Reader* (pp. 194–205). London and New York: Routledge.

Bose, J. (2005). Images of trauma: Pain, recognition, and disavowal in the works of Frida Kahlo and Francis Bacon. *Journal of the American Academy of Psychoanalysis and Dynamic Psychiatry* 33:51–70.

Bowlby, J. (1951). *Maternal Care and Mental Health*. Geneva: World Health Organization.

_____ (1973). *Attachment and Loss, Vol. 2: Separation: Anxiety and Anger*. New York: Basic Books.

_____ (1988a). *A Secure Base. Clinical Applications of Attachment Theory*. London and New York: Routledge (Routledge Classics Edition, 2005).

_____ (1988b). Developmental psychiatry comes of age. *American Journal of Psychiatry* 145(1):1–10.

Breier, A., Charney, D.S., and Heninger, G.R. (1986). Agoraphobia with panic attacks. *Archives of General Psychiatry* 43:1029–1036.

Breuer, J., and Freud, S. (1893). On the psychical mechanism of hysterical phenomena. *The Standard Edition of the Complete*

*Psychological Works of Sigmund Freud* 2:1–17. London: Hogarth Press.

Brody, R. (2011, October 3). Willem de Kooning: The new wave in art. *New Yorker*. Retrieved from https://newyorker.com/culture/ richard-brody-willem-de-kooning-the-new-wave- in-art.

Broll, T.B. (2005). *The Violent Brushstroke: Contributions from the Independent School of British Psychoanalysis to the Art of Willem de Kooning*. A dissertation submitted in partial fulfillment of the requirements for the degree of Master of Fine Arts to the Faculty of Humanities, Development and Social Sciences of the University of KwaZulu-Natal, Pietermaritzburg.

Bucci, W. (1997). *Psychoanalysis and Cognitive Science. A Multiple Code Theory*. New York: Guilford Press.

_____ (1998). Transformation of meanings in the analytic discourse: A strategy for research. *Canadian Journal of Psychoanalysis* 6(2):233–260.

Calabrese, M.L., Farber, B.A., and Weston, D. (2005). The relationship of adult attachment constructs to object relational patterns of representing self and others. *Journal of the American Academy of Psychoanalysis and Dynamic Psychiatry* 33(3):513–530.

Cateforis, D.C. (1991). *Willem de Kooning's "Women" of the 1950s: A Critical History of their Reception and Interpretation*. Doctoral dissertation submitted to the Department of Art History, Stanford University.

_____ (1994). *Willem de Kooning*. New York: Rizzoli International Publications, Inc.

Chasseguet-Smirgel, J. (1984a). *Creativity and Perversion*. New York: W.W. Norton.

_____ (1984b). Thoughts on the concept of reparation and the hierarchy of creative acts. *International Review of Psychoanalysis* 11:399–406.

Chu, J.A. (1991). The repetition compulsion revisited: Reliving dissociated trauma. *Psychotherapy* 28(2):327–332.

Clark, M. (2020). *The Woman in Me. Willem de Kooning. Woman I–VI.* Washington: Academica Press.

Clarke, G.S. (2006). *Personal Relations Theory.* London: Routledge.

Clyman, R. (1991). The procedural organization of emotions: A contribution from cognitive science to the psychoanalytic theory of therapeutic action. *Journal of the American Psychoanalytic Association* 39 (Supplement): 349–382).

Coates, R.M. (1953, April 4). The art galleries. *New Yorker*, pp. 94–96.

Coates, S.W. (2004). John Bowlby and Margaret S. Mahler: Their lives and theories. *Journal of the American Psychoanalytic Association* 52(2):571–601.

Crehan, H. (1953, April 15). A sea change: Woman trouble. *Art Digest* 27(14):5.

Curtis, C. (2017). *A Generous Vision: The Creative Life of Elaine de Kooning.* New York: Oxford University Press.

Damasio, A. (2003). *Looking for Spinoza: Joy, Sorrow, and the Feeling Brain.* Orlando, Fl: Harcourt.

Davenport, R.W., and Sargeant, W. (1948, October 11). A *Life* round table on modern art: Fifteen distinguished critics and connoisseurs undertake to clarify the strange art of today. *Life* 25, no. 15, pp. 56–68, 70, 75–76, 78–79. Cited in R.E. Krauss (2015), *Willem de Kooning Nonstop. Cherchez la femme.* Chicago: University of Chicago Press, p. 67.

Davies, J.M. (2016). A review of *Mended by the Muse: Creative Transformations of Trauma*, by Sophia Richman. *Psychoanalytic Perspectives* 13:230–235.

Davis, D. (1972, September 4). De Kooning on the upswing. *Newsweek*, p. 70. Cited in R.E. Krauss, *Willem de Kooning Nonstop: Cherchez la femme*. Chicago: University of Chicago Press, 2015.

De Carli, P., Tagini, A., Sarracino, D., Santona, A., Bonalda, V., Cesari, P.E., & Parolin, L. (2018). Like grandparents, like parents: Empirical evidence on the transmission of parenting styles. *Bulletin of the Menninger Clinic* 82(1):46–70.

de Hirsh, S. (1955, October). "A talk with de Kooning." *Intro Bulletin: A Literary Newspaper for the Arts* 1(1):11–13.

de Kooning, W. (1951a, Spring). Willem de Kooning, text of talk delivered at a symposium at the MoMA on February 5, 1951, on "What Abstract Art Means to Me: Statements by Six American Artists." *The Bulletin of the Museum of Modern Art* 18 (3):4–8.

_____ (1951b). "The Renaissance and order." *Trans/formation* 1(2):85–87. Reprinted in S. Yard, *Willem de Kooning. Works, Writings, Interviews*, pp. 111–113. Barcelona: Ediciones Poligrafa, 2007.

_____ (1963). Content is a glimpse. In G. Scrivani, (Ed.), *The Collected Writings of Willem de Kooning*. New York: Hanuman Books, 1988.

_____ (1988). *The Collected Writings of Willem de Kooning*, [Edited by G. Scrivani]. New York: Hanuman Books

Denby, E. (1964). My friend de Kooning. *ARTnews Annual* 29:82–99.

Devree, H. (1953, March 22). De Kooning. *New York Times*.

Dickerson, G. (1964, November 21). The strange eye and art of Willem de Kooning. *Saturday Evening Post* 237(40):68–71.

Dodes, L.M. (1990). Addiction, helplessness, and narcissistic rage. *Psychoanalytic Quarterly* 59: 398–419.

Duncan, C. (1977). The esthetics of power in modern erotic art. *Heresies* 1:46–50.

_____ (1989). The MoMA's hot mamas. *Art Journal* 48(2):171–178.

Eagle, M.N. (1981). Interests as object relations. *Psychoanalysis and Contemporary Thought* 4: 527–565.

_____ (1997). Attachment and psychoanalysis. *British Journal of Medical Psychology* 70: 217–229.

_____ (2011). *From Classical to Contemporary Psychoanalysis. A Critique and Integration.* New York: Routledge.

_____ (2013). *Attachment and Psychoanalysis. Theory, Research, and Clinical Implications.* New York: Guilford Press.

Ehrenzweig, A. (1961). The hidden order of art. *British Journal of Aesthetics* 1(3):121–133.

Elderfield, J. (2011a). The beginnings of *Woman I*. In J. Elderfield (Ed.), *de Kooning, a Retrospective* (pp. 246–254). New York: The Museum of Modern Art.

_____ (2011b). *Woman I* continued; *Woman II* and *Woman III*. In J. Elderfield (Ed.), *de Kooning, a Retrospective* (pp. 255–266). New York: The Museum of Modern Art.

_____ (2011c). Woman to landscape. In J. Elderfield (Ed.), *de Kooning, a Retrospective* (pp. 238–245). New York: The Museum of Modern Art.

_____ (2011d). Space to paint. In J. Elderfield (Ed.), *de Kooning, a Retrospective*, pp. 8–46. New York: The Museum of Modern Art.

_____ (2011e). The late paintings. In J. Elderfield (Ed.), *de Kooning, a Retrospective*, pp. 441–486. New York: The Museum of Modern Art.

Eliot, A. (1953, April 6). Big City Dames. *Time* 61, no. 4, p. 80. Cited in Cateforis, 1991, p. 331.

_____ (1954, June 28). Under the Four Winds. *Time* 63, pp. 74–77.

Erel, O. (2020). Vicissitudes in Winnicottian theory on the origin of aggression: Between dualism and monism and from back to front. *Psychoanalytic Quarterly* 89(2):259–279.

Esman, A.H. (1998). What is "applied" in "applied" psychoanalysis? *International Journal of Psychoanalysis* 79:741–752.

Espinel, C.H. (2007). Memory and the creation of art: The syndrome, as in de Kooning, of "creating in the midst of dementia." In J. Bogousslavsky and M.G. Hennerici (Eds.), *Neurological Disorders in Famous Artists — Part 2. Frontiers in Neurology and Neuroscience* 22:150–168.

Fitzsimmons, J. (1953, May). Art. *Arts and Architecture*, 70(5):8.

Flack, A. (2016). Audrey Flack on de Kooning's women. Retrieved from https://paintersonpaintings.com/audreyflack-on-de-kooning-women/

Flint, P.B. (1991, January 21). Juliet Man Ray, 79, the artist's model and muse, is dead. *The New York Times*, Section B, page 8.

Fonagy, P. (2001). *Attachment Theory and Psychoanalysis*. New York: Other Press.

Fonagy, P., Gergely, G., Jurist, E.L., and Target, M. (2002). *Affect Regulation, Mentalization, and the Development of the Self*. New York: Other Press.

Freud, S. (1894). The neuro-psychoses of defence. *The Standard Edition of the Complete Psychological Works of Sigmund Freud* 3:41–61. London: Hogarth Press.

_____ (1905). Three essays on the theory of sexuality. *The Standard Edition of the Complete Psychological Works of Sigmund Freud* 7:123–246. London: Hogarth Press.

_____ (1914) Remembering, repeating and working through (Further recommendations on the technique of psycho-analysis II). *The Standard Edition of the Complete Psychological Works of Sigmund Freud* 12:145–156. London: Hogarth Press.

_____ (1919). The "uncanny." *The Standard Edition of the Complete Psychological Works of Sigmund Freud* 17:217–256. London: Hogarth Press.

_____ (1920). Beyond the pleasure principle. *The Standard Edition of the Complete Psychological Works of Sigmund Freud* 18:1–64. London: Hogarth Press.

_____ (1922). Medusa's head. *The Standard Edition of the Complete Psychological Works of Sigmund Freud* 18:273–274. London: Hogarth Press.

_____ (1926). The question of lay analysis. *The Standard Edition of the Complete Psychological Works of Sigmund Freud* 20:183–258. London: Hogarth Press.

_____ (1927). Fetishism. *The Standard Edition of the Complete Psychological Works of Sigmund Freud* 21:147–158. London: Hogarth Press.

_____ and Jones, E. (1995). *The Complete Correspondence of Sigmund Freud and Ernest Jones*, 1908–1939, ed. R.A. Paskauskas. Cambridge, MA: Belknap Press.

Frosch, A. (1995). The preconceptual organization of emotion. *Journal of the American Psychoanalytic Association* 37:369–376.

Fuller, P. (1980). *Art and Psychoanalysis*. London: Writers and Readers Publishing Cooperative.

Fuller, P. (1981). *Robert Natkin*. New York: Harry N. Abrams.

Gabbard, G.O. (1986). A review of *Lives, Events, and other Players: Directions in Psychohistory, Vol. 4*, edited by Joseph T. Coltrera. *Psychoanalytic Review* 73(2):232–235.

Gabriel, M. (2018). *Ninth Street Women*. New York: Little, Brown and Company.

Garrels, G. (1995). Three toads in the garden: Line, color, and form. In *Willem de Kooning: The Late Paintings, The 1980s*. San Francisco: San Francisco Museum of Modern Art.

Gaugh, H.F. (1983). *Willem de Kooning*. New York: Abbeville Press.

Geist, S. (1953, April 1). Work in progress. *Art Digest* 27(13):15.

Gentile, J. (2016). On spatial metaphors and free association: Phallic fantasy and vaginal primacy. *Contemporary Psychoanalysis* 52(1):21–50.

Giron, K. (2019, June 6) Baby care in the 19th century. Retrieved from https//:www.hhhistory. com/baby-care-in-the-19th-century-6-6-19. (Online at: https://www.hhhistory.com/2019/06/baby-care-in-19th-century.html).

Glover, N. (2009). *Psychoanalytic Aesthetics: An Introduction to the British School*. London: Karnac.

Gombrich, E.H., and Kris, E. (1938). The principles of caricature. *British Journal of Medical Psychology* 17:319–342.

Goodman, G. (2002). *The Internal World and Attachment*. Hillsdale, NJ: Analytic Press.Ill

Greenberg, C. (1948, April 24) Review of an exhibition of Willem de Kooning. *The Nation* 166 (17). Reprinted in J. O'Brien (Ed.), *Clement*

*Greenberg. The Collected Essays and Criticism*, vol. 2, *Arrogant Purpose 1945–1949*, (p. 228). Chicago: Chicago University Press, 1986.

_____ (1955). American-type painting, in J. O'Brien (Ed.), *Clement Greenberg. The Collected Essays and Criticism, vol. 2, Affirmations and Refusals 1950–1956*, (p. 222). Chicago: Chicago University Press, 1995.

Grotstein, J.S. (1997). "Internal objects" or "chimerical monsters?" The demonic "third forms" of the internal world. *Journal of Analytical Psychology* 42:47–80.

_____ (2007). *A Beam of Intense Darkness. Wilfrid Bion's Legacy to Psychoanalysis*. London: Karnac.

_____ (2009). *"…But at the Same Time and on another Level…" Volume One: Psychoanalytic Theory and Technique in the Kleinian/Bionian Mode*. London: Karnac.

Hall, L. (1993). *Elaine and Bill. Portrait of a Marriage. The Lives of Willem and Elaine de Kooning*. New York: Harper Collins Publishers.

Heathcote, C. (2020, August 1). Willem de Kooning and his "Woman" series. *Quadrant Online*. Retrieved from https://quadrant.org.au/magazine/2020/07-08/willem-de-kooning-and-his-woman-series/

Heim, C., Shugart, M., Craighead, W.E., and Nemeroff, C.B. (2010). Neurobiological and psychiatric consequences of child abuse and neglect. *Developmental Psychobiology* 52(7):671–690.

Heiman, P. (1952). Certain functions of introjection and projection in early infancy. In M. Klein, P. Heimann, S. Isaacs, and J. Riviere (Eds.), *Developments in Psycho-Analysis* (pp. 122–168). London: Hogarth Press, 1973.

Hess, B. (2012). *Willem de Kooning. 1904–1997. Content as a Glimpse*. Köln, Germany: Taschen.

Hess, T.B. (1953, March). De Kooning paints a picture. *ArtNews* 52(1):30–33. Cited in J. Zilczer, *A Way of Living: The Art of Willem De Kooning.* New York: Phaidon Press, p. 280.

_____ (1959). *Willem de Kooning.* New York: George Braziller, Inc.

_____ (1965, March). De Kooning's new women. *ArtNews* 64(1):36–38, 63–65. Cited in J. Zilczer, *A Way of Living: The Art of Willem De Kooning.* New York: Phaidon Press, p. 280.

_____ (1967). *De Kooning. Recent Paintings.* New York: Walker and Company, in association with M. Knoedler & Co.

_____ (1968). *Willem de Kooning.* New York: The Museum of Modern Art.

Hofer, M.A. (2005). The psychobiology of early attachment. *Clinical Neuroscience Research* 4: 291–300.

Holmes, J. (2005). Preface to the Routledge Classics Edition. In J. Bowlby, *A Secure Base. Clinical Applications of Attachment Theory,* pp. xiii–xx. London and New York: Routledge Classics Edition.

Holt, L.E. (1894). *The Care and Feeding of Children: A Catechism for the Use of Mothers and Children's Nurses.* New York: Appleton & Co.

Horney, K. (1932). The dread of women. *International Journal of Psychoanalysis* 8:348–360.

Hughes, R. (1997a). *American Visions. The Epic History of Art in America.* New York: Alfred Knopf.

Hughes, R. (1997b, March 31). Desire as full stretch: Willem de Kooning: 1904–1997. *Time* 149 (13):87. Quoted in Zilczer, J. (2014). *A Way of Living: The Art of Willem De Kooning.* New York: Phaidon Press, p. 247.

Hunter, S. (1975, November). De Kooning: Je dessine less yeux fermés (I draw with my eyes closed). *Galerie Jardin des Arts,* 152:70. Cited in Richard Shiff, *Between Sense and Sensibility*. New York: Reakton Books, 2011, pp. 126, 287.

Hustvedt, S. (2016). *A Woman looking at Men Looking at Women*. London: Sceptre (Hodder and Stoughton Ltd).

Isaacs, S. (1952). The nature and function of phantasy. In M. Klein, P. Heimann, S. Isaacs, and J. Riviere (Eds.), *Developments in Psycho-Analysis* (pp. 67–121). London: Hogarth Press, 1973.

Katz, S.M. (2018). Prologue: Sex, gender, and identity. *Psychoanalytic Inquiry* 38(1):1–10.

Kennedy. R. (2010). Ruth Kligman, muse and artist dies at 80. *The New York Times*, March 6.

Kernberg, O. (1976). *Object Relations Theory and Clinical Psychoanalysis*. New York: Jason Aronson.

Khan, M. (1963). The concept of cumulative trauma. *Psychoanalytic Study of the Child* 18:286–306.

Knafo, D. (1991). Egon Schiele's self-portraits. *Annual of Psychoanalysis* 19:59–90.

_____ (2002). Revisiting Ernst Kris's concept of *regression in the service of the ego* in art. *Psychoanalytic Psychology* 19(1):24–49.

_____ (2012). Alone together: Solitude and the creative encounter in art and psychoanalysis. *Psychoanalytic Dialogues* 22:54–71.

Koob, G.F., Powell, P, and White, A. (2020). Addiction as a coping response: hyperkatifeia, deaths of despair, and COVID-19. *American Journal of Psychiatry* 177(11):1031–1037.

Krauss, R.E. (2015). *Willem de Kooning Nonstop. Cherchez la femme.* Chicago: University of Chicago Press.

Kris, E. (1936). The psychology of caricature. *International Journal of Psychoanalysis* 17:285–303.

Kris, E. (1952). *Psychoanalytic Explorations in Art*. New York: International Universities Press.

Kubie. L.S. (1974). The drive to become both sexes. *Psychoanalytic Quarterly* 43:349–426.

Kulish, N.M. (1986). Gender and transference: The screen of the phallic mother. *International Review of Psychoanalysis* 13:393–404.

Kuspit, D. (1994). Body of evidence. *Artforum International* 33(3):74–79.

_____ (1998). Venus unveiled: De Kooning's melodrama of vulgarity. In B. Beckley and D. Shapiro (Eds.), *Uncontrollable Beauty. Toward a New Aesthetics* (pp. 279–295). New York: Allworth Press.

_____ (2000). Freud and the visual arts. *Journal of Applied Psychoanalytic Studies* 2(1):25–39.

_____ (2011). Beauty and the beastly artist: Willem de Kooning's destructiveness. *Artnet Magazine*. Retrieved from http://www.artnet.com/magazineus/features/kuspit/willem-de-kooning-at-moma-10- 6-11.asp

Lanchner, C. (2011). *Willem de Kooning*. New York: The Museum of Modern Art.

Laub, D., and Podell, D. (1995). Art and trauma. *International Journal of Psychoanalysis* 76: 991–1005.

Lauter, E. (1976). Some psychological and cultural implications of Willem de Kooning's images of woman. *Soundings: An Interdisciplinary Journal* 59(4):426–446.

LeDoux, J.E., and Pine, D.S. (2016). Using neuroscience to help understand fear and anxiety: A two-system framework. *American Journal of Psychiatry* 173(11):1083–1093.

Levy, M.S. (2000). A reconceptualization of the repetition compulsion. *Psychiatry* 63(1):45–53.

Lewin, B.D. (1933). The body as phallus. *Psychoanalytic Quarterly* 2:24–47.

Lieber, E. (2000). *Willem de Kooning. Reflections in the studio.* New York: Harry Abrams.

Lippard, E.T.C., and Nemeroff, C.B. (2020). The devastating clinical consequences of child abuse and neglect: Increased disease vulnerability and poor treatment response in mood disorders. *American Journal of Psychiatry* 177:20–36.

Lopez-Corvo, R.E. (2014). *Traumatized and Non-traumatized States of the Personality.* London: Karnac.

_____ (2020). *The Traumatic Loneliness of Children.* London: Free Association Books.

Luscombe, B. (2021, October 11/October 18). 15 Questions [an interview with Jasper Johns]. *Time* 198(13–14):112.

Macmurray, J. (1995). *Persons in Relation*, vol. II of *The Form of the Personal.* London: Faber and Faber (first published in 1961).

Mander, G. (1996). The stifled cry or Truby King, the forgotten prophet. *British Journal of Psychotherapy* 13(1):3–12.

Matthews, C. (1993). Acts of aggression: Acts of obsession: A feminist perspective on Willem de Kooning's *Woman* series. In V.M. Bentz, and P.E.F. Mayes (Eds.), *Women's Power and Roles as Portrayed in Visual Images of Women in the Arts and Mass Media* (pp. 181–186). Lewiston, New York: The Edwin Mellen Press.

McDougall, J. (1980). *Plea for a Measure of Abnormality.* New York: International Universities Press.

_____ (1985). *Theaters of the Mind. Illusion and Truth on the Psychoanalytic Stage*. New York: Basic Books.

_____ (1989). *Theaters of the Body. A Psychoanalytic Approach to Psychosomatic Illness*. New York: W.W. Norton.

_____ (1995). *The Many Faces of Eros*. London: Free Association Books.

Molcard, E.S. (2019, February 19). 21 Facts about René Magritte. Department of Impressionist & Modern Art, Sotheby. Retrieved from https://www.sothebys.com/en/articles/21-facts-about-rené-magritte

Molino, A. (1997). *Freely Associated. Encounters in Psychoanalysis with Christopher Bollas, Joyce McDougall, Michael Eigen, Adam Phillips, Nina Coltart*. London: Free Association Books.

Neumann, E. (1963). *The Great Mother. An Analysis of the Archetype*. Princeton, NJ: Princeton University Press.

Ogden, T.H. (1983). The concept of internal object relations. *International Journal of Psychoanalysis* 64:227–241.

_____ (1984). Instinct, phantasy, and psychological deep structure. *Contemporary Psychoanalysis* 20(4):500–525.

_____ (1985). On potential space. *International Journal of Psychoanalysis* 66:129–141.

_____ (1992). The dialectically constituted/decentred subject of psychoanalysis. II: The contributions of Klein and Winnicott. *International Journal of Psychoanalysis* 73:613–626.

Paetzold, R.L., Rholes, S., and Kohn, J.L. (2015). Disorganized attachment in adulthood: Theory, measurement, and implications for romantic relationships. *Review of General Psychology* 19:146–156.

Pearlstein, P. (1989, Fall). "Re: De Kooning." *Art Journal* 48(3):233.

Peláez, M.G. (2009). Trauma theory in Sándor Ferenczi's writings of 1931 and 1932. *International Journal of Psychoanalysis* 90:1217–1233.

Pepper, C.B. (1983, November 20). The indomitable de Kooning. *The New York Times Magazine*, pp. 42–47, 66, 70, 86, 88, 90, 94.

Perelberg, R.J. (2018). The riddle of anxiety: Between the familiar and the unfamiliar. *International Journal of Psychoanalysis* 99(4):810–827.

_____ (2013). Paternal function and thirdness in psychoanalysis and legend: Has the future been foretold? *Psychoanalytic Quarterly* 82(3):557–585.

Piaget, J. (1951). *Play, Dreams, and Imitation in Childhood*. New York: W. W. Norton.

Polcari, S. (1991). *Abstract Expressionism and the Modern Experience*. Cambridge, UK: Cambridge University Press.

Portner, L.J. (1953, June 14). "Art in Washington: The abstract of the impression." *The Washington Post*, p. L3. Cited in Zilczer (2014). *A Way of Living: The Art of Willem De Kooning*. New York: Phaidon Press, pp. 128, 275.

Posèq, A.W. (2001). *Soutine: His Jewish Modality*. Sussex, England: The Book Guild, Ltd.

Poser, S. (2008). The life and death of the unconscious in modern and contemporary art. *Modern Psychoanalysis* 33A (1):128–141.

Rank, O. (1924). The trauma of birth in its importance for psychoanalytic therapy. *Psycho-analytic Review* 11(3):241–245.

Raskin, M., Peeke, H.V.S., Dickman, W., and Pinsker, H. (1982). Panic and generalized anxiety disorders. *Archives of General Psychiatry* 39(6):687–689.

Reiner, A. (2008). The language of the unconscious. Poetry and psychoanalysis. *Psychoanalytic Review* 95(4):597–624.

Rholes, W.S., Paetzold, R.L., and Kohn, J.L. (2016). Disorganized attachment mediates the link between early trauma and externalizing behavior in adult relationships. *Personality and Individual Differences* 90:61–65.

Richman, S. (2014). *Mended by the Muse: Creative Transformations of Trauma*. London: Routledge.

Rodman, S. (1957) *"Willem de Kooning." Conversations with Artists*. New York: Devon-Adair, Co. Cited in J. Zilczer (2014). *A Way of Living: The Art of Willem De Kooning*. New York: Phaidon Press, p. 275.

Rosenberg, H. (1952, December). The American action painters. *ArtNews* 51, no. 8.

_____ (1972, September). Interview with Willem de Kooning. *ArtNews*. Reprinted in S. Yard, *Willem de Kooning. Works, Writings, Interviews* (pp. 141–155). Barcelona: Ediciones Poligrafa, 2007.

Rosenblum, R. (1985, October). The fatal women of de Kooning and Picasso. *Art News* 84:98–103.

Saketopoulou, A. (2020). Thinking psychoanalytically, thinking better: Reflections on transgender. *International Journal of Psychoanalysis* 101(5):1019–1030.

Sakkal, G.J.E. (2015). *Cuvism. Cognitive Unconscious Visual Creativity. The Human Creative Response*. North Charleston, South Carolina: CreateSpace Independent Publishing Platform.

_____ (2021). *Whose Truth—Whose Creativity? A 21st Century Manifesto*. London: The Black Spring Press Group.

Salberg, J. (2015). The texture of traumatic attachment: Presence and ghostly absence in transgenerational transmission. *Psychoanalytic Quarterly* 84(1):21–46.

Schierbeek, B. (2005). *Willem de Kooning: A Portrait*. Leiden: Menken Kasander & Wigman Uitgevers.

Schjeldahl, P. (2011, September 26). Shifting picture. A de Kooning retrospective. *New Yorker*, pp. 122–123.

Schnier, J. (1950). The blazing sun. A psychoanalytic approach to Van Gogh. *American Imago* 7(2):143–162.

Sedivi, A.E. (2009). Unveiling the unconscious: The influence of Jungian psychology on Jackson Pollock and Mark Rothko. Undergraduate Honors Theses. Paper 284. Retrieved from https://scholarworks. wm.edu/honorstheses/284

Segal, H. (1952). A psychoanalytical approach to aesthetics. *International Journal of Psycho-analysis* 33:196–207.

_____ (1991). Art and the depressive position. In H. Segal, *Dream, Phantasy and Art* (pp. 85–100). Hove, UK: Routledge.

Seitz, W.C. (1983). *Abstract Expressionist Painting in America*. Cambridge, MA: Harvard University Press.

Shiff, R. (2011). *Between Sense and de Kooning*. London: Reaktion Books.

Shirey, D.L. (1967, November 20). "Don Quixote in Springs." *Newsweek*, pp. 80–81.

_____ (1978, February 5). De Kooning and the Island's spell. *New York Times*.

Siegel, D.J. (1999). *The Developing Mind. Toward a Neurobiology of Interpersonal Experience*. New York: Guilford Press.

Smee, S. (2017). *The Art of Rivalry*. London: Profile Books.

Snyder, R. (1960). *Sketchbook No. 1: Three Americans*. New York: Time.

Spector, J.J. (1973). *The Aesthetics of Freud. A Study in Psychoanalysis and Art*. New York: Praeger.

Spitz, R.A. (1955). The primal cavity — A contribution to the genesis of perception and its role in psychoanalytic theory. *The Psychoanalytic Study of the Child* 10:215–240.

Steele, H., and Steele, M. (1998). Response to Cassidy, Lyons-Ruth, and Bretherton. A return to exploration. *Social Development* 7(1):137–141.

Steinberg, L. (1955, November). Month in review. *Arts* 30:46. Republished as "De Kooning's Woman," in L. Steinberg, *Other Criteria: Confrontations with 20th Century Art* (pp. 259–262). New York: Oxford University Press, 1972.

Stevens, M., and Swan, A. (2004). *De Kooning. An American Master*. New York: Alfred Knopf.

Stokes, A. (1934). Carving, modelling and Agostino. In A. Stokes, *Stones of Rimini* (pp. 108–109). London: Faber & Faber.

Stoller, R.J. (1975). *Perversion. The Erotic Form of Hatred*. New York: Pantheon Books.

Storr, A. (1957). The psychopathology of fetishism and transvestitism. *Journal of Analytical Psychology* 2(2):153–166.

Suttie, I.D. (1935). *The Origins of Love and Hate*. London: Kegan Paul.

Sylvester, D. (1994). Flesh was the reason. In M. Prather (Ed.), *Willem de Kooning Paintings*, (pp. 15–31). Washington, DC: National Gallery of Art; New Haven: Yale University Press.

_____ (2001). *"Willem de Kooning, 1960,"* in *Interviews with American Artists* (pp. 43–57). London: Chatto and Windu.

Taylor, G.J. (1980). Splitting of the ego in transvestism and mask wearing. *International Review of Psychoanalysis* 7:511–520.

_____ (1984). Judith and the Infant Hercules: Its iconography. *American Imago* 41(2):101–115.

_____ (1987). The transitional object and disorders of regulation. In G. J. Taylor, *Psychosomatic Medicine and Contemporary Psychoanalysis* (pp. 143–167). Madison, CT: International Universities Press.

_____ (2016). Varieties of castration experience: Relevance to contemporary psychoanalysis and psychodynamic psychotherapy. *Psychodynamic Psychiatry* 44(1):39–68.

_____ (2019). Creativity and perversion: Waiting for the muse. *Journal of the American Psychoanalytic Association* 67:425–454.

Teicher, M.H., and Samson, J.A. (2013). Childhood maltreatment and psychopathology: A case for ecophenotypic variants as clinically and neurobiologically distinct subtypes. *American Journal of Psychiatry* 170 (10):1114–1133.

Turco, R. (1998). *The Architecture of Creativity: Profiles Behind the Mask.* Yachats, Oregon: Dancing Moon Press.

van der Kolk, B.A. (1989). The compulsion to repeat the trauma. *Psychiatric Clinics of North America* 12(2):389–411.

Viederman, M. (1987). René Magritte: Coping with loss—reality and illusion. *Journal of the American Psychoanalytic Association* 35:967–998.

_____ (1994). Edvard Munch: A life in art. *Journal of the American Academy of Psychoanalysis* 22(1):73–110.

Wallach, A. (1994, April 24). My dinners with de Kooning. *Newsday*, p. 9. Cited in R. Shiff, *Between Sense and de Kooning* (p. 247). London: Reaktion Books, and in J. Zilczer, *A Way of Living: The Art of Willem De Kooning* (p. 131). New York: Phaidon Press.

Waters, E., Merrick, S., Treboux, D., Crowell, J., and Albersheim, L. (2000). Attachment security in infancy and early adulthood: A twenty-year longitudinal study. *Child Development* 71(3):684–689.

Weiss, H. (2020). A river with several different tributary streams: Reflections on the repetition compulsion. *International Journal of Psychoanalysis* 101(6):1172–1187.

Werman, D.S. (1989). James Ensor, and the attachment to place. *International Journal of Psychoanalysis* 16:287–295.

Williams, M.H. (2014). Introduction. In M.H. Williams (Ed.), *Art and Analysis: An Adrian Stokes Reader* (pp. xi–xxv). London: Karnac Books.

_____ (2015, October 3). The aesthetic conflict in artistic process and in psychoanalysis as an art form. Paper presented at the 20th Annual Day in Applied Psychoanalysis, Toronto Psychoanalytic Society, Toronto, Canada.

Wilson, A., and Malatesta, C. (1989). Affect and the compulsion to repeat. Freud's repetition compulsion revisited. *Psychoanalysis and Contemporary Thought* 12(2):265–312.

Winnicott, D.W. (1953). Transitional objects and transitional phenomena. A study of the first not-me possession. *International Journal of Psychoanalysis* 34:89–97.

_____ (1960). The theory of the parent-infant relationship. *International Journal of Psycho-analysis* 41:585–595.

_____ (1962). Ego integration in child development. In *The Maturational Processes and the Facilitating Environment* (pp. 56–63). London: Hogarth Press, 1965.

_____ (1967). Mirror-role of mother and family in child development. In *Playing and Reality* (pp. 111–118). New York: Basic Books, 1971.

_____ (1969a). The use of an object and relating through identifications. In *Playing and Reality* (pp. 86–94). New York: Basic Books, 1971.

_____ (1969b). The use of an object in the context of *Moses and Monotheism*. In C. Winnicott, R. Shephard, and M. Davies (Eds.), *Psychoanalytic Explorations* (pp. 240–246). Cambridge, MA: Harvard University Press, 1989.

_____ (1971). *Playing and Reality*. New York: Basic Books.

Wintle, M. (2000). *An Economic and Social History of the Netherlands, 1800–1920. Demographic, Economic and Social Transition*. Cambridge: Cambridge University Press.

Wohl, R., and Trosman, H. (1955). A retrospective of Freud's Leonardo: An assessment of a psychoanalytic classic. *Psychiatry* 17:27–39.

Wolfe, J.L. (1994). "Van Wim tot Bill de Kooning: Zeven decennia thematiek en vorm." Translated by A. van Hoorn. *Jong Holland* 10(1):6–28. (English summary, pp. 62–63).

_____ (1996). *The Young Willem De Kooning: Early life, Training and Work, 1904–1926*. Dissertation, City University of New York, New York.

Wolfenstein, M. (1966). Goya's dining room. *Psychoanalytic Quarterly* 35:47–83.

Wollheim, R. (1974). *On Art and the Mind: Essays and Lectures*. Cambridge, MA: Harvard University Press.

_____ (1987). *Painting as an Art. The A. W. Mellon Lectures in the Fine Arts, 1984*. Princeton, NJ: Princeton University Press.

Wright, K. (1995). Painting and the self: A psychoanalytic perspective on art. Unpublished manuscript.

Yard, S. (1997). *Willem de Kooning*. New York: Rizzoli.

_____ (2007). *Willem de Kooning. Works, Writings, Interviews.* Barcelona: Ediciones Poligrafa.

Yovell, Y. (2000). From hysteria to posttraumatic stress disorder: Psychoanalysis and the neurobiology of traumatic memories. *Neuro-psychoanalysis* 2:171–181.

Zilczer, J. (2014). *A Way of Living: The Art of Willem De Kooning.* New York: Phaidon Press.

_____ (2016). Willem and Elaine de Kooning visit the Barnes Foundation. *American Art* 30(3): 76–91.

# Full Citations for Photo Images

**Frontispiece.** Willem de Kooning in his studio in New York, 1950
Gelatin silver print, 9 ½ × 7 ⅞ inches (24.1 × 20 cm)
Whitney Museum of American Art, New York
Gift of Alex Katz
Photograph by Rudy Burckhardt. Courtesy of the Tibor de Nagy Gallery, New York
Photo © Rudy Burckhardt Estate/ARS, New York /SOCAN, Montreal
Artwork © 2022 The Willem de Kooning Foundation /ARS, New York /SOCAN, Montreal

**Figure 1.** Willem de Kooning
*Woman I*, 1950–1952
Oil on canvas, 75 ⅞ × 58 inches (192.7 × 147.3 cm)
The Museum of Modern Art, New York
Purchase
Digital Image © The Museum of Modern Art /Licensed by SCALA/Art Resource, NY
Artwork © 2022 The Willem de Kooning Foundation/ARS, New York/SOCAN, Montreal

**Figure 2.** De Kooning contemplating one of his paintings in his improvised studio on the porch of Leo Castelli's house in East Hampton, New York in the summer of 1953
Photograph by Tony Vaccaro
© Tony Vaccaro/Getty Images
Artwork © 2022 The Willem de Kooning Foundation /ARS, New York /SOCAN, Montreal

**Figure 3.** Willem de Kooning
*Woman and Bicycle,* 1952–1953
Oil, enamel, and charcoal on linen, 76 ½ × 49 ⅛ inches (194.3 × 124.8 cm)
Whitney Museum of American Art, New York
Purchase
Digital Image © Whitney Museum of American Art/Licensed by SCALA/Art
Resource, NY
Artwork © 2022 The Willem de Kooning Foundation/ARS, New York/SOCAN,
Montreal

**Figure 4.** Willem de Kooning
*Woman II,* 1952
Oil on canvas, 59 × 43 inches (149.9 × 109.3 cm)
The Museum of Modern Art, New York
Gift of Blanchette Hooker Rockefeller
Digital Image © The Museum of Modern Art/Licensed by SCALA/Art Resource, NY
Artwork © 2022 The Willem de Kooning Foundation/ARS, New York/SOCAN,
Montreal

**Figure 5.** Willem de Kooning
*Woman III,* 1952–1953
Oil on canvas, 68 × 48 ½ inches (172.7 × 123.2 cm)
Collection of Steven A. Cohen. Photo courtesy Gagosian
© 2022 The Willem de Kooning Foundation/ARS, New York/SOCAN, Montreal

**Figure 6.** Willem de Kooning
*Woman V,* 1952–1953
Oil on canvas, 60 ⅞ × 45 inches (154.6 × 114.3 cm)
National Gallery of Australia, Canberra
Photo © National Gallery of Australia, Canberra/ Purchased 1974/Bridgeman
Images
Artwork © 2022 The Willem de Kooning Foundation/ARS, New York/SOCAN,
Montreal

**Figure 7.** Willem de Kooning
*Woman VI,* 1953
Oil on canvas, 68 ½ × 58 ½ inches (174 × 148.6 cm)
Carnegie Museum of Art, Pittsburgh
Gift of G. David Thompson
Digital Image © Carnegie Museum of Art, Pittsburgh
Artwork © 2022 The Willem de Kooning Foundation/ARS, New York/SOCAN,
Montreal

**Figure 8.** Willem de Kooning
*The Kiss*, 1925
Graphite on paper, 19 × 13 inches (48.2 × 34.7 cm)
Photo courtesy of the Allan Stone Collection, New York
© 2022 The Willem de Kooning Foundation/ARS, New York/SOCAN, Montreal

**Figure 9.** Willem de Kooning
*Women and Tree*, ca. 1924
Conté crayon and pencil on paper, 13 ⅝ × 10 inches (34.5 × 25.4 cm)
Private collection
Photo courtesy of Judith L. Wolfe
© 2022 The Willem de Kooning Foundation/ARS, New York/SOCAN, Montreal

**Figure 10.** De Kooning at work in his studio, Springs, East Hampton, New York, 1967
Photograph by Ben van Meerendonk
© Ben van Meerendonk/Getty Images
Artwork © 2022 The Willem de Kooning Foundation/ARS, New York/SOCAN, Montreal

**Figure 11.** Willem de Kooning
*Woman in the Water*, 1972
Oil on canvas, 59 ½ × 54 inches (151.2 × 137.2 cm)
Collection Siegfried and Jutta Weishaupt, Germany
Photo courtesy of the Kunsthalle-Weishaupt Gallery, Ulm, Germany
© 2022 The Willem de Kooning Foundation/ARS, New York/SOCAN, Montreal

**Figure 12.** Willem de Kooning
*. . . Whose Name Was Writ in Water*, 1975
Oil on canvas, 76 ¾ × 87 ¾ inches (195 × 223 cm)
The Solomon R. Guggenheim Museum, New York
Digital Image © The Solomon R. Guggenheim Foundation/Art Resource, NY
Artwork © 2022 The Willem de Kooning Foundation/ARS, New York/SOCAN, Montreal

**Figure 13.** Willem de Kooning
*Portrait of Elaine*, 1940–41
Pencil on paper, 12 ¼ × 11 ⅞ inches (31.1 × 30.2 cm)
Photo courtesy of the Allan Stone Collection, New York
© 2022 The Willem de Kooning Foundation/ARS, New York/SOCAN, Montreal

**Figure 14.** Willem and Elaine de Kooning, 1953
Photograph by Tony Vaccaro
© Tony Vaccaro/Bridgeman Images

**Figure 15.** Willem de Kooning and Emilie Kilgore in his studio in Springs, East Hampton, New York, 1975
© Nancy Crampton
Artwork © 2022 The Willem de Kooning Foundation/ARS, New York/SOCAN, Montreal

**Figure 16.** Willem de Kooning
*Untitled XIX*, 1977
Oil on canvas, 79 ¾ × 70 inches (202.6 × 177.8 cm)
The Museum of Modern Art, New York
Gift of Philip Johnson
Digital Image © The Museum of Modern Art/Licensed by SCALA/Art Resource, NY
Artwork © 2022 The Willem de Kooning Foundation/ARS, New York/SOCAN, Montreal

# INDEX